Copenhagen Seminars for Social Progress

Building a World Community
Globalisation and the Common Good

No public body, group,
I speak seriously,
has undertaken a more important
and germane effort in our time.

JOHN KENNETH GALBRAITH

Building a World Community

Globalisation and the Common Good

Edited by Jacques Baudot

Royal Danish Ministry of Foreign Affairs
Copenhagen

in association with

University of Washington Press
Seattle and London

Royal Danish Ministry of Foreign Affairs
Department of Public Information
Asiatisk Plads 2
DK-1448 Copenhagen K
Denmark

University of Washington Press
PO Box 50096
Seattle, Washington 98145-5096
U.S.A.

Editor:
Jacques Baudot

Design:
Designgrafik

Library of Congress Cataloging-in-Publication Data
  Building a world community : globalisation and the common
good/edited by Jacques Baudot.
   cm.
  ISBN 0-295-98099-0 (alk. paper)
  Globalization. 2. International relations. 3. Common good.
  I. Baudot, Jacques.
JZ1318.B85 2001
327.1--dc21   00-069080

The paper used in this publication meets the minimum requirements
of American National Standard for Information Sciences—Permanence
of Paper for Printed Library Materials, ANSI Z39.48-1984.

Contents

In March 1995 Denmark hosted the United Nations World Summit for Social Development. Attended by a large number of world leaders and representatives from non-governmental organisations, this conference adopted the Copenhagen Declaration for Social Development, a text committing governments to pursue the eradition of poverty, the promotion of full employment, and the fostering of stable, safe and just societies.

To contribute to the implementation of these goals, the government of Denmark, at the initiative of Poul Nielson, then Minister for Development Cooperation, decided to organise the Copenhagen Seminars for Social Progress. International in their composition and global in their purpose, focused on a reflection and dialogue on the moral principles and political orientations required by social progress for all, four seminars and their preparatory meetings took place between 1996 and 1999. Their subjects were successively *A World Economy for the Benefit of All*, *Humane Markets for Humane Societies*, *Political Culture and Institutions for a World Community*, and *Defining, Measuring, and Monitoring Social Progress and Social Regress*.

This book presents a synthesis and interpretation of the work undertaken by these seminars. Prepared by the Secretary of the Copenhagen Seminars, it does not commit the responsibility of those who participated in this endeavour, nor does it reflect the policy of the Royal Danish Ministry of Foreign Affairs on the matters under discussion. It also includes specific contributions and commentaries from eight participants in the seminars.

The hope of the organisers of the Copenhagen Seminars is that this book will make a contribution to the international dialogue on social progress between the various actors engaged in the building of a peaceful, fair, and sustainable world community.

Foreword

The Copenhagen Summit on Social Development brought together over a hundred political leaders and several thousand activists from non-governmental organizations, parliaments, trade unions, cooperatives and business enterprises. It reflected a sense of disquiet with the prevailing view that market-oriented reforms should be the principal goal of public policy to the virtual exclusion of the objective of equity and solidarity, within and between countries.

The ten commitments made by governments at Copenhagen were far-reaching. They sought to move economic policy beyond the objectives of growth and stability towards a concern for equity and also to extend social policy beyond a preoccupation with welfare programmes for the vulnerable towards a concern for social cohesion and solidarity. Yet the impact of these commitments on policies and programmes was modest, partly because of continued triumphalism about the potential of free markets and liberalisation, at least until the financial crisis of 1997-98, and partly because the philosophy and practice of the approaches advocated in Copenhagen was not fully spelt out. The Copenhagen Seminars for Social Progress were an attempt to address the latter gap, to provide, if you like, a coherent ideology for the middle way.

Ideology matters far more in the shaping of policy than is commonly recognized. It is true that public policy is shaped largely by the interplay of interest groups. But interest groups seldom argue simply in terms of costs and benefits of alternatives. Whether it is trade unions, cooperatives and businesses or rural and urban interests or developed and developing countries, interest groups articulate their demands as consequences of abstract principles of what is right and good. A compromise is possible when there is some common ground in these principles *and* a procedure for finding this common ground. In the absence of

9

such shared values, the more powerful of the interest groups will prevail with perhaps some modest concessions to moderate discontent. The Copenhagen vision of a society for all requires that economic and political procedures move beyond bargaining and bullying towards a shared framework of rights and obligations.

The Copenhagen Seminars sought to bridge this gap between self-interest and solidarity, between economics and ethics. They were, in essence, an intellectual exercise in the best sense of the term. A group of people who, in some sense belonged to this or that interest group, but who were willing to explore differences and look for commonalties, were brought together in a joint search for principles and policies that would reflect the common good. The atmosphere of the seminars was often argumentative but always constructive. The set of participants changed from one seminar to the next but with enough of an overlap to provide some continuity of thought. These seminars were a dialogue conducted in good faith, that is to say, a dialogue which one enters not just to convert but also to be converted, not just to talk and persuade but to listen and be persuaded.

Over the years a certain synthesis emerged and the participants started to agree more often than not. This synthesis has been captured in this volume by Jacques Baudot, the principal organizer of the Copenhagen Summit and the Copenhagen Seminars. The synthesis is built around three substantive goals – democracy, a humanist political culture and an economy oriented to meeting human needs in the widest sense. The fulfillment of these goals requires two further procedural goals – the development of a coalition of social forces with a global agenda and a more fully articulated structure of multilateral governance. These five elements are the framework within which this volume spells out an ideology for the pursuit of the common good in a globalising world.

The vision that emerges from this synthesis is of a society that places a far higher value on equality of opportunity and outcomes than most do at present, that requires of its citizens an active engagement in the political process not just from the perspective of group interests but with a concern for the common good, that recognizes individual rights but requires social responsibilities in the exercise of these, that celebrates differences and respects dissent, that orients the pursuit of private profit so that it serves the public good, that tempers the workings of self-interest with the spirit of solidarity. This is a vision not just of how societies can be organized within the boundaries of political jurisdictions but also a framework for relations between these jurisdictions and, at some future time, a vision for a single global community of the human race.

The synthesis presented in this book is only a beginning. There are others who are working towards the same end. In many ways the political processes of the United Nations, particularly the cycle of great global conferences of the nineties, can also be described as a massive continuing meeting of the global village that has helped to define a substantial agenda for public policy in a globalising world. Even more than that, all of these processes are helping in the emergence of an international civil society, a transnational network of issue oriented activists and advocacy groups and of more traditional elements of civil society like trade unions, cooperatives and business associations. The dialogue in good faith must continue and this book, which reflects the outcome of one such dialogue, will help to provide us with a framework for the continuing exploration of globalisation and the common good.

Nitin Desai
Under-Secretary General
for Economic and Social Affairs,
United Nations

The views expressed in this foreword are those of the author and should not be taken to represent the views of the United Nations.

Findings of the Copenhagen Seminars

by Jacques Baudot

« _La démocratie favorise le goût des jouissances matérielles._
Ce goût, s'il devient excessif, dispose bientôt les hommes à croire
que tout n'est que matière ; et le matérialisme, à son tour,
achève de les entraîner avec une ardeur insensée vers ces mêmes
jouissances. Tel est le cercle fatal dans lequel les nations
démocratiques sont poussées. Il est bon qu'elles voient le péril
et se retiennent. »

ALEXIS DE TOCQUEVILLE

Introduction

Today the world is not a community. Plagued by violent conflicts and violations of fundamental human rights, it lacks the political institutions and the shared values that could replace a culture of competition and mistrust with a culture of cooperation and peace. Such a community has to be carefully constructed with deliberate effort. It would be imprudent to rely on the "natural" evolution of humanity from group to global solidarity to achieve this end.

This is a project whose first intellectual elaboration can be said to have been initiated by Emmanuel Kant with his design for "perpetual peace". Two centuries later, and after a number of subsequent initiatives, including the League of Nations, the United Nations was created, in the words of the Preamble of its Charter, "to save succeeding generations from the scourge of war", "to reaffirm faith in fundamental human rights", "to promote social progress and better standards of life in larger freedom", "to employ international machinery for the promotion of the economic and social advancement of all peoples". At the regional level, the members of the European Union, and before it the Nordic Countries, put in place laws and structures that seem to set them on a path towards political unity. And there are social movements and citizens of the world who, sometimes at great personal peril, testify of the human spirit in their determination to fight oppression and obscurantism, corruption and greed.

The struggle for a safer and better world is taking place in the midst of a technological revolution of enormous magnitude. The physical distances between continents and peoples have shrunk dramatically. In an ideological context dominated by liberalism, new techniques of communications have made possible the current process of globalisation. Supported by a number of governments, notably those of Europe and the United States, powerful financial and economic forces are seeking global markets and propagating a model of development and progress based on freedom of the individual and the acquisition and consumption of increased quantities of goods and services. As proclaimed by the Social Summit, the elimination of poverty on earth and the enjoyment of social development by all appear to be within reach. Openness to change, initiative, growth and creativity, and the liberation of humankind from old constraints are the virtues of this process that has great promise and appeal.

By themselves, however, the globalising forces leading to economic expansion and better standards of living are not sufficient to create an harmonious world community. Their contribution to the betterment of the human condition will remain limited to a few – individuals, social classes and countries – unless controlled and oriented towards the common good by appropriate public authorities and institutions. Their Promethean drive to master planet Earth and the universe will ultimately be destructive unless tempered by respect for humanity and nature, their bounties and mysteries. The appeal of these forces to acquisition and consumption will generate unsustainable materialism unless illumined by the recognition that human beings also have spiritual and other non-material needs and aspirations. The dominant ideology that drives global capitalism has to be corrected, enriched, and in a number of instances replaced by a modern humanist political philosophy centred on the person and the common good of humanity. Necessary to the creation of a viable world community are a new form of global democracy, economies serving equitably needs and aspirations, a compassionate political culture, social forces pursuing the general interest, and institutions responsible for protecting the common good. The development of these ideas and elements, introduced in the following paragraphs, constitutes the main purpose of this book.

The future world community needs to be democratic. As an international community, it should involve all nations. As a global community, it should implicate all citizens of the world. There are at least four sets of reasons for engaging in a quest for global democracy.

- First, *keeping under control the dangers threatening a globalised world requires the cooperation and commitment of a maximum number of states and other institutions.* Threats to the welfare and future of humankind range from the availability and constant "improvement" of weapons of mass destruction to the spreading of epidemics, and include damages to the natural envi-

15

ronment, the misuse of scientific and technological ingenuity, as well as the development of various forms of criminality. A civilisation dependent on an extensive array of techniques is fragile. And a world open to multiple forms of communications is vulnerable. Security, in its individual and collective forms, is bound to become a major concern. Authoritarian ideas and regimes, the domination and "protection" by a few over the many, including through technocratic and "efficient" world institutions, do not constitute an acceptable nor practical approach to this question of security. Only a mix of laws, regulations, enforcement and control procedures at different levels of legitimate authority, and a debated and evolving culture of care for the common good can reduce the severity of those global threats. Since their complete elimination, however, is not feasible, there remains the necessity to continually promote the rule of law at all levels, as well as to establish new global institutions such as the International Criminal Court.

- Secondly, *the process of globalisation itself is in need of control, and orientation, notably in its financial and economic facets.* It is a process which is partly the automatic result of technological innovations and revolutions of great magnitude, and partly the expression of the political and societal project of actors with great power. This process has mixed consequences for democracy. Nationally, it is a dissolver of authoritarian regimes. These regimes have great difficulty maintaining a suppression of individual freedom while liberalising their economies and being exposed to the mass media. Regression of these regimes towards more severe totalitarianism is economically costly and means international isolation, especially if the country concerned is not militarily powerful. More freedom, however, does not mean more equity and equality, nor more effective participation in public life beyond the casting of an occasional vote. There is credible evidence of aggravation of inequalities in the distribution of income, assets and perhaps also sentiment of social integration, notably in affluent countries, during the last decades of the 20th century. The process of globalisation reinforces or generates powers in the public and private spheres that have a formidable influence on the lives of people and the functioning of governments. Global capitalism is not a democratic affair. But the essence of the market economy system is a fair and broad distribution of opportunities for work, entrepreneurship and acquisition of various types of assets. And this issue of distribution of opportunities now applies within as well as among countries. To democratise the world economy is to bridge the gap between the current avatar of global capitalism and the raison-d'être of the market economy system.

- Thirdly, *peace and cooperation will only prevail over conflicts and wars through shared values of greater scope and depth.* In this globalised and yet fragmented and conflictual world, only strong moral values can provide a sound basis for global democracy. The great religions and philosophies that humankind has developed along its history have basic moral values in common. For instance, the moral prescriptions of the New Testament and the Analects are quite similar. At this point, the Charter of the United Nations and the Universal Declaration of Human Rights represent the most complete secularised expression of these common values defining the dignity of the human person and the quality of government and society. At the level of international debates and relations, however, both the discourse on universal values and its coherent translation into effective policies are seriously hampered by a complicated mixture of unforgotten and unforgiven historical events and artificially created or all too real differences in views and deeds. In very simplified terms, the Western powers are not always credible in their advocacy of democracy and human rights, and the Southern and Eastern powers are not always credible in their claim for cultural diversity and defence of national sovereignty. Progress in shared values will be achieved only through patient and rigorous work requiring research, debates and negotiations, and involving a maximum number of actors.

- The fourth *set of reasons justifying the search for a global democratic community stems from the very nature and appeal of democracy as the only morally and politically acceptable form of social organisation.* Democracy is an ensemble of procedures and institutions, such as elections and representative assemblies, a regime aiming at the protection and promotion of the human rights of the individual, and a culture giving content and quality to the relations between those in power and the citizens. Democracy is the most demanding political philosophy. It requires continuous efforts to implement its founding principle that all human beings are equal in dignity and worth. And it is the only political doctrine based on faith in the human capacity to reconcile liberty and solidarity, equality and creativity.

Such an ideal, nowhere fully implemented, has to remain as the main mobilising political utopia. It has to be the system of reference justifying rejection of authoritarian doctrines that still prevail in a number of countries and that represent a recurrent temptation to democracies themselves especially in times of hardship. As it relies on freedom and habits of the mind and heart rather than simply on laws and coercion, democracy can easily degenerate into anarchy and oligarchy. At present, democratic regimes tend to suffer from excessive laxism. Short-term expediency appears more frequently than the patient search for the general interest. Democracy has become more often identified with the exercise of individual freedom than with participation in public decision-making. For example, there is the avid consumer limiting his/her sense of responsible citizenship to an occasional vote for candidates to public offices who have been sold to the public through the media. There are other reminders that the *vox populi* is not necessarily respectful of the principles on which democracy is based. Support can be "democratically" given to politicians with non-democratic views. This is the image of the angry citizen ready for simple answers and radical "solutions". In addition, there appears to be in the world in general, and in Western democracies in particular, a weakening of the principle and objective of equality. Questions of distribution of income and assets, for example, receive less attention than thirty years ago. And yet, there is no democracy without equality in rights, opportunities and recognised dignity. Thus, democracy has to be both reinvented and promoted. It has to be imagined internationally and globally, while being defended in local, national and regional settings.

Critical to the task of strengthening and promulgating global democracy are economies that serve human needs and aspirations. The market economy system is a social arrangement for the production and exchange of goods and services that is both natural and desirable. It responds to the fundamental needs of individuals to have an economic activity, to exert their freedom of initiative and to possess and transmit the fruits of their labour. It enables societies to attain a sufficient level of prosperity while respecting human rights and the exercise of liberty. It is a system that link political and economic democracy. But, as have democratic regimes, market economies have varied enormously, both historically and geographically. Some market economies have a great number and proportion of small enterprises and businesses, while others are dominated by large companies. A relatively narrow range of personal income and assets in some, is contrasted by a concentration of wealth in others. The practice of honesty and trust in transactions is prevalent in a few, while corruption and litigation are conspicuous features of many. In seeking to establish humane market economies that would serve best the welfare of individuals and the harmony of the community, be it a nation, a region, or the world, the Copenhagen Seminars have identified four criteria that appear to be of particular significance in assessing the quality of an economy.

- *Economic participation refers to the involvement of individuals in productive activities, either through independent entrepreneurship and craftsmanship, or as workers and employees.* The essence of the market economy system is to offer opportunities for creativity and work to a maximum number of people. A market economy fails if a man or a woman with an entrepreneurial spirit is discouraged by too many obstacles. It also fails if unemployment or underemployment affect more than a small minority of those who desire to work. Globally, the domination of markets by a few transnational companies and the concentration of economic and financial power among a few countries are impediments to economic participation. So are all forms of discrimination in employment and work, notably against women. The question of economic participation of people across borders and continents has become a major issue of the global economy to be addressed by governments and international organisations.

- *Economic justice is achieved when individuals and communities, for example a nation, receive fair rewards for their activities.* Unjust is a market economy that does not sufficiently reward entrepreneurship, for example because of excessive or unfair taxation, or that offer too low salaries to its unskilled workers, or that has a highly skewed distribution of primary income. The global economy is also unjust if the prices of certain commodities are too low, if trade barriers are discriminatory, or if some currencies are battered by speculative decisions. Notions of fairness and justice are obviously rooted in cultures and are always evolving. But there has been, at least since the creation of the ILO in 1919, the progressive emergence of internationally recognised conceptions and definitions of what is fair and unfair, tolerable and unacceptable in various aspects of economic activities. Exploitation is a fairly well understood notion across continents. Again comparing present trends with the situation thirty years ago on the eve of the great surge of liberal ideas at the beginning of the 1980s, economic justice appears to be regressing. The emphasis on measures of a protective nature, such as "safe-ty-nets", or the targeting for assistance of groups in situations of extreme poverty, run counter to the necessarily large scope of the distributive and redistributive policies required by the pursuit of economic justice.

- *Economic morality addresses the behaviour of all the actors in the market economy, not only entrepreneurs, companies and workers, but also public authorities and other groups such as consumer's movements.* It is as immoral to advertise a product that is harmful to its consumers as it is immoral to pollute the atmosphere or the sea. It is as immoral to escape taxation through location of one's headquarters in a tax haven, as it is to dismiss workers simply to increase profit and the value of shares in the stock-market. Uncertain historical comparisons are not necessary to observe a divorce between legality and morality in the dominant economic culture and a weakening of norms of basic decency in the behaviour of numerous economic actors. On the other hand, concern with corrupt practices is mounting in a number of societies and international organisations are taking steps to place on their agendas issues of morality in economic and financial transactions.

- *Economic moderation is likely the most difficult virtue to attain in a market economy.* The modern economy not only responds to the needs of individuals and families but creates such needs through advertising and the propagation of an overall materialistic culture. Goods that used to be classified as "durables" have an increasingly short life, as obsolescence is one of the main engines of growth. Increased and, in some cultures, quasi complete secularisation of ideals, aspirations and institutions – including sometimes religious institutions themselves – is another cause and effect of the imperalism of economic elements in modern societies. Money and the mercantile rationality have imposed their dominance in most spheres of life and society. Market societies are precisely those that leave no room for pursuits other than acquisition and consumption.

This criticism of market economies becoming market societies has to be replaced in its historical context. Thinkers of the utilitarian persuasion, including Adam Smith, saw the market society as the liberation of individuals from various artificial constraints hampering the virtuous pursuit of their well conceived self-interest. The struggle against political absolutism and the power of established religions, the enlightenment movement that led to the French revolution, the militantism of trade-unions and other movements that gave birth to the social gains of the 19th and 20th century and to the welfare society, all had the noble ambition of making societies more peaceful and individuals happier and freer, first through the liberation of economic forces impeded by various powers and then through democratic control of these same forces. Generations of politicians, generally on the left of the polical spectrum, helped people to acquire and consume more and better goods. And today, throughout the world, many persons, families and countries are longing for the benefits of market societies. What is questioned here, therefore, is still part of a legitimate aspiration in poor and/or oppressed societies and is also the unintended but logical consequence of economic progress. That does not alter the fact that globally, and starting with affluent and energy hungry societies, economic moderation is imposed by the preservation of the environment and by the need of the human person to pursue other than materialistic goals. There are many signs that the current style of global capitalism, notwithstanding the "knowledge economy", is unsustainable in physical, moral and political terms.

Critical also to the emergence of a viable world community is a humanist political culture that would provide an alternative to the prevalent ideology associated with the current process of globalisation. This humanist culture, sought by many people throughout the world, has to be fully elaborated and has to find expression in a political movement with significant force. A humane global market economy, shaped not only by competition and the drive for growth and expansion but also by participation, justice, morality and moderation, is part of this overall humanist political culture. In its future manifestations, this culture ought to be enriched by the virtue of stability in some spheres of life and society, and by values essential to human interactions and social harmony. Compassion, generosity and hospitality, currently considered as "soft" and relevant only to the private realm, are to be emphasised. Solidarity, among regions and nations, among social groups between the fortunate and the poor, and between the current and future generations, was seen by the Seminars as central to a global humanist culture. Self-interest is a strong but insufficient basis for partnership and cooperation in the building of a viable and democratic global community. National interest has to be increasingly challenged in the search for the common good.

This view of the desirable emergence of a different political culture, less predatory and more in empathy with the world and its wonders, is based on the conviction that ideals, even utopias, are necessary to guide political action and orient human aspirations. To deny a role to compassion, generosity, religion and spirituality, art and conviviality, is not only mutilation of the human adventure, but lack of realism. And, of course, this sort of reductionist realism is self-fulfilling. What is suppressed and denied can die. Relentless appeals to the lower tendencies of human nature and the less demanding features of social relations lead easily to collective stupor.

The struggle for democracy and progress involves not only ideals but also humble statistics and indicators. The predominance of mercantile logic and the imperalism of a materialist conception of the betterment of the human condition are reflected in the data that are collected, published and debated on matters of development and progress. Innovations in the domains to be measured, reflections and debates on what constitutes social progress and social regress, less emphasis on comparisons of performance and more on specific conditions and problems, are among the steps that should accompany the elaboration of a new humanist political culture.

Among the forces with a global agenda and, in some cases a global reach and power, are the new world capitalist elite, the media, the new idealists and citizens of the world, the public servants, and the members of social movements and non-governmental organisations. The very brief evocation in this book of such forces aims to stimulate documented reflections on groups that are participating in the emergence of a globalised world. The new world capitalist elite has a sense of reaching the universal, is opposed to any form of fundamentalism and to traditional modes of exploitation, believes in the virtues of competition, has mixed feelings with regard to speculative transactions and concentration of power through mergers and acquisitions, and is genuinely deeply sceptical of the capacity of public authorities, national or international, to regulate the economy without destroying the spirit of initiative and enterpreneurship. The logical conclusion of this diagnosis is that, notwithstanding the social responsibility of the private sector, the main burden and duty to identify and pursue the common good remains with the politicians and public servants, from the local to the global domains of action. To blame global capitalism for its excesses and the materialistic culture it propagates, and for its blindness to the problems it creates in its wake, is in fact to say that for a variety of reasons those in charge of the general interest have failed in their mission. A number of social movements and non-governmental organisations are now in a position to put pressure on private and public authorities and to contribute to the difficult struggle for a decent world order.

A fair and peaceful world community requires strong public institutions seeking the common good. In the spirit of the time, institutions tend to be identified with public institutions and to have a rather negative image. The Western world, which, notably through the media with a global reach, shapes the modern ethos, forgets that institutions such as the United Nations are the only access of many countries to the international community and the only hope of many people for relief for their misery. Institutional diversity is an objective in itself, at all levels of social life. This point is in line with the recognition that human beings have various aspirations, that only totalitarian societies are simple, and that the international community has to be built on both cultural and political diversity and instruments suited to address global problems and respond to common aspirations. Humane and effective states, and increasingly regional organisations, are the necessary building blocks of this international and global community. A vague universalist culture based on the weakening of national entities and on the unchecked power of private organisations is not a sound basis for a new world order. The global world economy has to be oriented and regulated by public authorities acting on behalf of all countries, accountable to assemblies representing the people of the world, and involving in their decisions, representatives of all economic forces. This is a central aspect of a global democratic regime. New institutions ought to be established when the need arises and when the management of global issues is not possible at other levels of legitimate authority. By its charter, by its traditions and culture, the United Nations has the vocation to be the center of the political institutions that are required to establish and protect a global democratic community.

The five chapters on the main ideas expressed by the Copenhagen Seminars are followed by a number of specific contributions and commentaries by persons having participated in the seminars and their preparatory work. These are briefly introduced in the following paragraphs.

In his commentary, *Richard Falk* calls for a "feasible political project" that would reconcile "the continuing growth and integration of the world economy" with firm commitment to the "humanisation of globalisation". He believes that the "second predatory cycle of capitalism" – the first having occurred during the 19th century – is coming to an end after the Asian crisis and the events

23

in Seattle in November 1999, and that the critics of globalisation have now "a capacity for a more nuanced opposition that does not trap itself into an allegience with largely outmoded ideals about self-reliance and territorial sovereignty". Globalisation is not intrinsically linked with neo-liberal economics. It is the significance of globalising technologies that need to be understood and used to work for the advent of "compassionate globalisation" that would "enhance the material, moral and spiritual well-being of people". Richard Falk explains the distinction between "globalisation from above" and "globalisation from below", evokes the "new internationalism" created by alliances of NGOs with like-minded governments, and support "institutional experiments that embody the spirit of global democracy", such as a Global Peoples Assembly.

The commentary of *Peter Marris* starts with the observation that a "world which is economically integrated, overwhelming cultural and political boundaries, but socially divided at every level by ethnic and religious differences and growing inequality, risks being torn apart". Also, "in its relentless search to accumulate new wealth, global capitalism progressively destroys the natural environment on which it ultimately depends". Participants in the Copenhagen Seminars were caught in a fundamental contradiction. While criticising global capitalism, they did not intend to "deny its benefits, or exclude its access to any part of the world", they "did not challenge the potential of a global market economy to enhance the quality of life", and they did not "tackle directly neo-classical assumptions about human nature". For Peter Marris, an alternative world begins with the realisation that "meaning is crucial". The "preservation of meaning is more fundamental than biological survival", first through "attachment to parenting figures", then as a "constantly elaborated structure of purposes and attachments, seeking to make good sense of whatever happens to us". And, "we all need respect and a sense of worth that only a stable connection to some social groups can provide". It follows that the emphasis of the dominant economic model on consumption is misplaced because "we find the meaning of our lives in the part we play as producers, not consumers, and the work we do is not a thing but – a relationship through which we are connected, with dignity or in humiliating squalor, to the rest of society". Peter Marris makes comparable observations on "uprooting" and "social disruption in the interest of competitive production", and asserts that "food and clothes, shelter and tools, entertainment and crafts can be produced in many different ways (...) than capitalistic manufacture". He rejects the idea that "a competitive economy implies a competitive society", and stresses the fact that "alternatives will not survive without policies that protect and invest in them". "Real needs of real people" have to be reinserted into "a dauntingly inhuman economic equation".

Saad Nagi develops four propositions. "As dismal and intractable" current problems may seem, "the real world today is far better than it was half a century or a century ago". "Progress in human affairs is largely powered by the forces of modernisation". These forces "are also propelling a fast trend towards globalisation in many aspects of life". And, becoming the "community of solution", the global level will need "to develop institutions appropriate for managing these responsibilities". He believes that the course of human history is "tied to modernisation" and that "the lack of access of large proportions of the world population to the fruits of change is due to institutional weaknesses and dislocations". A community of solution refers to "boundaries within which a problem can be defined, dealt with, and solved". At this juncture, global institutions have to overcome four types of difficulties to be able to handle properly their functions: there is "dissonance in values held in different parts of the world"; "national governments are responsible for multiple difficulties", including because "national interests" and "power politics" continue to dominate the scene; there is "institutional hegemony or dominance", as the "values and norms of certain institutions have overpowered those of others", creating an ethos that "encourages an exaggerated emphasis on monetary achievements"; and, the "performance of international organisations at the national level" is also an issue, with a need to examine development assistance. Then Saad Nagi identifies six "leverages", or "foundations" for the process of development. These are education, justice, accountability, the role of non-governmental organisations, information, and "access to affiliation with regional and global communities". On information, he states that it "may turn out to be one of the most significant contributions of international organisations". Saad Nagi concludes that problems may proliferate and increase in intensity in the short term, but "the long term trend is towards more effective institutions at the various communal levels and better human conditions".

The contribution of *Deepak Nayyar* is a historical perspective on globalisation and development. First, he defines globalisation "a process associated with increasing economic openness, growing economic interdependence and deepening economic integration in the world economy". Economic openness pertains to trade flows, investment flows, financial flows, and includes services, technology, information and ideas, but "the cross-border movement of people is closely regulated and highly restricted". Economic interdependence is "asymmetrical", as there is a dependence of the South on the North and limited interdependence among countries of the South. Economic integration is in part "integration of markets" and in part "integration of production on the supply side". Deepak Nayyar provides data on the globalisation of world trade, international investment, and international finance. He points out that globalisation was possible through the dismantling of barriers, the development of enabling technologies, and new forms of industrial organisation. He then considers the process of globalisation that took place between 1870 and 1914 and finds "striking parallels" between that period and the present situation. The fundamental difference resides in "labour flows", which were enormous before World War I. Most critical is the point that "uneven development" is the order of the day, as it was a century ago. Deepak Nayyar analyses "mechanisms through which globalisation may have accentuated inequalities". He cites data on the unequal distribution of its benefits and costs. He concludes that "the concern for efficiency must be balanced by a concern for equity" and that "more freedom for the cross-border movement of people is both feasible and desirable in this age of globalisation".

In his commentary on "the realm of politics" *Ignacy Sachs* first recalls the tremendous changes that occured during the 20th century notably in terms of population and growth of the global GNP. He also recalls the "dismal social and humanitarian condition of our planet" and observes that "growth through inequality with perverse social effects" is a common situation. He advocates strategies centered on "full employment and its equivalents" and with "need oriented" components. He contends that "genuine development" requires "socially responsive, environmentally prudent and economically "viable" solutions, responding to the "double ethical imperative of synchronic solidarity with future generations and diachronic solidarity with future generations. Ignacy Sachs considers that the reconciliation of economic growth with social development "resides in the realm of politics", with a "system of regulation of the public and private spheres of our lives". He explains that special attention must be given to "the interface between the national and the global economy" and concludes that "the development age is still ahead" and that "direct democracy" ought to be given a greater scope.

The contribution of *Nafis Sadik* is on population and gender issues. She recalls that by the end of the 1950s "the global population growth rate was at its historic peak, at 2 per cent per year", with "2,5 per cent per year and an average of six children per woman" in the developing countries. Thirty years later "fertility has fallen by half" in developing countries and "as a result population growth rates have begun to slow". During that period, "population has changed from a highly divisive and controversial issue to one of the few development questions on which there is a detailed global consensus". This consensus was elaborated at the International Conference on Population and Development in 1994 and confirmed five years later through a Special Session of the United Nations General Assembly. It includes a number of benchmarks on illiteracy rates for women and girls, primary health care and family planning facilities, birth assistance by skilled attendants, availability of contraceptives, and reduction of vulnerability to HIV/AIDS infection. Nafis Sadik notes that a "total of 67 countries have made policy changes affirming a commitment to reproductive rights and reproductive health". She states that, globally, "we have seen remarkable progress in women's collective status and individual prospect over the last 30 years". At the same time, however, "much of humanity remains caught in a web of poverty, ill health and inequality". Currently, half of the world population is made of people under 25 years of age, but the proportion of people over the age of 50 will rise to 22 per cent by 2050. Nafis Sadik sees as priorities for action an "increase in access to reproductive health", the integration of "a gender-sensitive human rights perspective in reproductive health programmes", "the empowerment of women" and the "securing of gender equality", a "reduction of the HIV/AIDS pandemic and other sexually transmitted diseases", more "investments in the social sectors", an effective use of "operational partnership to build country capacity", the mobilisation of additional resources, and more "consensus building" through the United Nations.

Peter Townsend concentrates his contribution to "social polarisation and the growth of poverty". He ascertains that "the widening of living standards across and within countries began to accelerate in the final decades of the 20th century". He emphasises that "widening inequality has to be addressed at both ends of the spectrum", with attention being given to "the pay of executives" and "the disposable income and wealth of the richest people in the world". He notes that poverty, "a recognised evil, has lacked precise international definition and scientifically constructed remedy". He endorses the concepts of "absolute" and "overall" poverty and the objectives and strategies formulated by the Social Summit. Peter Townsend provides in this paper the first results of a large scale survey undertaken recently in the United Kingdom. One of the findings is that "22 per cent of the people surveyed, representing nearly 13 millions, ranked themselves in overall poverty". A "new international social strategy" is advocated. It would be "intimately connected with measurement". It would involve "equitable tax and income policies within an internationally sanctioned framework of socially responsible accumulation of wealth and income", "an employment creation programme", "a measure of social control of transnational corporations and international agencies". Peter Townsend advocates also a "halt to indiscriminate privatisation" and "collaborative scientific and political action to establish a more democratic and internationalised legal framework to protect human living standards".

For *Tu Weiming*, "if social development is seen as an aspiration and a promise for human flourishing, we need to address the fundamental ethical and spiritual issues confronting the global community". For this pursuit, "the old triumphant or confrontational Western mindset is counter productive". They are a number of ethical questions, requiring a "learning attitude" and a "critical self-consciousness among the reflective minds of the world". One of those questions is "can liberty as an intrinsic value generate a humane society without distributive justice?". Another question: "can instrumental rationality alone fight inequality without sympathy and compassion"? For Tu Weiming, "we should accept a plurality of models of sustainable development", "global interests must not be subsumed under national interests", "multiple modernities" have to be sought, "fruitful comparisons across geographic, linguistic, ethnic, cultural and religious boundaries will enrich our understanding of social development", and "change can only occur through mass mobilisation of social forces, including non-governmental organisations". He considers that "the possibility of an authentic American internationalism is still there" and that "if the American mindset evolves to encompass responsibility, civility and compassion as well as freedom and rights, and take a global perspective in defining national interest, the United States can significantly enhance the UN agenda for social development".

* * *

Most of the ideas mentioned in this book are not new. Some, such as the need for compassion and generosity of the spirit, are probably as old as the capacity of humankind to rise above the "state of nature". The description it gives of the world situation is partial. Any attempt to describe this complex and chaotic world is a terrible simplification. But the central message that the Copenhagen Seminars tried to convey is that a renaissance is needed and possible, that ideas, old or new, matter and that moral values determine the quality of an economy and society, national or global.

To criticise global capitalism is not to express indignation against technological change and modernity. It is a reminder that means should not be confused with ends and that the essence of a true market economy system is not concentration but dissemination of power, of initiative, of work and its fruits.

To call for compassion and love for fellow human beings is not to indulge in sentimentality. It is to stress that egoism, personal or collective, is not a virtue and cannot be the founding value of a viable world community.

To insist on responsibility, as indispensible to the enjoyment of one's rights, is not to preach reform with the assumption that morality has declined since a mythical "golden age". It is to note that basic decency is a readily understandable moral attribute cutting across all cultures and that responsibility for the welfare of the community increases with wealth, talent, and power.

Critical is the realisation that market economies and societies cannot function properly without public laws, regulations, and institutions. There is no decent society without public authorities and public services. A laissez-faire economic and political philosophy is tantamount to promoting domination of the strong and exploitation of the weak. Market economies cannot function properly and harmonious societies cannot emerge and flourish without moral norms and values. Markets are social constructs at the service of the welfare of individuals and the prosperity of communities. States are at the service of their citizens.

Critical also is the understanding that social progress applies to individuals and societies, and has material, intellectual, and spiritual facets. An economic base is an absolute necessity, for individuals, families, and communities. But there is a strong relationship, in economic, political, and moral terms, between excessive wealth, excessive income inequalities, and the persistence of poverty in the world. More consumerism will not eliminate material deprivation. It will only aggravate spiritual vacuity. A good education system is as important for a society as the efficient functioning of markets. Moral values are indivisible. They apply to individuals, to public institutions, as well as to corporations and other private institutions. Self-interest, unless understood as the fulfilment of the person through creativity and generosity, does not provide a sufficient base for harmonious societies. Similarly, the securing of national interest increasingly needs to be subsumed into the search for the universal common good.

Chapter I
Dimensions of Global Democracy

Democracy is a set of procedures and institutions through which citizens participate directly or indirectly to the elaboration and implementation of the laws that govern the community; it is also a regime protecting and promoting human rights; and it is a culture shaping individual and collective behaviour. Each of these dimensions is indispensable to the others.

As a set of procedures and institutions, democracy is subject to variations in time and space. There are forms of direct democracy, that is of decisions being taken directly by all the assembled citizens of a specific area, that ought not to be dismissed as remnants of a bucolic agrarian past. Referenda stem from the same belief in the capacity of individuals to make sound judgements on sometimes complicated matters. There are also many ways of setting institutions with legislative, executive and judicial power. Lately, however, Western arrangements involving elections of candidates selected by the administrations of political parties operating on a national scale have received a sort of "imprimatur" from international organisations and the global media. Progress in democracy tends to be identified with the holding of "free elections" on the basis of competition between at least two political parties. The rationale for this insistence on elections is the notion of "accountability" of those, individuals and institutions, that have the privilege to lead and administer public affairs. The fact that somebody can be removed from office by the will of the electorate is a minimum guarantee that he or she will exert power in accordance with the law and hopefully with honesty and dedication. Given the present state of the art on the practice of political democracy, there is no convincing alternative to free elections to ensure a modicum of accountability of public officials. More complicated than the organisation of parliamentary or presidential elections, democracy is, at this juncture, not possible without it. To the accountability of those in power, is attached the notion of "transparency" of public decisions. Democracy implies legal and institutional arrangements for orderly debate on conflicting views and interests, and for implementation of decisions through transparent administrative procedures.

As a regime protecting and promoting the rights of the individual, democracy has an immediate and universal appeal. It means freedom in its most basic dimensions, including freedom to have an activity, to establish a family, to travel, to learn, to express one's views and to create. It means personal safety and security, the right not to be arbitrarily arrested, detained, mistreated by public authorities, and the right to have a recourse in case of personal injury, damage, or tort. It means also the provision of an adequate level of living to all and equality of opportunities in terms of work, income, education, health and other aspects of individual and social welfare recognized in the Covenant on Economic, Social and Cultural Rights. It excludes any form of discrimination. It implies respect for the rights of the minority(ies), the recognition that the "other" has the same rights as I, and the active conviction that a plurality of views, opinions, and beliefs is natural and good for a society. This is why democracy is antinomic with theocracy and with any form of fundamentalism. Democracy is secular. But laicism does not mean hostility to religion, and, even less, indifference to morality and the spirit of humanity. Across cultures, levels of economic development and levels of civic education, people aspire to democracy, so equated with freedom and equality of rights. It is the equivalent of respect for human dignity, and the opposite of oppression and deprivation.

As a culture shaping individual and collective behaviour, democracy relates to attitudes, working methods, ways of exercising power, and even intellectual and emotional reflexes. An elected parliament, or a government responsible to an assembly, is unfortunately no guarantee against corruption, or against the abuses of a police treating citizens and a fortiori non-citizens such as foreign workers in a coercive manner. True democracy implies civility and ingrained respect for the dignity of the "other person", irrespective of wealth, status knowledge, and power. Democracy is the daily and humble practice of fundamental equality between all human beings. Democracy calls for participation, at all levels of society, and therefore requires debates and time. A democratic culture is antinomic to a narrow conception of efficiency. Democracy is receding when "time is money", not only in private corporate organisations but in all spheres of society and in the psyche of the individual.

There is a continuum in the human moral capacity to practice democracy at different levels of political interaction, from the local to the global. The democratic culture required to manage local affairs with integrity and equity is also necessary to envisage the treatment of the global commons with respect for the welfare of future generations. Democratic virtues are indivisible. But the concepts and institutional arrangements required at these different levels vary so significantly that it would be imprudent to count on an automatic passage from national to global democracy. If, in a future which does not have to be very distant, most countries and regions of the world would deserve to be considered democratic, this would not be a guarantee that the world economy would be managed democratically and that different cultures would have a role on the world scene. Specific efforts would still be needed. Issues of relative power and nationalism are obviously relevant. This is why a world dominated by the United States of America, a country with democratic traditions and institutions, is not *ipso facto* a world democratic community. Issues of intellectual and political imagination are also relevant. How for example regulate global capitalism with the participation of small and large enterprises, trade-unions, consumers, environmentalists, national governments and international organisations?

In a humanist and voluntarist perspective, it is therefore necessary to work for democracy simultaneously and at all levels. All the more so because positive and negative influences operate in all directions. Large countries with authoritarian regimes are obstacles to global democracy. So are international institutions with elitist and restrictive modes of operation. Benevolent democratic countries demonstrating concretely their solidarity with the rest of the world, through financial transfers or hospitality to people in search of work or home, contribute powerfully to the construction of a global community, as does the General Assembly of the United Nations when it launches world conferences on global problems and aspirations.

But the task ahead is enormous. In addition to the fact that entire regions and large countries are still ruled by governments and social groups hostile to democratic principles or unable to put them into practice, there is a patent lack of democracy at the international and global level. The most important decisions in the economic, financial, political and military domains are taken in institutions that are neither democratic in their intent nor accountable to the public. Often, these decisions are secret or published in a manner that excludes serious debates. The attempt at ruling the world economy by the Group of Seven Most Industrialised Countries symbolises this oligarchic organisation of world affairs. International and national financial institutions, including ministries of economy and finance largely escape the control of representative assemblies of the people. Decisions of transnational corporations affecting directly or indirectly the economic well-being of millions of people are taken at best with the participation of a few shareholders. Huge movements of short-term capital, again affecting sometimes dramatically the living conditions of large numbers of people, are decided upon by a few banks and stockholders, not to mention speculators. Even on matters of peace and security, for which the Charter of the United Nations has significant precautions against democratic excesses, the possibility of dissent and veto by governments with a different agenda has lead the currently most powerful countries to entrust the main responsibility for war and peace to their own organisation, NATO.

It is as if there was a trade off between democracy and the search for effectiveness and efficiency. The issues at hand – on matters of security, finance, trade – have an urgency, magnitude and complexity that appear to defy democratic processes of decision. A frequently held view is that questions of relevance to humanity as a whole are better understood and better addressed through technocratic, elitist, or even authoritarian methods than through democratic consultations and deliberations. It seems to be taken for granted that representatives of different regions, cultures, and interests would have great difficulty agreeing on measures required to manage the supply and consumption of water, ensure the renewal of fish stocks, protect the ozone layer, or combat violence, impose a truce on belligerents or levy taxes, and distribute humanitarian assistance. While democracy implies the sharing of power, the world seems to be heading in the opposite direction.

Among the other obstacles to global democracy are three that deserve special mention. These are the difficult relations of the current practice of democracy with Truth, Order and Commitment; the double temptation of laxism and fundamentalism in moral and political philosophy; and, perhaps above all, the decline of interest in the principle and goal of equality of all human beings.

Democracy, Truth, Order and Commitment

Not only with regard to the treatment of international and global issues, but also on the national level, the present political culture is more authoritarian and technocratic than opened to participation and organised dissent. The spreading of some of the practices of the Western liberal democratic model, notably the organisation of elections, should not mask this tendency. As governments are increasingly dominated by economic issues and increasingly sensitive to the needs and demands of powerful economic and financial corporations, the prescriptions of democracy in terms of information and open debates are perceived as obstacles to quick decision-making rather than normal features of transparent political processes. The unformulated objective of most governments and public administrations seems to be to avoid discussions rather than to benefit from different viewpoints. The question of corruption is also linked to this excessive proximity between the public and the private sectors and to the blurring of the still necessary distinction between collective and corporate interests. Then corruption is allowed to become a cancer that penetrates political institutions and gravely undermines their credibility and legitimacy. In poor countries with underdeveloped governmental and administrative structures, the capacity of public authorities to resist external and corporate measures is so limited that it endows democratic procedures such as elections with characteristics of rather pathetic smokescreens. Modern democracy seems to have ambivalent relationships with some key concepts for the functioning of society, notably Truth, Order, and Commitment.

In the search for the common good of a community, why should decisions of a majority, or of a government responsible before that majority, have a better chance to approximate the Truth – defined here as the long-term interest of this community in a peaceful world – than decisions of an enlightened monarch or informed civil servant? The same applies to the reliance on opinion polls to identify a vox populi determing policy orientations. It is difficult to reconcile attentiveness to the opinions of the electorate with guidance and leadership from those who govern. Complexity of the issues, lack of proper information, emotions and passions stirred by demagogues, and intellectual comfort fed by prejudices, often lead democratic institutions to decisions at odds with the common good, or to paralyses.

These rather traditional questions are taking a new acuity because of the complexities of the globalisation process. The fact that many contemporary problems have an objective global and often threatening dimension is an encouragement for reflecting on the merits of modern versions of the "Confucian Guide" or the "Enlightened Despot". And one is immediately reminded that people can vote for a potential dictator, and that democratically consulted majorities can be in favour of the death penalty, or of the "ethnic cleansing" of their neighbours. Prejudices and manipulations often have dramatic consequences. In the search for a better world community, there is a tenuous dividing line between constructive criticism of the limitations of current democratic practices and an apologia of non-democratic doctrines. But modern democracy cannot be based only on the search for compromises. It has to be rooted on intellectual integrity and enlightened by a humanist conception of society and progress.

Order has a conservative connotation. It evokes a society with a division of responsibilities and status between its members. Democracy conveys images of free expression of opinions, however extreme or extravagant, of discussions without conclusions, and of decisions carried out without planning and follow-up. Democratic regimes have great difficulties addressing social problems such as drug abuse, violence and insecurity. And yet, it is necessary to associate the two concepts of order and democracy, because a non-democratic world order would be oppressive and because a global democracy without order would not be able to address the problems of the coming century. But, at present, the two currents, one favouring order to reduce uncertainties, the other favouring a form of democracy to promote freedom and other fundamental rights, are divergent. Related is the apparent incapacity of democratic regimes to take the long-term perspective called for by many contemporary issues. The protection of the environment is a case in point. The current obsession of the Western ethos with short-term political and financial gains, linked to consumerism, is a major obstacle to the building of a viable world order.

The same difficulty arises with the level of Commitment required to begin addressing properly the problems of a world fragmented along a multiplicity of economic, cultural and political lines. Democratic regimes are not famous for their determination and capacity to follow a straight political line. There are domestic or national conflicts that would have a better chance to be solved if solutions could be imposed by elected leaders without the involvement of some of the groups concerned. Parliamentary democracies have been criticised for their dubious record in avoiding or terminating conflicts. The fact that dictators or pseudo democratic leaders do initiate conflicts, treat human rights with contempt, and impose social order through coercion does not absolve democratic regimes from lack of resolve and consistency. In times of danger, the best or most fortunate of these regimes have given power to inspired and courageous leaders. Others have collapsed. The 20th century has not had a very encouraging record in terms of the capacity of democracies to handle adversity and pursue ambitious goals.

Laxism and Fundamentalism

The concern for democracy is often identified with Western thinking on human affairs and Western propaganda. The universality of the appeal of the democratic ideal does not alter the fact that Western powers are often seen as trying to impose a world order fitting their political and economic interests. And, they are perceived as "selling" their culture to the entire world while their political institutions are at a low point in terms of prestige and recognised legitimacy. Democracy is advocated when everything public is weakened in affluent countries. A most important element of the privatisation movement has been a brain drain from the public to the private sector. And the view that governments should do less, should use and transfer less resources, and should interfere less with the functioning of markets and society has gained considerable credence.

Moreover, political parties have problems attracting people, notably young persons interested in working for political ideas and the public interest. Young idealists would rather dedicate their energy to social movements and organisations of the civil society. A number of political parties have become essentially propaganda machines to sell candidates. In a number of countries, notably the United States, less than half of the electorate actually participates in the election of their representatives. And is it "democratic" to select candidates for elected positions through processes involving large amount of money and requiring "high tech" advertising? Political confrontations to win the favour of the electorate, especially between two champions on a television screen, are entertaining. Especially when one of the protagonists is embarrassed and defeated. But is this the best way to select leaders? Why, for instance ignore the ancient and not entirely vanished traditions of Asia and Africa to associate the legitimacy of power with wisdom and experience?

In the streets of a city of a typical Western affluent liberal democracy, the passer-by is more frequently offered pamphlets from religious or pseudo religious sects and advertisements for beauty products than solicited to participate in a political rally. At the same time, groups voice and defend their interests more frequently and seemingly more successfully through street demonstrations than through parliamentary debates. Extremist groups predicating violence and rejection of the "other" as the enemy are enjoying some success. Parliaments have great difficulties to resist pressure groups, to catch up with experts, and to handle properly their traditional responsibilities, including in the fiscal and financial domains. Their deliberations seem sometimes to serve primarily the purpose of endorsing decisions taken elsewhere in a secretive and elitist manner. Financial and security issues are hardly subjects of public debates in Western democratic regimes. How could such practice of democracy with weakened parliaments, executives highly sensitive to the interests of banks and large corporations, and disinterested citizens be usefully carried over to the international and global level?

The confusion of some advocates of democracy between fundamental principles and their specific current Western avatar which is a brand of elitist and libertarian democracy, often leads non-democratic leaders to a convenient rejection of "democracy" as an expression of Western imperialism and insensitivity to cultural diversity. The popular culture disseminated by the West, with its noisy and vehement rejection of all constraints and taboos, is used to justify the maintenance of oppressive structures and policies. It generates a counter propaganda associating liberalism with licentious conduct and democracy with decadence. The difficulty of liberal democracies to build a moral foundation and to reconcile rights and responsibilities provides a fertile ground for the development of anti-democratic ideologies. Then the identification of democracy with global dissemination of a culture of immediate satisfaction of individual impulses feeds various expressions of fundamentalism.

Historically, fundamentalism appeared within the Christian faith as a reaction against modernism and liberalism. It has clear antecedents in Puritanism and other doctrines that, along history, have stressed the need to keep the individual within the strict constraints imposed by institutions preserving traditions and morality. Fundamentalism expresses the fear that freedom is destructive of social cohesion and of the virtues that define human nature and human dignity. It is anti-democratic in its rejection of individual liberty and in its insistence that norms of behaviour are not for debate and questioning. Today, fundamentalism remains a strong current in branches of Christianity, including the Orthodox Church, and has gained greater visibility because of its militancy and success in establishing theocratic states in parts of the Muslim world. Fundamentalism of all types represents a serious challenge that will not be met by more laxism and libertarian attitudes in Western democracies. The future of the democratic ideal still depends on the reconciliation of individual freedom with responsibility for the welfare of the community.

Decline of the Principle of Equality

To treat individuals, or rather citizens as equal in terms of political participation – one person, one voice, one vote – and equal in terms of rights, is the essence of democracy. In that sense, one can observe continuous progress in the Western liberal regimes, from the time of participation limited to men with property, money and knowledge, to the time when every citizen has the right to vote and to be elected. And current efforts to extend such rights to non-citizens and to revise the notion of citizenship in a more liberal direction are part of that progress. Here, there is great consistency between the Western democratic model and the project of building a global democratic community.

But democracy means also the reduction of concrete and tangible inequalities between individuals. The article of the Universal Declaration of Human Rights stating that "everyone has the right to a standard of living adequate for the health and well-being of himself and of his family" has been part of the Western culture since more than a century, at least as an aspiration and a claim of left inclined political forces. Taking a long historical perspective, the evidence of such a reduction of inequalities, in all domains, is overwhelming in the Western countries, and in fact in most parts of the world. In that very general but very fundamental way, the world is more democratic now than a century ago.

The question, however, is to determine whether or not this identification of democracy with economic and social equality of individuals and groups is persisting or weakening, particularly in the affluent countries. If such were to

39

be the case, a legitimate conclusion would be that the dominant model of democracy is turning into plutocracy or some new form of domination of the few over the majority, and that such a model ought to be readjusted to serve as a valid foundation for a world community.

A trend towards more equality was very pronounced after World War II, notably through the establishment of systems of social security and protection with a universal coverage and through redistributive policies. Among the many reasons for the reversal of this trend since the beginning of the 1980s are the greater emphasis on the free interplay of market forces, the weakening of workers and employees in their dialogue or confrontation with managers and capitalists, and the shift from Keynesian to monetarist macro-economic and financial policies. Probably cause and effect has also been a significant change in the societal objectives of the Western world. Equality in income and opportunities for personal growth, status and social recognition is a much less prominent value than a few decades ago. Perhaps not in the hearts and minds of those who are deprived of material means and social prestige, but unquestionably in the public discourse and in this intangible but powerful set of views, mental reflexes and prejudices that constitute the spirit of the time, the importance of equality is regressing.

Is this only an ephemeral trend reversal? Liberalism focuses on the right of every individual to be free, particularly from oppression, and on equality before the law, but not on equality in opportunities and living conditions. Market forces operating on their own tend to transmit and create inequalities. Some decades ago, Western democracy was being attacked by the Soviet Union and by thinkers of Marxist obedience as being "formal" rather than "real" because of its emphasis on procedures such as elections and multipartyism at the expense of social and economic objectives of justice and equality. Such criticism would be more justified now, as a number of Western states have abandoned the instruments they had to regulate the economy and distribute equitably opportunities and benefits. In Europe and the United States, there is currently more relative poverty than ten or twenty years ago. But the denunciation of this state of affairs is weak, at least for the time being, partly because the main political source of criticism has disappeared with the Soviet Union. Voices from the former "Third World", joined by intellectuals and religious and civil organisations of the North, are deploring the lack of commitment of the affluent countries to the solidarity that could bring economic and social democracy to all, as evidenced by the decline of the amount of Official Development Assistance being provided to developing countries. These voices are, however, much weaker than those – coming from the North and from the South – proclaiming that democracy means the freedom of individuals from constraints and that free markets alone provide the foundations for better living conditions and acceptable societies. The current neglect of the principles and objective of equality and social justice should not be allowed to continue.

There are other reasons to work purposefully for the construction of a global democratic community. Global threats to humankind and its future are real and have to be addressed. And there is need for public guidance into the workings of capitalism itself. The process of globalisation as well as the current mode of competition need to be tamed and put at the service of the community. Financial transactions have to be controlled. And common values need to be found.

Reduce the Severity of Global Threats

Peoples of different regions and cultures share the impression that a new world is in the making and that ideas, beliefs, living conditions as well as political arrangements through which groups and nations transact, compete and cooperate, are rapidly being altered and will continue to be so in the foreseeable future. This transformation is perceived as global and out of control of the "common man". The traditional conviction that "destiny" is ruling human affairs, strong and precise in some cultures and vague in others but pervasive everywhere, combines with the immeasurable distance that separate most people from the modern sources of knowledge and power to generate a sense of fatalism.

At the same time, the wide dissemination of information on the problems, tragedies, and threats that plague the world endows this phase of history with grey and dark colours, rather than the radiant features promised by the eschatological thinkers of the past or the true believers in the virtues of technological change. The prodigies of science are heralded by some modern positivists, but the awe they inspire in the popular psyche is only overshadowed by the fear created by undesirable consequences of technological ingenuity in domains affecting health and life in its various forms. The realisation of the deterioration of the environment has fundamentally altered the modern ethos. People are trying to improve their lot and control their lives and more income for better living conditions remains a sound and often achievable aspiration for many individuals and families. But, on a collective level, there is the feeling that the future of the world is determined "somewhere else". And deep scepticism on the durability of material progress as presently conceived is not limited to a few intellectuals.

While the "average world public opinion" has no obvious sense of a "natural" evolution towards a better world, the political and corporate establishment has quite naturally a more dynamic and optimistic discourse. In the speeches of leaders of dominant countries and in the influential world press, global capitalism is presented as the path towards a world of prosperity and peace. The creation of a global market and economic integration through free flow of capital, technologies and goods and services, are heralded as sources of continuing progress. Even before the events that marked the meeting of the World Trade Organisation in Seattle at the end of 1999, this discourse, however, was not as triumphant as might be expected from a project currently enjoying great success. Global capitalism, often perceived as a phase in the evolution of humankind that is logically unfolding in the wake of the European Renaissance and Enlightenment, has nevertheless a sober and pragmatic Anglo-Saxon cultural heritage. Its proponents are not inclined to grandiose schemes. For them, global capitalism is the "only game in town" because it rests on the freedom of the individual and because possible alternatives involving grand planned designs have failed. Their esteem for global capitalism is not as vehement as their dislike for a world government.

To advocate deliberate and purposeful construction of a world democratic order, be it humanist, communitarian, socialist, or even capitalist with a "human face" is therefore to respond to a diffuse malaise and to risk facing a deeply rooted scepticism.

But, many problems requiring ambitious political solutions on a global scale are currently insufficiently controlled or left unaddressed. Examples include the availability of weapons of mass destruction, several aspects of the protection of the environment and the management of resources such as water and fisheries, the control of genetics manipulations and other scientific and technological developments that respond to profit and power rather than the welfare of humankind, the rise of international crime, the spreading of communicable diseases, and in other domains the reduction of poverty and inequalities, the management by all concerned of the question of migrations, and the universal enforcement of the basic rights of the human person.

Such global problems confronting humankind are not necessarily new. As economic globalisation can be traced back to 19th century capitalism, or even to the traders of the Silk Road and the mercantilists of the European Renaissance, problems of pollution across national borders started with the Industrial Revolution almost two centuries ago and the spreading of communicable diseases devastated entire continents, including through imperialism and colonialism. New to the second part of the 20th century, however, is the dramatic historical event that was the development and use of atomic bombs. It showed that humanity had the capacity to put into question its own survival. This threat is still present half a century later, notwithstanding the "end of the cold war". It has in fact been aggravated by the use of science to develop other equally lethal weapons. And technologies for such weapons can be mastered by governments or private groups and individuals. Moreover, many nuclear energy plants are unsafe and represent an enormous threat to vast regions of the planet. The world remains, and is perhaps increasingly a dangerous place.

Also new, and related to the first human step on the moon and the "conquest" of space, is the realisation that the earth is only a fragile and minuscule part of the universe. It is a realisation with profound philosophical, religious and cultural consequences. It can lead to exacerbated forms of anthropomorphism, or to a diffuse fear and sense of futility of human endeavours. For those in search of a renewed humanism with universal ambition, the fragility of earth and life is an added reason for humility, care for fellow human beings and determination to increase solidarity and cooperation in pursuing the human adventure. Such attitude should colour the approach to questions such as demographic perspectives and population policies. The legitimate interrogation on the capacity of the planet to sustain the lives of some seven billion persons in a few decades cannot be addressed as at the time of Malthus.

Major threats to the future of humankind are not mentioned every day in the news and people "live with them". In addition to the "banality of evil", there is in the modern psyche a "banality of doom", that is a mix of self deception

43

and fatalistic cynicism. There is also, a diffuse feeling that science and technology is all powerful and that somewhere are competent and benevolent leaders who will be able to take care of "me" – person, family or nation – if the worse occur. There is no alternative but to dissipate illusions and to increase the knowledge and awareness of both the possibilities and threats that are confronting the future of humanity. Ignorance and escapism have never been sources of progress. In the same manner as local and national communities are learning to confront their problems, the global community has to address its specific issues. In this effort more democracy means more transparency from scientific public and corporate authorities, more research financed by a variety of sources, and more debates in institutions like the United Nations that have a responsibility for the common good. With the exception, albeit timid, tentative and reversible, of the protection of the environment, more consciousness has not led yet to the fundamental changes of perceptions and policies that could eliminate at least some common problems and menaces. Even if this is partly an article of faith, more democracy should help reduce global threats.

Tame and Enrich Economic Globalisation and Competition

There is a difficult but necessary distinction to be drawn between globalisation as a stage in the historical evolution of humanity, and globalisation as a political project steering the world economy in a particular direction. Calling the first a "trend" is to state that the narrowing of physical distances between peoples and the growing interdependence of countries represent both an unstoppable course of history, moved essentially by the application of human reason to the development of science and technology, and a general direction of change that can be navigated by human decision. The "project" is global capitalism, or the application of the ideas and institutions of the market economy to the world as a whole. It is actively pursued by the United States and a number of other governments, from large and small countries, by the most powerful international organisations, and by economic and financial elites. Globalisation is not moved by an invisible and benevolent hand. It is shaped by powerful actors and influenced by a multitude of forces, not all operating in the economic realm. It has tensions and contradictions.

The distinction between the trend and the project is difficult to make because judgements as to what is determined by the evolution of humanity and what is subject to deliberate choices differ enormously on both objective and subjective grounds. Quite naturally, a proponent of global capitalism will tend to blur the distinction, presenting the free circulation of goods, services, and capital as natural a stage in the ineluctable advent of global market, economy and society. Also logically, an opponent of global capitalism will be inclined to play down the weight of the trends and to emphasize the role of decisions taken by transnational corporations and governments favourable to global markets. This distinction, however, is necessary to create space for human thinking and human action. Without it, the "end of history" would be accompanied by the "end of politics". There would be only one polity and one form of political organisation best serving the interests of global capitalism and leaving governments and societies with little room for manoeuvre.

A trend can be slowed down and a project can be debated, modified and enriched. It would seem that part of the malaise which permeates the world, and notably the feeling of impotence that many governments have, is due to the speed and apparently blind force of the process of economic integration and globalisation. There is a seeming no-alternative syndrome. Precautions, objections and possibilities for autonomous actions appear to be swept away. Powerful governments and institutions are setting deadlines and establishing demanding agendas which most other actors have to follow. Limited and strict deadlines always favour the most powerful and penalise the least equipped in knowledge and capacity to mobilise assistance. The alternative to participation, as it now goes, is marginalization. This is one of the major reasons for the protests against globalisation and the role of the WTO and the main international financial institutions that started to mount at the end of 1999.

Should there be a pause to reflect? A pause to build democratic rules of the game and institutions whose raison d'être and survival will not be dependent on a capitalist vision of the world economy and its future? Why not give to the concept of "transition" a richer and more universally applicable meaning that it has now? If no country or region can afford to refuse participation in the common venture, there is a clear need for selective linking processes, according to national circumstances and cultures. The timing of the process of globalisation requires more thinking and more democratic decision-making.

An added reason for a more reflective and prudent attitude is that globalisation, however strong a trend, is not irreversible in its positive aspects. Despite history's repeated examples of collapses of ideas, structures and institutions that were intended to be made to last forever, it remains a common illusion that contemporary achievements are indestructible. The more so for those who are in control of current events. And yet, the process of globalisation in economic and financial domains has serious problems of credibility and durability. Global capitalism creates inequalities and strives on the distinction between winners and losers. The unmitigated power of transnational corporations, the imperialism of financial markets, the dilapidation of public assets and the often grotesque enrichment of some private hands under the guise of the "privatisation movement", the "downsizing" of jobs and the reduction of social protection, the aggravation of disparities between economically affluent and poor countries, and the fading out of the political dialogue and cooperation between the "North" and the "South" – all negative features of the contemporary scene – do not evoke a viable world community. Analysts with no ideological hostility towards globalisation of economic transactions and markets, believe that this movement might generate increasingly widespread and violent opposition, and eventually collapse, if not rapidly complemented by a global social contract and the building of welfare systems at the world level. In other words, the global market economy needs to be rescued from social and political bankruptcy, in the same manner that Lord Beveridge and his disciples contributed to spare Western societies from unrest and revolutions after World War II through the implementation of social welfare and social security schemes. According to this perspective, globalisation, unless controlled and enriched, would be a destructive rather than integrative force, creating dual societies and a dual world.

Competition is a very prominent concept in the modern culture. To be "competitive" is a stated strategy and rationale for action, not only for business but also for nations. Critical domains of domestic and foreign policy appear to be shaped by the need for "competitiveness on the world market". Often presented as a healthy and peaceful alternative to military confrontation, economic competition is indeed less dangerous for neighbours than sheer military nationalism and expansionism.

Yet, a harmonious world community assumes civilised competition. Competition implies rules, whether in personal life, in sports or in the economic realm. Unless controlled, competition degenerates into warfare and leads to the death or destruction of the loser.

Competition should be a means, never an end. A means for the athlete, to push his or her limits, in endurance, skill or talent. A means for a company to improve the quality of its products or services, of its productivity and efficiency. A means for a country, to foster the quality of life of its citizens and to become a responsible member of the international community.

Of much importance are the terms of economic competition. Firms tend to compete with wages and costs. This has strong negative effects on employment, and mergers and concentration of economic and financial assets are presented as required by competition. This approach is not satisfactory neither for the company, nor for the collectivity. "Safety-nets", presented as remedies, are not only costly but disruptive of the social fabric when they involve more than a small minority of the population. An alternative to competition through wages and costs, is competition through value-added. The development of such alternative would require elaborate policies and strategies from the companies themselves and from public authorities.

Control and Orient Financial Transactions

One of the major characteristics of the world economy at the turn of the 21st century is the formidable and uncontrolled expansion of the financial speculative sphere. Financial flows are constituted mostly by short-term capital movements in search of capital gains, and sensitive to exchange and interest rates. Depending on political orientation, this is called "financial liberalisation" or "casino economics" and there is a great temptation for ordinary citizens to consider that the world is presently organised to favour capital and to allow a great accumulation of income and wealth into a few hands. Moreover, fluctuations of financial markets tend to be identified with blessings and catastrophes affecting the welfare and future of humankind. This distorted outlook on human affairs introduces an element of insecurity in the minds of many individuals, including those who have neither stocks nor knowledge of the world of finance. Any situation of factual or coming crisis adds to this diffuse sentiment to create an atmosphere of radical uncertainty.

Financial crises of the 1990s with their dire social and economic consequences have confirmed the misgivings of those who have been saying for years that "financial liberalisation" has been excessive, imprudent and anarchic. In its 1998 Trade and Development Report the United Nations Conference on Trade and Development recalled what it wrote in 1990: "The ascendancy of finance over industry together with the globalization of finance have become underlying sources of instability and unpredictability in the world economy. Financial markets have for some time had an independent capacity to destabilise developing countries; there are now increasing indications of the vulnerability of all countries to financial crisis. The evidence indicates that the costs of financial liberalisation and deregulation can be quite high (...). Overall, there appears to be a need for more collective control and guidance over international finance. (...) So long as the international monetary and financial system remains structurally vulnerable, the potential for an extremely costly crisis will remain" (page 1). At the end of the 1990s, objectives of transparency of financial transactions affecting the world economy and of democratic control of the policies of public and private authorities managing global finance, were still generally considered unrealistic and undesirable. It is difficult to imagine the emergence of a world democratic community as long as the most powerful actors on the world economic and financial scene are not accountable to an institution of elected representatives.

In 1972, the economist James Tobin proposed a levy on international currency transactions in order to discourage short term speculation and introduce some stability on financial markets. The "Tobin Tax" would be on spot transactions in international currency markets. It would to some extent, lessen the problem created by floating exchange rates. Then the idea came that the revenue from such tax could be used for development projects. Estimates made in 1994 suggested that a 0.01 per cent levy could yield revenues of approximately 150 billion United States dollars a year. Different proposals have been made on the collection and control of the proceeds. It would seem important, for moral, economic and financial reasons to revive the idea of such a tax on international currency transactions, to link its use to problems and objectives reflecting a shared perception of the common good, and to base its management on a partnership between nations at different levels of economic development.

More democratic control of financial resources in the world is highly desirable. A case in point is the management of pension funds. Control of these funds is a critical issue in light of the magnitude of the capital involved and the levels of savings required to sustain economic growth. There is also need to explore ways beyond traditional public funding, to broaden responsibilities for public and private investment, and to make links between the public and the private initiatives. As transactions and problems become more international, the question of taxation will become increasingly difficult. Beyond the Tobin Tax, it would be useful to enter into a phase of serious negotiations among the various partners, to open new avenues for shaping the future global society, and to base this construct on a strategy reflecting democratic values.

The dominating role of the media-finance complex has to be replaced by open and transparent governance of the process of globalisation. At this point of time, the "global market" is far from being a universal well functioning market economy. The rise of global capitalism is not a democratic affair. A good market economy is not only an economy of a few producers and a multitude of consumers, but also of people being given an opportunity to make their contribution to growth and the welfare of society. Such a market economy is a most democratic form of social organisation. But, for all sorts of reasons, including the propensity to acquire as much wealth and power as possible, this democratic nature of the market economy has to be constantly protected, restored and promoted through regulations, and incentives. The challenge for the state, and also for regional and international organisations is to keep as good a balance as possible between such regulations and freedom of initiative.

Develop Shared Values

It is necessary and useful to debate the values that are sustaining contemporary societies and that should provide a basis to a democratic world community. This is not an obvious statement. When values are lived, they are not discussed. In an exemplary society, values are interiorised and embodied in codes of behaviour, transmitted from one generation to the other through teaching and through rituals, and there is no need for public debate. In secularised and liberal societies attaching prime importance to the freedom and rights of the individual, to probe into the philosophical foundations of the common perception of what constitutes a good life and a good society is often seen as futile. And even dangerous, as there are always demagogues and false prophets lurking in the shadows of society and ready to exploit uncertainty and fear.

49

Besides, there are institutions with complementary roles: the churches and philosophical societies are made to talk about values, governments are made to govern, enterprises to produce, and media to inform and entertain.

This line of reasoning is strengthened on the international scene by the diplomatic culture. References to beliefs, feelings and values complicate relationships and negotiations and are perceived as slightly impolite. It is with great reluctance that the diplomatic community has accepted to let values be more or less openly discussed in some of the major United Nations conferences, including the Social Summit. And, often, formal "reservations" negate the moral and political obligations contained in the texts adopted by consensus. This is an accepted practice suggesting some cynicism, but also the conviction that it would not serve any useful purpose to expose differences in sensitive subjects, and the hope that the governments who have made reservations may eventually be influenced by mainstream thinking.

Yet, there are a number of compelling arguments for putting values and their evolution on the agendas of national and international fora as well as in the curricula of schools and other institutions of learning.

Most contemporary societies suffer from a number of social problems – criminality, insecurity, violence, drug addiction, alienation of youth, corruption, lack of civic virtue and sense of responsibility – which are symptoms of a bad functioning of the social fabric. Among the causes, is the loss of a clear understanding in the modern soul of the right and the wrong, the good and the bad, the morally acceptable and the morally reprehensible. To consider questions of values is to be realistic and to increase the capacity to address these problems. Justice requires a sense of injustice. Some tendencies, such as a social Darwinism, ought to be denounced. There is virtue in the capacity for indignation, and moral quality in the rejection of cynicism. A debate on values does not aim at "desincarnating" social issues and promoting social engineering.

There are absolute values, derived from the common humanity of all human beings which have to be restated, taught and learned. All barbarian acts, be it torture, murder, slavery, racism, the holocaust, or ethnic cleansing, implies a denial of the humanity of the other – individual, community or race. This denial appears sometimes cold and easy as if all humanity had disappeared from the mind of those who order or commit atrocities. When such collapse of a civilisation occurs, there is no alternative but to start rebuilding, step by step, using all means and institutions, from the school to the media, from debates in all fora to international justice. The universal conscience should not be allowed to be muted, even temporarily. There is need for shared values in the "global village" that has yet to be constructed. The Charter of the United Nations and the Universal Declaration for Human Rights provide a sound basis for the elaboration and continuous improvement and adjustment of the political and moral philosophy that is indispensable to a democratic world community. There is little doubt that these texts meet the approval and active support of all persons of good will. Their universalism is currently hampered by their use as political weapons of domination by the most powerful and by the reactions of those who need excuses and alibis for the perpetuation of their non-democratic methods of government or governance. Also, the development of shared values requires avoidance of double-standards, hypocrisy and selective reading and use of these international treaties and agreements. For example, debates on rights and responsibilities and on individualism versus civic virtues would gain from a full use by all concerned of Article 29 of the Universal Declaration which defines very clearly the obligations of citizens vis-á-vis their community.

It is impossible to exaggerate the role of education in maintaining and constructing humane economies and societies. For the teaching of rules and attitudes conducive to basic decency in social relations, primary schools as well as business schools and universities have critical roles to play. In the past and in all cultures, education involved the learning of a trade and the learning of moral principles and rules of conduct. It is only in modern times that these two areas of learning have been separated. And yet, no society can prosper or even endure without a basic sense of duty and responsibility shared by its members. Societies are humane when individualism merges into community spirit.

Learning to be human is to apply to all spheres of life – economic transactions or political negotiations, personal or social relations – the general principle at the core of all great philosophies and religions that "good must be done and evil must be avoided". Contrary to the claims of ethical relativism, concepts of "good" and "evil" do not vary significantly over time and space. Learning to be human is to give an idealist content to self-improvement. It is to understand that the human person is endowed with infinite possibilities for self transformation and self improvement and to realise that this spiritual and moral quest is as relevant in the conduct of market transactions as in the management of a public agency. It is to recognise that human beings are not merely profit-seekers, political consumers and news-eaters. Learning to be human is to comprehend that the quest for true personal identity and for an open and creative selfhood is predicated on one's ability to transcend egoism. Both for the individual person and for the community, including the world community, learning to be human is to transcend the homo economicus that provides but the mere basis for a culture and a civilisation.

Cutting across these various reasons for adopting a voluntarist and normative approach to the construction of a global democratic order is the fact that there is no example in human history of a laissez faire political philosophy bringing more equality and more fraternity. Laissez faire is above all a theory to secure the positions of the mighty and powerful. All social conquests of humanity, be it the abolition of slavery or the equality between women and men have been initiated against the "normal" and "dominant" current. The immense virtues of the market economy system do not obviate the need to challenge, correct and balance global capitalism.

Before discussing criteria to assess the functioning of market economies, including the global economy, and their contribution to human aspirations, a detour is needed to explain the choice of the word "community", rather than "society" to express the desirable setting of a global democratic order.

Global Democratic Community or Society

The concept of society applied to the world evokes a system with clearly defined and visible institutions and structures setting relationships between its members. A world society implies a world administration, a comprehensive body of laws and regulations with universal intent and reach, a set of procedures for settling conflicts in a variety of domains and enforcing decisions of arbitrators, and a shared understanding of critical moral norms of behaviour. A world society does not necessarily mean the disappearance of nation-states and regional organisations. However, it would require a large transfer of sovereignty from these entities to a world authority. A society, including a world society, is not merely a cold body of legal rights and obligations. But it certainly evokes a world government. A world society also implies decent relations between the citizens of the world, as suggested by the Latin "societas" derived from "socius", meaning "companion", and as still conveyed in some languages.

The interplay of the various actors and forces shaping the current process of globalisation can be seen as a crude prelude to an organised world society. The combination of roles of national and international public authorities, corporations, new world elite, public intellectuals and organisations of a growing international civil society can be interpreted as the beginning of a global system of checks and balances, as the sketch of a constitutional infrastructure for a world government. It is tempting to consider that humanity has been slowly, often through tragic means, but steadily moving its political organisation from the village to the nation, and then the region and the entire world.

Those who prefer to evoke a world community rather than a world society often share such a mix of voluntarism and faith that history has direction and purpose. But community sounds more humane, more spontaneous, less structured, less complex and less coercive than "society". It evokes togetherness, the sharing of a land, or a project, or a faith, the communion in a celebration, the joy of festive conviviality. A community is ambitious in human terms, as it demands tolerance and generosity from its members. But it is respectful of the freedom of each, and relies more on shared values and accepted social mores than on laws and institutions. Members of a community are not expected to fight each other and it is difficult to imagine a community at war with another community. The word has a soothing quality. It calls for consensus and the muting of conflicts of interests.

A world community is a concept and aspiration compatible with different political philosophies. It is acceptable to both the advocate of liberalism and the proponent of national sovereignty. Significant is the fact that representatives of secular or religious organisations with a humanist and generous outlook on human affairs are generally very reserved on the concept of world society. They believe that only a strong civil society – at the local, national, regional, and global levels – can alleviate human suffering and bring to reality an acceptable world order. They do not share the view that a world government would bring good solutions to current problems. They see cooperation among various groups and institutions, including national states, as the only workable and safe path towards a better and more harmonious world. Also attracted by the gradual improvement of a world community, as opposed to the deliberate construction of a world society, are those who are very sensitive to the virtues of regional cooperation and arrangements. They see the emergence of constructive regionalism as providing a sense of security, a buffer to the vagaries of the globalisation process, a sense of direction given to people linked by common undertakings, and a most useful apprenticeship to cooperation on a world scale.

Thus the concept of "world community" reflects widely shared aspiration. It is a concept compatible with the conviction that national states have to be strengthened or even in many cases constructed to respond to the needs of their citizens. Nation states also have to gain or regain enough autonomy and margin of manoeuvre to control economic and financial forces with global reach and power. A future world community should be able to exert a sufficient amount of world governance while respecting the autonomy of its members. The distinction between "world community" and "world society" should, however, not be over-emphasised. To do so would be tantamount of depriving the notion of community from any kind of legally binding obligations between its members, and of identifying a society with the triumph of a rigid rule of law.

Chapter II

Economies to Serve Human Needs and Aspirations

Markets are social constructs. They are institutions that developed throughout history from the realisation by individuals that exchanges of goods and services were necessary for survival and useful for prosperity. Markets are elements of the social fabric shaped by laws, regulations, and the ideas, attitudes and interests of the actors involved. They operate with a mix of trust and legal contracts that vary with ways of thinking and traditions.

Markets are made of people operating within a specific historical context. People, not markets, innovate and use new techniques of production and devices for sale and trade. People, not markets, exploit others, or speculate and manipulate prices or exchange rates.

There are many different types of local, national, regional, and global markets. A market on the town square brings together buyers and sellers of farm and other products. A financer or lawyer participates in the management of the oil market, or the operation of the stock market. There is the "wheat market", the "steel market", or the "computer market", and the "car market". The "Market", as often evoked in contemporary parlance is an expression with an ideological connotation. Of late, this "Market" has been out-fitted with "forces", "constraints", "imperatives", "necessities", "requirements", and even "laws". Such mix of reification and deification of the "Market" does not contribute to the quality of market economies.

A market economy is more than a "Market". As a social arrangement rooted on private property and freedom of initiative for the production and distribution of goods and service, a market economy is a complex and constantly evolving system of institutions, regulations and patterns of behaviour, with many actors, including public authorities. Market economies are instruments to serve human needs. As such, and similar to some other institutions, notably the state and the family, they are indispensable to society. Even at the height of its attempt to centrally control all economic activities, the regime of the Soviet Union had to tolerate some market transactions. And, so far, no Utopian community based on the replacement of economic transactions expressed in monetary terms by another system of distribution has managed to acquire any political significance. At this point of history, the market economy system offers the best possibilities for improved standards of living in a context of respect for the fundamental civil and political rights of individuals.

Market economies, again as other necessary institutions, can function well or less well, can be efficient or wasteful. They can be improved, be made more efficient, more democratic and more humane, through changes in the behaviour of the economic actors. The assessment of the quality and performance of a market economy depends on the perspective and criteria that one adopts. Here, the perspective is the well-being of people throughout the world, the harmony of social relations within and among communities, and the welfare of future generations, particularly with regard to the protection of the environment and the "sustainability" of patterns of production and consumption. A good economic system, or humane market economy, ought to provide opportunities for sufficient income to all people, generate enough resources to enable public institutions to fulfil their responsibilities and promote the common good, and permit participation by citizens, national governments, and other public and private actors in decisions that affect society as a whole.

From this perspective, four criteria are of particular importance to assess the quality of a market economy, including the emerging global economy. These are economic participation, economic justice, economic morality, and economic moderation.

Economic Participation: Promises and Uncertainties

Economic participation is the offering of economic opportunities to a maximum number of people. This means availability of jobs, as well as possibilities for entrepreneurship. Such economic opportunities are meant to enable people to earn an income, have access to the basic necessities of life, and the possibility to make meaningful contribution to the economy and society in which they live. Obstacles to equal opportunities for economic participation include various forms of discrimination, notably on the basis of sex, colour, religion, or social origin, and concentration of economic power, property, knowledge, and other assets.

In traditional economies, where the great majority of adult men were engaged in subsistence farming with the help of their spouses and offsprings, economic participation was neither a matter of individual choice nor an issue for public policy. Only a few crafts-men could think in terms of employment for their apprentices and a few merchants in terms of economic opportunities for themselves and their children. Most people were simply trying to survive. Only the loosening of the regulations and constraints imposed by guilds and corporations, followed by the dramatic social transformation brought about by the industrial revolution, gave a widespread meaning to the notions of employment, entrepreneurship, and opportunities for career development.

Economic historians are competent to analyse and assess levels of economic participation that different societies have experienced since economics became an autonomous discipline and economic policy a priority of governmental action. Here, in terms of historical perspective, it might simply be argued that by mid-twentieth century work and employment opportunities and levels of living were steadily improving in those societies which combined representative democracy and market economy system. The prosperity of industrialised countries after World War II was founded on dynamic markets oriented and supported by public policies. The doctrine of development elaborated in the aftermath of the decolonisation process was also built on the idea that private property and individual initiative should be shaped and complemented by government intervention and international cooperation. Economic "take-off" and employment creation would lift people of "developing" countries out of their subsistence living conditions.

In the 1980s, however, the overall political landscape and the economic outlook of developed and developing countries changed dramatically. Reliance on mixed economies gave way to increased reliance on free markets. Opportunities for entrepreneurship increased in most parts of the world, but unemployment also grew in many affluent societies and the proportion of people of poor countries employed in the modern sector stagnated at a low level. At the same time, the "informal" or "parallel" economy grew everywhere. Financial stability and reduction of public debt became dominant objectives. After the collapse of the Soviet Union, a wave of deregulation, liberalisation and privatisation swept the world. Today, on the eve of the 21th century the market economy system is spreading, but the provision of economic opportunities to a maximum number of people and countries appears problematic. Economic participation can be assessed from four angles:

- Opportunities for entrepreneurship
- Opportunities for employment
- Opportunities for co-management
- Opportunities for involvement in the world economy

Opportunities for Entrepreneurship

The opening of opportunities for a person to exert initiative and creativity in the production and exchange of goods and services and to participate in the economic life of the community is the essence of the market economy system. This entrepreneurship has been recently enhanced by the removal of bureaucratic and other obstacles to private initiative in many countries, including the former Soviet Union, Central and Eastern Europe, as well as China and Vietnam. In a number of already affluent countries, the deregulation and privatisation movement of the last part of the 20th century has unquestionably given more space to entrepreneurship. In particular, the United States, the United Kingdom and a few other countries with a long standing pro-capitalist ethos have become again lands of opportunities. New professions are appearing and in some leading industries, notably the electronic industry, small businesses are flourishing and entrepreneurship is much alive.

Such positive developments for economic participation need however to be nuanced. The "small is beautiful" proclaimed by David Schumacher in the 1970s continues to have a strong appeal in the modern psyche, but with nostalgic or utopian connotations. Concrete decisions of public authorities are generally not favourable to small enterprises. There are, in many societies, administrative and fiscal disincentives, problems of access to credit, knowledge and technologies that are common impediments to small entrepreneurs. Frequently, the "death rate" of small enterprises is, on an annual basis, comparable to their "birth rate". They have difficulties competing with large companies. Political choices, in democratic or authoritarian regimes, tend to systematically favour a concentration of economic and financial power.

The result is that entrepreneurship is associated in the popular psyché with global capitalism and its transnational corporations. By the end of the 20th century there were approximately 40,000 such corporations, with 250,000 foreign affiliates. The 300 most powerful of these corporations accounted for approximately 25 per cent of world wide assets. A large proportion of world trade is done by a few powerful players. Mergers, acquisitions, hostile takeovers became a dominant feature of the 1990s. The most prestigious and influential entrepreneurs constitute an international class of managers, bankers, and financiers operating within the same type of economic rationality and speaking the same language. For them, "big and global is beautiful". And, for a majority of men and women in the world trying to make a living and exert their entrepreneurial spirit "small is difficult and precarious". Together with global capitalism and global entrepreneurship is an "informal sector" whose persistence was not foreseen.

A few decades ago the popular view was that the informal sector, comprising economic activities not officially registered nor taxed, reflected the transition from an agrarian society to an economy in which people would be predominantly employed in the modern sector. Informal, that is small, precarious, and hardly lucrative activities would progressively disappear with development. The actual slowness of this process was attributed to demographic pressures, lack of investment and credit facilities, inefficient public administrations, unfavourable terms of trade and a generally unsupportive external environment. Very few voices suggested that this informal sector was perhaps there to stay.

In fact, the informal economy is still prevalent in the developing world. In Latin America, for example, 85 per cent of the jobs created during the 1990s were in the informal sector. In India only about 10 per cent of the work force is currently part of the formal public and private sector. Overall, half a century after the doctrine of development came to prominence on the agenda of most governments, a majority of the world's population is still trying to make a livelihood from economic activities classified as informal. On average, living conditions have improved in terms of the consumption of a variety of goods and access to basic services. And, there are television sets, movie theatres and the ubiquitous advertising of mass products. But, techniques of production and exchange have, for this majority of people, remained unchanged for centuries, and markets for the sale of products or labour have traditional characteristics which have little in common with the textbook features of a modern market economy.

More surprising is the fact that unregistered and untaxed economic activities have been growing since the end of the 1980s precisely in those economies classified as developed and market oriented. The "parallel" economy, previously considered the picturesque anomaly of a few affluent societies with a relaxed attitude towards regulation and taxation, is now a widespread phenomenon representing probably 30-40 per cent of the national income of a number of developed countries. In these societies, there are people in urban areas who have never known anything but precarious jobs on the fringe of the modern economy. Many are migrant workers. A new phenomenon, however, is the passage backward from the formal to the informal economy which has taken a significant dimension in some societies. Because only a few countries with a socialist or social democratic tradition have comprehensive systems of assistance for those who are not participating in the mainstream economy, lack of opportunities for regular or remunerated employment and increased inequalities in many domains of social life have marginalised numerous individuals and families into an unstable and painful search for livelihood. This social exclusion has been particularly brutal and widespread in those former socialist countries having undertaken "reforms". Many individuals were pushed into the informal sector by losing their jobs in a "downsized" public sector. Under these conditions, the growth of the informal economy suggests not only problems of economic participation but a possible breakdown of social structures and a threat to social cohesion. Opportunities for entrepreneurship ought to be promoted in organised economies and societies. The growth of the "informal", "parallel", "underground" economy is not a positive development.

Opportunities for Employment

To the demographic and cultural factors pushing upwards the demand for jobs are added the ambivalent effects of technological changes on the supply of work opportunities. The prevalent view has long been that innovations in techniques of production, organisation, and commercialisation suppress jobs in some domains and create more jobs in others. Moreover, gains in productivity permit higher wages, shorter working hours, lower prices, and more consumption and comfort for a greater number of people. In turn, the demand for goods and services generates more activities, more investment, more innovations through entrepreneurship. And this virtuous cycle perpetuates itself. Thus, the global proportion of people working in agriculture can decline to less than 50 per cent, while food consumption can grow in quantity and diversity. And, as economies become more diversified, people can demand services – from education and health to insurances, sports, tourism and restaurants – and can find work in activities axillary to these services. Present statistics substantiate this common view. Tourism represented 255 million jobs in the world at the end of the 20th century. In the United States, in the context of a sharp rise in civilian employment – 24 per cent since 1980 – the proportion of people employed in services had reached 73 per cent by the end of the 1990s.

And yet, unemployment and underemployment remains one of the most serious problems in the world. Apart from the increased demand for jobs and apart from the overall problems of underdevelopment in many countries of the South, relatively low economic growth in the North – apart from the United States at the end of the 1990s – and structural adjustments or reform in the South and the former socialist countries, explain at least in part the widespread dearth of socially recognised productive employment. In addition, it is widely asserted that big enterprises will not create additional employment in the foreseeable future; that the employment prospects of persons with low skills are threatened by patterns of production and trade dictated by technological changes; and that, in short, the process of economic transformation has lately become more destructive than creative. The computer revolution has, for example, both created and suppressed jobs.

Moreover, technological progress tends to be concentrated in countries or enterprises which have already achieved technological leadership. Techniques made to replace human beings are more frequently and more massively developed than techniques intended to assist men and women to accomplish their tasks. At the root of this trend is the culture of modern capitalism. Costs are reduced essentially by labour-saving techniques.

Free trade, or the progressive elimination of financial, quantitative and qualitative barriers to the circulation of goods and services across national borders, generates increased competition among the economic actors. Competition in the interest of whom? Beneficiaries are essentially the winning firms, their executives and shareholders. Private investments which, apart from already affluent countries, tend to concentrate in regions with cheap and sufficiently qualified labour, has presumably positive effects on levels of employment in these regions. However, local activities are often destroyed by modern foreign companies with which they cannot compete. But, on balance, global capitalism can claim to offer work and income to people who had remained outside the process of modernisation.

It remains true, however, that the easiest way for international capital to make profit and offer cheaper goods and services is to reduce labour costs, partly by keeping wages lower than productivity gains, and mainly by dismissing people or not replacing those who leave or retire. Not only transnational companies, but all enterprises exposed to competition from businesses benefiting from any type of comparative advantage try to remain competitive on their local or national market by downsizing and trimming their labour costs. The argument, for example, that globalisation has no negative impact on employment in the countries of the OECD because imports from developing regions with the comparative advantage of low salaries represent a small proportion of total imports, ignores the fact that companies "adjust" and "adapt" precisely to resist this competition and to keep their share of national markets. Short of a perfect international division of responsibilities for the production of goods and services and short of perfect international mobility of labour, it is difficult to envisage how global capitalism can have by itself an overall positive effect on work opportunities. It is up to public authorities to set the conditions for full employment through economic, financial and social policies. Key to a humane and efficient economy is a renewed and active partnership for full employment between the private sector and the state. The prerequisite to reducing unemployment and underemployment is to make it a priority and intrinsic dimension of all economic and financial policies.

Opportunities for Co-management

Partnership between the owners of a company, its management, and its employees and workers is often a recipe for economic success and, in itself, a contribution to a humane economy. Many private companies go beyond the law of their land to establish far-reaching forms of participation, co-ownership and co-management. In doing so, they make a most significant contribution to the social fabric. Also, there is a growing part of the economy which is shifting from the production of physical goods to the production of knowledge, information and communication. It would seem that there are elements in the very nature of this type of industry that call for innovative forms of management with loose structures, networks rather than hierarchy, and a premium on the "human factor" and on the capacity to mobilise the best in the brains and hearts of people. During the last decades of the 20th century, however, much more emphasis has been placed on participation of workers and employees in the finances of enterprises and corporations, than on participation in decision-making. Shareholders are no longer exclusively from the upper and middle class of society. But strategic corporate decisions are made by a few, and the growing informal and parallel sector is obviously not conducive to organised forms of co-management. It should also be noted that nowhere in the world have public services played a leading and innovative role in the promotion of meaningful forms of participation for workers and employees. Now that the private sector is focused on short-term profit and expansion and advocates "flexibility" in working conditions, the interest for democracy at the level of the firm or plant is at low-ebb.

Opportunities for Participation in the World Economy

A limited number of countries are involved in the globalisation process. Even if the trend is towards the participation of a growing number of economies in the "global market", the extent of economic integration in the world should not be overstated. In addition to the OECD countries, less than a dozen developing countries were active partners in the process of globalisation by the end of the 20th century. About 80 per cent of world trade was conducted between the OECD countries. The share in world exports of non-oil producing developing countries had remained roughly at 20 per cent during the last thirty-five years. The United States was receiving approximately as much foreign direct investment as it was providing, and the share of Africa was only 5 per cent of total foreign investment.

The leadership of a few affluent countries in shaping the current process of globalisation and economic integration is symbolised and officialized by the annual meeting of the seven major economic powers, known as the G.7 Meetings. The other countries, whether affluent but small or, for the great majority, poor and struggling with a large array of economic, social and demographic problems, are only marginally involved in the management of the international part of the world economy. Many of them are trying to join the movement towards an integrated and open world economy, but they have a limited say and a narrow or inexistent degree of initiative. Together with transnational corporations, and with the participation of some international organisations, a few governments are running the world economy. In that sense, the economic participation of the people of the world and their representatives is very limited. There is currently a huge global democratic deficit.

Economic Justice: Evidence of Regression

Economic justice implies fair reward for one's economic activity, in pecuniary terms, as well as in relation with dignity and social status. Economic injustice stems from exploitation and from excessively skewed income and wealth distribution. A fair distribution of economic benefits is a notion that has evolved considerably over human history and remains subject to various interpretations in different cultures and political systems. Yet, there are some sign-posts, such as the ILO Conventions and the provisions of the International Covenant on Economic, Social and Cultural Rights, regarding for example, "fair wages and equal remuneration for work of equal value". And, the concept of "excessive" in respect to wealth, income or remuneration of capital versus remuneration of work, is possible to circumscribe. Economic justice differs from social justice, as the latter includes the results of redistributive policies through taxation and transfers in cash and kind.

Economic justice evolved during the last part of the 20th century in an unfavourable political context, with social justice and the reduction of inequalities no longer major objectives of most governments. As noted above, in many respects, and with the critical exception of greater equality for women, the secular trend towards a lessening of differences among human beings in terms of opportunities, income, knowledge, and power seems to have reversed in the last decades of the 20th century. From a universalist and humanist perspective this development is morally unacceptable and politically dangerous.

64

The quest for more equality in the distribution of income begs to be resumed for philosophical and political reasons. The concept of a common humanity implies that all individuals are given equal opportunities to exert their rights and responsibilities and to realise their full human potential. From this perspective, reduction of poverty and reduction of inequalities coincide. Politically, no society, short of becoming totalitarian, can survive when some of its members are treated as discardable commodities and as a dangerous group for whom more and more jails are built. The increasing marginalization of people and the increasing social dualism in many societies – and to some extent in the world – are morally indefensible and are threatening not only political stability but the essence of modern civilisation. More economic justice in the world means above all better levels of living and more economic security for all those, communities, families and individuals that suffer from material deprivation.

Reduction of Poverty: Ambivalent Tendencies

Defining the reduction of poverty in modern and essentially quantitative terms, there is no doubt that over the last fifty years a spectacular progress has occurred in the world. Increases in income have brought reduction of material poverty. Social indicators, notably reduction of infant mortality, increased life expectancy and lower morbidity confirm that levels of living have dramatically improved in all regions of the world and for most countries and people.

Over the shorter period of the last twenty years, facts and impressions are contrasted. Though data are scanty, fragile and often nothing more than very rough estimates, it is probable that, as traditionally measured by poverty lines expressed in dollars available per day, the number and proportion of poor people has decreased in China, India, and other large and small countries of East, South, and South Asia. Though gains were offset by the consequences of the financial crisis that occurred in the mid-1990s, notably in Indonesia, Thailand and South Korea, a steady improvement in material levels of living was rapidly resuming in that part of the world. There is opposite evidence for most countries of Latin America and Africa. There, the number of poor people appears to have increased during the last two decades of the 20th century and, in some countries and communities, poor people have seen their condition worsened.

Perhaps most significantly for an assessment of trends, there is little doubt that poverty has increased during the same period in most economically developed regions and countries. In the worst cases, notably in Russia, widespread deprivation is already reflected in aggravation of morbidity and mortality rates and decline of life expectancy, especially for the male population. In other cases, including the United States and Western Europe there is both statistical and visual evidence that the number of destitute people has increased over the last decades.

Overall, there is still a very large number of materially poor people – perhaps around one billion – in the economically developing world, and poverty and economic insecurity are rising in the majority of the economically developed countries.

Reduction of Inequalities: Reversal of a Secular Trend

For the purpose of relating economic trends and arrangements with movements in the level of inequalities, income is a good proxy and its distribution a good indicator. The availability of a personal and disposable income is a requirement for dignity and participation in society.

Among people, during the last part of the 20th century, income inequalities have increased. Over the past thirty years the share of global income of the world's richest 20 per cent rose, while the share of the poorest 20 per cent fell. In developing countries with high rates of economic growth, there is a visible and growing gap between an urban and affluent new class of entrepreneurs and the lowest income groups. In developing countries with low or negative economic growth and policies of structural adjustments and reduction of public services, inequalities have also increased as part of the population – urban and rural – has been further marginalized. In most of the economically developed societies and in the former socialist countries, inequalities in income, job opportunities and access to services have become conspicuous. Often, deprivation and inequalities of all types are compounded by the lavish life style of a new capitalist class and by growing criminality and insecurity. With very few exceptions in small countries with a social-democrat tradition, the last decades of the 20th century have been marked by a reversal of the drive for more equality which was initiated with great strength after World War II. Within the middle-class, women have improved their situation in terms of rights and income, but inequalities between groups have lately become more acute. Obvious distinctions between social classes and lack of upward mobility are again becoming features of modern societies.

Income inequalities between countries are increasing. The gap in per capita incomes between the industrial countries and the developing countries tripled from US$ 5,700 in 1960 to US$ 15,400 by the mid 1990s. By 1994-1995, the GNP per capita in the world was US$ 4,600. This average meant a GNP per capita of US$ 24,000 in the richest countries with a total population of 849 million, and a GNP per capita of less than US$ 400 in the poorest economies where more than 3 billion people live. Such inequalities were still deepening at the beginning of the 21st century.

Exploitation in the Informal and Formal Sectors

The immense majority of people involved in the informal sector are, by modern standards, barely making a living. Struggle for a livelihood and survival is their shared condition. There are no reasons for romanticising economic and social structures and activities outside the formal economy. The informal sector is not without regulations and constraints from a variety of sources, including traditions. Some are humane and helpful to individuals. Others are not. Both employers and employees exist in the informal sector. Some employers are benevolent and fair. Others are exploitative. Forms of "private" taxation by the "boss" of the trade or district can be terribly oppressive.

Overall, labour standards such as minimum working age, minimum wage, health protection, or the right of association, are more frequently ignored and more difficult to enforce in the informal than in the formal sector. Many of these standards were elaborated to protect the workers involved in the manufacturing sector created by the industrial revolution. This historical context does not mean that internationally recognised norms and standards are not valid in different economies and sectors at different levels of modernity. But they are certainly not easily applicable to the small urban shopkeeper in a city of a developing country, or to the worker exploited in a sweatshop. The dignity and freedom of the human person are the decisive criteria for economic and social justice. The fact that fair labour standards are mainly enforceable in the formal sector of the economy is a powerful argument against the spread of the informal sector.

The modern sector, however, is not immune from exploitation and there is disturbing evidence that working conditions in this part of the world economy are deteriorating rather than improving. In the "Export Processing Zones", for example, companies often benefit from tacit agreements that labour standards and workers' rights can be ignored. There were by the late 1990s about 170 such zones, mostly in the developing world, employing 4 million persons, the great majority being young women. Coming from poor families and having no other options, these women accept excessively low salaries. For them, any income represents improvement. In "sweatshops", usually in the manufacturing sector, workers, again often women, are kept in conditions of quasi-slavery with low pay, no security and no rights. People subjected to such exploitation in poor and affluent communities are often illegal immigrant workers. Many sweatshops are known to public authorities and tolerated. Some sweatshops are connected with established national and transnational companies.

In general, with exception of societies with strong trade unions, working conditions appear to have deteriorated in many places. Various forms of exploitation have always coexisted with sophisticated, participatory and enlightened management which instil in employees a sense of trust and involvement in a mutual quest for growth and quality. In contrast to a few decades ago, however, many individuals are more and more isolated and powerless in their working environments. There is little a worker on a short term contract obtained through a private agency can do but accept with equanimity the pleasant and unpleasant decisions of the hierarchy. Between 10 and 13 per cent of workers were in this situation in Western Europe by the mid-1990s and the trend is sharply upward. Also more and more frequent in economically advanced societies, part-time work is often the only alternative and an expedient for those seeking jobs. Though practised in countries with healthy economies, collective bargaining between representatives of workers and employers at the levels of branch, industry, or nation, is under attack. Dismissals are easier, sometimes through changes in regulations, sometimes by contempt for such regulations. I.L.O. conventions embodying the results of hard fought battles for human dignity and freedom are not central enough to the agendas of governments, investors or managers.

Predominance of economic utilitarianism is obvious where neglect of basic worker's rights is condoned for the sake of "comparative advantage". Free trade unions are often prohibited or even persecuted by governments and employers. And unions have difficulties adjusting their structures and strategies to the necessities of modern economies. One reason for this is the decline of the industrial sector where most of the unions emerged during the industrial revolution and the rise of the service sector where workers and employees are more scattered and more isolated. Other explanations are the relative decline in employment in the public services, and the growing importance of enterprises where, with the exception of the Nordic countries, there is little unionisation. Perhaps above all, the widespread rejection of intervention by the state in the functioning of the economy and the belief that market forces have to operate freely are strong elements of the dominant ideology that tend to disfavour the trade union movement. Strengthening the unions and globalising their strategies and networks would provide a countervailing power to global capitalism.

A Modern Version of the Iron Law of Wages

It is sometimes asserted that competition in a context of free trade and free circulation of capital is reactivating Ricardo's Iron Law of Wages, according to which wages will automatically tend to stabilise at the minimal subsistence level. This did not happen until now, as this reasoning goes, because, contrary to the assumption of Malthus, population growth was curbed in the societies experiencing the industrial revolution and workers were able to protect their interests, albeit through fierce struggle, riots, and revolutions. Subsequently, workers organised themselves in trade-unions and political parties. Today, however, through expanding trade, the free circulation of capital and the resulting competition, workers and employees are in a global competitive situation with consequences not only for employment but also for wages and security.

Governments argue that the modern version of the Iron Law of Wages is rendered necessary by the control of inflation. "Downsizing" is defended by employers as required by the rigours of competition on a global market. The resulting stability or decline in real terms of wages, and increased salary differentials within the same company, are hardly discussed. Broadly, salaries of workers and employees have remained stable or have declined in relative terms. In the United States, for example, at the end of the 1990s, wages were on average and in real terms below their 1989 level. Truly enough, the middle-class of these affluent societies did not lose the income gains made in previous decades. But many people are experiencing the unpleasantness of a disintegrating social fabric with its extremes of wealth and poverty, insecurity and violence. Profits have soared at the same time. Capital has been amply rewarded and gains in productivity have been inequitably shared between capital and labour.

A minority of people are unquestionably becoming richer, in the North as in the South and in the former socialist countries, and consumers are gaining greater access to a number of goods at cheaper prices. Most consumers, however, are workers and employees often living on credit and preoccupied with their security and the future of their children. They see that their systems of social protection are under threat, and that there is impunity for some and hardship for others. Those who are laid off are told that times are difficult, competition hard and sacrifices needed, as if it was a privilege to be employed. In addition to frequently high unemployment and income stagnation or decline, there are indeed many reasons for labour to complain about the size and quality of its share of the economic pie. So far, the price of adjusting to increased competition has been paid by labour. Global capitalism has created nouveaux riches and destitutes, overpaid executives and underpaid workers. Since the beginning of the 1980s, the traditional values of equity, equality and justice have been poorly reflected in the spirit of the time and have had a low ranking on the political agenda of most countries. This is not a sound moral and political basis for the emergence of humane market economies.

Economic Morality: A Weakening of Norms

Economic morality is achieved if the economy is ruled by ethical principles, if competition is fair, and if contracts are respected. Market economies are ethical when integrity is a shared value, rather than expediency and corruption; when legitimate economic motives and interests are immersed in a quest for the useful; when the health of the consumer is a respected objective; when technical innovations and new products contribute to the beauty of the world; and when the natural environment is treated with deference. Economic morality means also that taxes are levied in accordance with a fair and progressive system and are used by the state in an efficient and transparent manner, including to promote social justice through redistributive measures.

Economic morality depends on the behaviour of the various economic agents, and this behaviour is in turn subject to a variety of influences, including from public authorities. Decency in economic transactions and social relations cannot be enhanced through legislation alone. It is heavily influenced by examples. Markets, as other fundamental institutions of society, need to be shaped by norms that economic actors are aware of and practice. As a minimum, the sharing of a perception of what is right or wrong in the functioning of markets enables societies to assess the quality of their economic life.

The morality of markets and market economies has many facets, but the modern divorce between legality and morality is at the root of severe problems. Also mentioned here are the lack of morality in the treatment of the natural environment, the moral laxism in attitudes towards taxation, and the growth of criminal economic activities.

The Split between Legality and Morality

Cynicism and morality are at opposite poles with varying degrees of attractiveness for individuals in different cultures. Cynicism is the deliberate and remorseless neglect of morality. Cynics respects the law, but use it to their best advantage and look actively for loopholes through which they can push their interests. The complexity of modern societies and the expansion of markets and economic and financial transactions beyond national borders have created a fertile ground for this behaviour generating a separation between legality and morality. Emphasised by Daniel Bell in the context of a society where lawyers have gained great pre-eminence in most spheres of economic, social and personal life, this split is a most important characteristic of modernity.

Like a few other negative and unintended consequences of the Enlightenment, such separation between law and virtue has its origins in the determination of the Western European philosophers and scientists of the 17st and 18st century to liberate Man and his Reason from the constraints imposed by temporal and religious powers. Freedom and social progress required secularisation of political institutions and laws. These thinkers, however, were deists or humanists who found the moral source of the law in the notion of human nature transcending personal and social differences. Law, reason and conscience were intertwined. Under the influence of different philosophies this link weakened over the last two centuries. Reason lost Conscience and became instrumental rationality. Positive law lost the inspiration it had received from prophets and sages and became a mere codification of human relations.

This split between what is legal and what is moral, as well as between self-interest and the happiness of "the other", and between knowledge and wisdom, was already pronounced when the vision of what constitutes a good society was articulated. Broadly speaking, this occurred after World War II, when ideas on growth, development and the centrality of economic rationality became dominant at the world level. Economics gained econometrics and sophisticated predictive models but lost its philosophical and ethical dimensions. Successively, State, Planning, then Market and Competition were deified. None of these institutions or instruments having the pursuit of morality as a natural objective, cynicism, indifference to anything but the self, and corruption could quite naturally proliferate. It became common for ethical concerns and efficient markets to be conflicting pursuits. There were only a few intellectual and political steps from this perception to the conviction that economics and morality had no common epistemological roots and preoccupations.

Laxism in the Treatment of the Global Commons

The understanding that there are limits to the use and misuse of the planet is one of the few major achievements of the second half of the 20th century. With the help of the United Nations conferences in Stockholm in 1972 and Rio de Janeiro in 1991, many initiatives have been taken, at all levels and in most countries, to modify and tame the traditional Promethean and destructive attitude vis-á-vis the resources that make life possible on earth.

Yet, the battle for more respect for the planet and its bounty is far from finished. It can still be lost in a variety of domains which are critical for the welfare of future generations. The text adopted in Copenhagen by the Social Summit refers to "unsustainable patterns of consumption and production, particularly in industrialised countries". There is still overexploitation and degradation of common property resources with overfishing, overgrazing, excess cutting of timber, air pollution, water pollution and the use of dangerous chemical products. While a number of private companies are pioneering products and types of production respectful of the integrity and beauty of the planet, the average tendency of the firm is to externalise the social and environmental costs of production. The realisation that humankind ought to have respect and love for other species and for nature is a slow process. To this is added the fear that a still rapidly rising population at the world level will bring an intolerable pressure on resources, the ecology, and the human community. Modern and less advanced market economies, including those that have kept a strong central planning, are far from having reconciled growth and productivity with respect for planet Earth.

Avoidance of Taxes Seen as an Acceptable Practice

At least in affluent societies, part of the growth of the informal sector is attributed to the deliberate avoidance of taxes. From an ethical standpoint, a distinction ought to be made between those who are in the non-taxed sector of the economy because of marginalisation and lack of options and those who operate in the same sector mainly to avoid taxes. There is the moonlighter who needs to make a living and to complement his income through rendering services such as painting or plumbing. At the other extreme is the company seeking a tax haven for the official headquarters of its activities. In between are the transactions which, by mutual agreement of the partners, are kept unregistered to escape taxation, notably the value-added-tax.

Legal measures and actual practices to discourage these types of behaviour vary enormously. There are, within societies, inconsistencies suggesting a significant amount of hypocrisy. Lucrative professions have emerged whose open function is to look for all possibilities for profit and avoidance of taxation while remaining in the scope of the legal. This is taking place together with a frequent questioning of the integrity and legitimacy of public authorities and governments, and wide dissemination of stories of fast and large profits in legal and illegal activities. Tax evasion tends to be perceived, in the North as in the South, as a normal undertaking. Governments often tolerate tax evasion by the most powerful individuals and institutions, and tax havens are still regarded as normal features of the world economy. This is a source of political alienation whose consequences for the stability of societies are currently grossly underestimated. Taxation is a form of social integration and an obvious necessity for the financing of public goods required by modern and humane societies. One of the marks of a good market economy and harmonious civilisation is a well-functioning, fair and respected tax system.

The Growth of Criminal Activities

In many societies, illegal activities are growing alongside structured markets. Sometimes, the formal sector feeds on criminal activities. Recorded in national accounts, the building and maintenance of prisons represent positive contributions to economic growth. The huge costs incurred by some countries in enforcing narcotic laws generate jobs and income. There is sometimes too smooth a continuum between economic activities with different degrees of legality and morality. The continuum can be through the same individual: the regularly employed manual worker who moonlights to improve his income, the housewife who cleans apartments or baby-sits for non-declared fees, or the lawyer who provides services to both established companies and narcotraffickers. This continuum is perceived as symptomatic of the complexities of modern life. Realism and profit are also the motivations of the farmer who alternates in his fields one row of grapes with one row of cannabis. A United Nations report estimated the annual turnover of narco-traffic to be 400 billion dollars, or 8 per cent of total world trade, around 1995. In addition, the rise of criminality through the operations of international gangs is another facet of globalisation.

These few illustrations of a pervasive lack of morality in contemporary economies would seem to suggest that global capitalism represents the triumph of the egocentric perception of "self"-interest over the general interest. Issues already mentioned above such as salaries of chief executives, financial speculation, mergers of companies with dismissal of employees, corruption of individuals, companies and public authorities, contribute to this perception of blind and callous pursuit of money and power. Even the states, though deriving their legitimacy from the protection and promotion of the general interest of their citizens, seem more often preoccupied with the preservation of the power of an elite than with a moralisation of economic and financial transactions. There are, however, a number of signs that economic morality is gaining visibility and legitimacy in the modern psyché.

There is awareness that to impose a conception of morality and the common good from above and in a coercive manner, leads to cynicism and exasperation of corruption, and that only a mix of legal obligations and interiorized values leads to personally responsible and socially useful economic behaviour.

The publicity given in various parts of the world to corruption and to the fight against it, is perhaps an indication that it is a widespread phenomenon, a cancer of modern societies. It also strongly suggests that there is a conscience at work in the same societies and that limitations on greed and cynicism are possible. Similarly the related emphasis on ethics, ethical behaviour, ethical codes, business ethics, social responsibility, even ethical accounting, could be interpreted as evidence that greed and global capitalism are trying to sell morality and virtue. A more helpful interpretation is that once more, humanity is trying to find new balances between the mix of constraints and aspirations, weaknesses and virtues that shape the human condition.

Economic Moderation: The Monetisation of Societies is Pervasive

Economic moderation prevails when economic rationality, the logic of market mechanisms, and the use of money as a medium of exchange remain restricted to economic transactions and do not invade all spheres of life and society. Economic moderation implies that enough space is available in the psyche of individuals and the ethos of institutions for the gratuitous, the spontaneous, the generous, the artistic and the religious. It implies that persons not directly active on the economic scene, but pursuing other ventures in the intellectual, artistic, aesthetic, spiritual and contemplative realms, be recognised as contributing to the overall welfare and harmony of society. Consumerism is a form of economic immoderation. So is the obsession with profit. So is the concentration of scientific research in organisations seeking profit and expansion. And so is the focus of public policies and public debates on the avatars of financial markets. Economic moderation relates to the virtues of self-discipline, self-denial, and frugality. Without moderation, market economies slide into market societies.

At present, some of the ideas shaping market economies are not consonant with this humanist ethos of moderation, self-control, and social harmony. The free market ideology treats "the Market" as the organising principle of society, as the ultima ratio of social relations and as the only guide that individuals, seen as consumers, have at their disposal to reach happiness through the satisfaction of needs, appetites and desires. Assuming that the "natural" distribution of good and bad, noble and mediocre moral propensities is fairly stable over time and space, it is the spirit of the time that explains why a society would become more egalitarian or more greedy, more fraternal or more selfish, more harmonious or more inclined to extremes. Today, global capitalism creates and feeds its growth on values which permeate the mentality of people across the world, notably through the mass media and advertising. These are not only attractive but seemingly good values for all individuals. They evoke freedom, initiative, openness, competition and rewards in income and comfort. Even if it were viable, however, this utopia is shattered when means are confused with ends and when profit and economic expansion become dominant goals for individuals and societies. Sound market economies turn into oppressive market societies when states are governed by market forces, when there is monetisation of scientific research, and confusion between happiness and the unrelenting search for satisfaction of individual wants.

The Control of States by Market Forces

Many governments have become docile instruments of market forces, have been instrumentalised by such forces, and have maintained but the semblance of institutions responsible for the general interest and the common good. With technological developments and improvements in comfort and levels of living, the notion of "progress" inherited from the Enlightenment has become identified primarily with economic gains and material achievements. One consequence is that the most important task of public authorities has become the promotion of economic growth. When Keynesian economics, requiring an active role of the state in the management of the economy, fell out of favour to be replaced by monetarist and liberal doctrines, the door was open for the view that the only legitimate role of government was to facilitate the interplay of market forces. Powerful leaders propagated the belief that governments and their bureaucracies, as well as trade-unions were only obstacles to the dynamism of the private sector and that the desire to accumulate wealth and power was a perfectly adequate foundation for a good society. "Deregulation", "liberalisation" and "privatisation" became the pillars of an aggressive ideological drive that transferred to market forces not only the control of economic policies but also the determination of a number of aspects of social life. At the same time, the revolution in communications, notably the Internet, led to the emergence of a new ethos according to which self-organising systems are the best and work to their maximum potential when there is the least interference from outside. This neo-libertarian approach to life and society has very strong anti-government overtones. And yet, only public authorities can reconcile the virtues of the market economy system with social agendas of equity, solidarity and participation.

The Monetisation of Scientific Research

Scientific research is a public good. Currently, this fundamental principle is doubly ignored: in many cases science is dominated by money and the pursuit of profit and is heavily concentrated in the most powerful countries. Scientific research tends to be predominantly financed and oriented by corporations operating according to a capitalist ethos. New products are launched which are not automatically useful to humanity. The monetisation of science and of intellectual property is one of the glaring evidences of the rise of a world market society. The proper mix between the marketing rights of inventors and innovators to profit from their efforts and the ability of the collective to freely enjoy them cuts to the core of the state versus market dichotomy.

A related aspect of this issue is that governments have, over time, assumed a significant role in education and in financing scientific research and development. But the products resulting from such support are increasingly privatised and the recipients of government largess are unfairly benefiting at the general public's expense. Many scholars, composers, physicians and even inventors traditionally created and innovated for the pleasure of doing so and out of concern for the welfare of their fellow human beings, rather than mainly for monetary reward. The current shrinking of public support, the aggressive policies of many transnational companies and the resulting emphasis on markets and financial incentives create a situation where money is the major source of creativity and the major criterion for the application of scientific and technological innovations. This situation leads to absurdities such as scientific journals restricting the intergenerational flow of knowledge by charging fees to graduate students for the right to photocopy scientific papers that are essential reading for career development. And, not only have scientists been given the right to patent new life forms, but more recently they have also been given patents for decoding the functions of various genes found in nature. The monetisation of knowledge and the capture by private actors of functions more equitably carried out by the state and international organisations on behalf of the collectivity can only be reversed through a formidable political and cultural effort to reshape perceptions. The notion of moderation, in economics as well as in politics, would help promoting such cultural renaissance.

Human Dissatisfaction as a Source of Economic Growth

At the core of the conception of progress prevalent during the last half century, are the two central notions of individual freedom of initiative and satisfaction of human needs. Initiative to create products and markets is entirely compatible with responsibility vis-á-vis the community as long as it remains within the confines of a reasonably demanding legal and ethical framework. The concept of "satisfaction" is more problematic. In its original meaning it has the acceptance of something dependable and true, and even the act of doing penance, but self gratification corresponds to the modern connotation of the term. Desires and appetites are never satisfied, except momentarily. This illusive notion of satisfaction is the rational basis for the growth of the market economy. In social and psychological terms, the engine of market economies is fed with increased consumption, rapid obsolescence of goods and services and creation of needs and demands through advertising.

In such culture, satisfaction has nothing to do with individual wisdom, individual creativity and even individual happiness, except in the sense that every human being must have a minimal material and economic base, and a source of livelihood to survive and flourish. Is the obsessive emphasis on satisfaction of individual needs compatible with social responsibility, social cohesion and a peaceful world society? Assuming that technologies will progress rapidly enough to harmonise increased consumption by a growing population and the physical health of the planet, it is unclear whether a world society dominated by consumerism can remain creative and viable. There is no known "sustainable civilisation" without moderation, the search for harmony with the self and the other, and the pursuit of excellence in non-material quests. As repeatedly emphasised by the proponents of global capitalism, to strive for money and more material comfort is infinitely better than to kill one's neighbour – be it an individual or another nation – or to take his land and assets. But a civilisation cannot flourish, offer enough to its members, demand enough from them, and probably cannot last if built only on the satisfaction of materially defined human wants or desires. The main question is whether or not the capitalist ethos can leave enough room for the other pursuits and achievements that are indispensable to peaceful communities and a relatively harmonious world society.

An aspect of this question is that the current understanding of modernisation and development involves a very utilitarian conception of time. Expressions such as "this is waste of time", "time is money", "time saving" actions or strategies, imply a culture with a predilection for achieving a maximum quantity of results within a minimum amount of time. A monetised notion of time is one of the characteristics of a market society. One reason to advocate the use of a less impatient and less materialistic conception of time, notably in public institutions and international relations, is that, as already noted above, limited and strict deadlines always favour the most powerful and the least equipped in knowledge and capacity to mobilise assistance. Another reason for being more lenient with time is that the individual requires time for education and for endeavours which are not strictly related to livelihood. People need time and space for intellectual artistic, spiritual, or simply convivial pursuits. Often, individuals do not give enough time to each other, lose the capacity to listen or to impart empathy because the modern psyché tends to be dominated by short term objectives, to be prisoner of too many obligations and constraints. Freedom is often de facto reduced to illusion under the dictates of the clock. Time is an asset that should often be used with prodigality.

Confusion between a Market Economy and a Market Society

The virtue and superiority of a market economy over other types arrangements is to enable individuals to exert freely their initiative and to work productively to fulfil their needs and enjoy the fruits of their efforts. A market economy is conducive to individual freedom, exchanges of goods and services, and better levels of living. Today, such positive characteristics are well recognised. But there is in the spirit of the time confusion between the market economy system and its virtues and a clear and reasonably comprehensive perception of what life is about and what a good society should look like. Lack of economic moderation transform market economies into market societies. A market society emerges when the attitudes, norms and values attached to economic transactions and economic efficiency invade all domains of public and private life and permeate social relations, normally governed by different codes of behaviour, and when policies are neither informed nor oriented by an ideal and a coherent set of moral principles. In this degenerative process, governments are overly focused on economic and financial indicators and are predominantly influenced by the most powerful economic actors; academic and research activities become dependant on provision of financial resources and contracts from private corporations; public services are privatised and profitability prevails over social objectives; sports and leisure activities are transformed into businesses; and, progressively, individuals have few personal and social relations that are not of a commercial nature and that respond to generosity, love, or simply conviviality.

Market societies suffer from an excess of pragmatism and "realism". Market societies promote social Darwinism, as success is defined in quantitative and monetary terms, personal accomplishment is reduced to acquisitiveness, and institutions responsible for the common good are vitiated by a short term and narrow perception of self or national interest. A global social Darwinism at the service of a global market society leads to global fragmentation, within nations and in the world as a whole. To illustrate this "counter-utopia" a "perfect" market society would have the following features:

The pursuit of material well-being would be a dominant and, for some, exclusive objective; or, in more philosophical terms, a reasonable utilitarianism would be transformed into a narcissistic hedonism.

There would be a cult for money, spreading in all spheres of life and society; informal and spontaneous forms of exchanges between individuals, would disappear and there would be a "legalisation" of most relationships; corruption would be widespread. There would be a weakening and destruction of activities, organisations, and associations of various types which, based on the dedication and generosity of individuals, provide the moral "fuel" without which society and its major institutions cannot function.

Political institutions and processes would decline, together with the notion of service; the function of teaching and educational institutions would also decline. And, the medical profession and health services would be entirely commercialised. Science would be dominated by objectives of profit and power and scientific achievements would be made to serve the same purposes. Traditional cultures and forms of social intercourse based on trust and rituals would be destroyed and replaced by a race for money and material comfort. Various forms of irrationality would flourish together with bizarre cults offering to individuals the false security of a pseudo-community. Crime and violence would plague societies. Ultimately, the market economy itself would be hampered, for it requires, to be efficient, trust and interiorized norms and values.

Chapter III
A Humanist Political Culture

Democracy, local, national, regional or global, requires organised and civilised debates between different political doctrines expressing different interests and perceptions of the common good. On the eve of the 21st century the liberal capitalist doctrine enjoys a strong dominance. As other doctrines with universal ambition have either disappeared, perhaps temporarily, or are not yet offering a real challenge to global capitalism, the dissent it generates has yet to be translated into a coherent political alternative.

A number of countries with socialist and social-democratic traditions that succeeded in combining economic efficiency and social equity offer an alternative to unbridled capitalism at the national level. Contrary to the predictions of neo-liberal extremists, welfare states and welfare societies have resisted pressures to dismantle systems that valorise solidarity, social security and social protection. But, at the turn of the 21st century, and in spite of its remarkable record since the end of World War II, this vision of economy and polity is still in a somewhat defensive position. It does not benefit from the attention of media with a global reach. It is largely ignored by the economic profession. It has limited influence in the major international organisations. Above all, its proponents have so far not succeeded in formulating a set of principles and objectives that would not only denounce the excesses of global capitalism but convey a new message on a just and sustainable world order. At the end of 1999, the protests that marked the meeting of the World Trade Organisation in Seattle showed that the prevalent type of economic and financial globalisation was questioned by many. But this challenge was diverse and diffuse and the intellectuals, social movements, religious organisations which, in the North and the South, are critical of the dominant ideology do not constitute a political force of sufficient strength and coherence to influence significantly the decisions of the world powers.

This situation is illustrated by the regional responses to global capitalism. Leaving aside the United States of America, which is spearheading global capitalism, the other regions are essentially supportive and anxious to join and benefit, or too weak economically and politically to have a voice.

Having recently extricated themselves from oppressive political systems the countries of the former Soviet Union and Central Europe cannot be expected at this juncture to have original views on economic and social arrangements conducive to economic growth and freedom of the individual. They identify capitalism with freedom, democracy, and the standards of living reached by the middle-class of North America and the European Union. Most of these countries are still trying to build their economic and institutional infrastructure. They see their social problems as temporary or as normal features of market economies.

The European Union, as an entity, appears to be essentially trying to build its identity and to establish an economic position on a par with the United States. Some of its members, notably France, see the dominant capitalist order more as a phase of human history than as a solution to social problems. With a long tradition of state involvement in economic matters, they seek to be "modern" and if possible at the forefront of technological change, while wishing to keep their political, social and cultural identities and some of their traditions. Western Europe seems interested in advocating "global capitalism with a human face", or "humanist global capitalism", but the features of this vision of the world economy are still very impressionistic.

The national economies of Latin America are fairly well integrated, regionally and to a lesser extent internationally. Well aware of the shortcomings of global capitalism the intellectual and political community of Latin America is anxious to find a genuine path to the construction of its own style of economic development and integration into the global community. But growing inequalities and social fragmentation are serious problems. It remains unclear whether this region will be able to elaborate a response to global capitalism through a doctrine comparable in its scope and appeal to the "dependency theory" or, in a slightly different domain, "liberation theology".

Before the financial crisis which developed in the region by the end of 1997, the behaviour of Asia on the world economic scene and the level of economic performance of some of its countries were sources of admiration and, occasionally, fear. Images ranging from the "Asian miracle" to "tigers" were mixed with references to the Asian culture and the role of Confucianism and Buddhism to suggest a part of the world with enormous resources, notably human, and the capacity to elaborate and implement very successful economic and political strategies. After this crisis, which affected seriously only a few countries, there is no doubt that a high level of entrepreneurship and economic activity will resume in most of this region. Social structures and styles of development will continue to vary greatly, from Japan to India. And it is uncertain if the "market socialism" of China will have lasting specific features. The "capitalist spirit" is particularly high in that part of the world. Neither in terms of attitudes vis-á-vis the environment, nor with regard to the social inequalities generated by the interplay of market forces, is there much evidence that Asia will offer to the world a different and attractive vision of harmonious development. Asian values have yet to be debated and defined in a universal perspective.

Many African intellectuals are searching for a path to economic, social and political development based on their history and cultural roots. At present, Africa is fearful of being by-passed by the process of globalisation. There is recognition that economic competition is required in many domains of activity, that sound macro-economic policies are necessary, but that those requirements do not account for the totality of the development process. There is the conviction that answers to problems of the human condition cannot be found only in more efficient economies and that Africa can bring to the world more solidarity and richer human relations. Ultimately, the elaboration of an African path to progress is a question of ethics and moral philosophy.

The paradox that has yet to be properly formulated in conceptual and political terms, is that Africa, as other regions, needs to participate in the globalisation process, to be "developed", in the current connotation of the term to influence and modify the world's emerging culture and civilisation, but in the process risks to "jettison" its beliefs and values and therefore its very capacity to play a genuine role. In some sense, all continents and regions, including North America, are caught in the same dilemma. Can for instance the North-American values of individual freedom and entrepreneurship maintain their original virtue when burdened with consumerism and greed?

In any domain, a situation of monopoly in the intellectual, political and economic domains is conducive to complacency and sclerosis. The sentiment that there are no limits to economic expansion and wealth, that truth has been reached, that history has given its verdict, and that there is only one path to progress, is certain source of decline. An alternative to neo-liberalism would help to tease out the many positive aspects of market economy systems from the dangerous oversimplifications and excessive claims of an ideology that currently guides and supports the most aggressive and destructive aspects of global capitalism. It would restore an understanding in the world public opinion of what constitutes a healthy political process. There is need for political reflection and political debates. The question of distribution and redistribution of power has to be seen as an essential aspect of normal political struggle. "Win-win" situations are not common occurrences. A government too anxious to secure painless solutions to problems will systematically favour the most powerful and most vocal social groups. The same applies to international organisations. It is only through dialogue and sometimes confrontation between different political views that the claims of various groups have a chance to be heard and addressed with a tolerable approximation of the common good.

At present humanity is greatly divided in terms of wealth, influence and power. There are profound differences between the rich and the poor, the dominant and the marginalised, the articulate and the silent, the included and the excluded, the informed and the uninformed, the connected and the isolated. When interdependence is accompanied by extreme inequalities and various expressions of resentment vis-á-vis the most powerful, it becomes imperative to discuss norms, values, the concept of modernisation, and to strive for a new political vision of the future of the world. A humanist political culture with a global ambition and a balance between respect for principles and pragmatism has to be elaborated.

Give Power to "Soft" Values

In the dominant culture, "soft" values are compassion, care, generosity, and detachment from worldly affairs. These values are seen as "non-operational". In the Vulgate of the time, what is important and serious, interesting and stimulating, excludes the prosaically fair and just and the genuinely good

85

without anticipation of return for the self. Important values include work, efficiency and the acquisition of money and power. The realist tends to identify sentiments and sensibility with romanticism and weakness. To question the current hierarchy of values is to be a dreamer and irrelevant Utopian. Realists and neo-realists might admit that generosity or conviviality are indeed "nice" virtues whose practice make social intercourse more pleasant, but this would be to add immediately that, unfortunately, "reality" is too rough for responsible people to indulge in such thinking.

Courage tends to be associated with roughness and efficiency with over-simplification. Too often, ethical outlooks and compassionate attitudes are excluded from the agendas of governments and other public and private institutions, as if these virtues were signs of effete idealism and naiveté. And yet, humility and the capacity for compassion have been closely associated with seriousness in many cultures throughout human history. Today, across the world, are many individuals and institutions testifying to a humanistic philosophy of life and society. But they are rarely in positions of power. They are in a pleasant but marginal realm that serious decision-makers like to visit, when time is available, after having made the hard choices imposed by the "necessities of the market" or the "realities of international life". From an Enlightenment philosophy that attempted to bind reason and conscience, freedom and altruism, the Western culture and gradually the world as a whole has evolved an instrumental type of rationality consisting of calculated self-interest, faith in material progress and constant awareness of one's rights.

The current hierarchy of soft and serious values is at the root of the conception of economic rationality and at the origin of the marginalisation of "social" concerns. The "social" is "soft". It is understood as what is relevant for the people who are not in power. It is a "problem" or a mere "consequence" of economic decisions. Hence the quasi marginal status of the WHO, the ILO and the UNESCO on the international scene, as compared with the Bretton-Woods institutions and the WTO. This also explains why major powers tend to downplay the role of the United Nations on matters of economic development and concede to this organisation only some corrective programmes.

The building of a global democratic community requires profound changes in this dominant ethos and a revisiting of the distinction between "soft" and "hard", "core" and "subordinate" values and policies.

The first reason is that societies operating with a capitalist, liberal, and "Darwinian" political culture are confronted with societal problems leading to "solutions" that are in contradiction with the very essence of those same societies. Violence and criminality arising from misery or from a weakening of secular and religious moral norms lead to repression, sometimes the incarceration of a large proportion of the young male population, and increasing recourse to the death penalty, and the disintegration of communities into separated, hostile and fearful groups. As a comparable spiral of exclusion and repression might be unfolding on a global scale, it would seem obvious that, for its own survival, liberal capitalism ought to be balanced by a different, non-competitive, more compassionate political philosophy.

The second reason for seeking enrichment of the dominant ethos is that the values of altruism, care for the beauty of nature and interest in the artistic and spiritual dimensions of life, are as fundamental to he human person as are the values of competition, economic initiative and desire to improve one's material conditions. The relegation of the need for love and harmony to the private sphere and to the realm of the gratuitous and superfluous is not a sign of "progress" in rationality and maturity. Rather, it is a mutilation of human nature and of the requirements of life in society.

The very old and famous "Do not do unto others what you do not wish others to do to you", was taught by Confucius and Jesus in strikingly similar terms, and by other lesser prophets as well. This is a principle of morality stated in the negative that greatly facilitates life in society. In addition, however, since this golden rule of morality has the potential for ambiguous interpretations and can be lived as an encouragement to the pursuit of selfish interests, in both the Analects and the New Testament it is shaped and oriented by an exigent demand for generosity of the spirit, love for fellow human beings, and appreciation of the joy of giving and sharing.

A rediscovery of such basic ideas and precepts of the great religions and moral philosophies invented by humankind would imply a reversal of the current hierarchy between "soft" and "serious" values. This is the line taken by radical ecologist movements. One cannot exclude the future emergence of such a culture, either because of environmental or social catastrophes, or as the "by-product" of technological changes that would liberate humanity from the old Promethean drive.

Short of such a revolution, already fundamental changes would result from consideration being given to both the values that make social life possible and harmonious and the values that enable transnational corporations to conquer new markets and meet more individual needs and appetites. A graduation of equality, civility, solidarity and responsibility from the level of "soft" to "serious" values would provide a strong foundation for a democratic global community. The difficulty in this task should not be overemphasised. It is true that the domination of the neo-liberal ideology since the beginning of the 1980s has been so complete and pervasive that a return to a moderate, middle of the road political doctrine takes on the appearance of a Herculean enterprise. But, after all, some societies with a social democratic or socialist tradition still practice some balance between individualist/productivist and collective/redistributive values. And, ideological change can be rapid.

Leave Room for Stability

As modernity is identified with social change, stability has become one of the "soft" values evoked above. Modernisation is the process through which societies achieve a sufficient level of "routinisation" of the transformation of their structures, knowledge and values. Under the formidable push of scientific and technological developments and drive for individual freedom and well-being, affluent societies are in constant turmoil. They have ignored stability since the shedding of their agrazian structures. Poor countries are requested to "transform", "adopt", "adjust", and "reform" their economies and cultures. Development is equated with change. Neither economic growth, nor entirely beneficial social objectives such as equality between women and men are compatible with stability of beliefs, values and social and human relationships.

During their lifetime, individuals commonly change residence several times and are asked by public authorities and the corporate world to update their skills and to be in permanent disposition for new training and new jobs. Tenure and long term contracts are the dwindling privileges of a few. The merits of long term attachment to a firm or to a public service are questioned. Productivity and individual fulfilment have become associated with mobility. Capacity for innovation, competitiveness and flexibility are highly valued individual and institutional attributes. The predilection for what is new is associated with a cultural emphasis on youth, dynamism, performance in various domains – from sports to the conquest of new markets – versus experience, moderation and fidelity to established beliefs and social mores.

It would be imprudent to attempt any sort of generalisation on the adaptability of human beings to valid and multiform societal change. And even more fallacious to suggest a relationship between individual happiness and change or stability of social structures and mores. At the utmost can it be ascertained that to keep a reasonable psychological balance in a changing environment, individuals need to have intellectual, moral and emotional markers. Localism, or the strong attachment to familiar physical and mental horizons, is often explained by this need.

For societies, however, history and common sense indicate that some elements of stability are always necessary. No community can survive if constantly threatened by novelty in all its norms, values and institutions. Even the United States of America, rightly seen as a society particularly apt at generating and adopting technological and other changes, has so far kept a number of traditional values and institutions. The problem with the current process of modernisation and globalisation is that it seems to sweep away those attitudes, values and institutions providing that "resistance to change" without which societies risk becoming purposeless. When change becomes a value in itself and is automatically identified with progress, there is need for deliberate intellectual and political efforts at finding a balance between the "creative destruction" evoked by Schumpeter and the sort of conservatism, or respect for what has been acquired and socially tested that was clear to political and moral thinkers as Edmund Burke. At this point, the acceptance of change is generally the easy path. The search for elements of stability is a more demanding task.

Accept Different Types of Modernity

A global democratic community should not be exclusively based on the currently dominant conception of modernity. Rooted in the utilitarian and liberal political philosophy of the promotion of self interest, modernity entails a most fundamental and beneficial emphasis on human rights, but also insecurity, inequalities, and difficulties in maintaining the social and ethical fiber of communities. Social pathologies of various types accompany individualism and affluence. A global community would probably be more viable, certainly more interesting, and unquestionably more acceptable to all, if made of a mosaic of "multiple modernities". At this point, debates on various paths to development and objectives of progress tend to be dominated by self-fulfilling prophecies on the "clash of civilisations" and by suspicion of the Western countries that other parts of the world question modernisation and democracy only to justify their lack of commitment to human rights. In such a context, debates on "Asian Values", or on an "African vision of progress", or on a "Latin American style of development" can only be superficial and damaging to international cooperation. But other reflections and discussions are taking place here and there to nurture the seeds of a truly global community respecting various cultures and striving for a joyful acceptance of different views on life and society. In the Western countries themselves are many different conceptions of modernity.

Modernisation has no a-priori positive moral qualities. It is a neutral concept. What is "modern" is what is contemporary, what belongs to the present, or what is of now in its characteristics and attributes, and, often in its intentions. Modernisation can intensify as well as lessen economic, political, social, cultural and religious conflicts in both national and international contexts. For example, the sense of relative deprivation that individuals and social groups can experience is greatly intensified by the glorification of conspicuous consumption propagated by the media. And at the extreme end of the spectrum, weapons of mass destruction are products of scientific development and the modernisation of the military industry.

Modernisation is neither a panacea nor a linear process. It is only a foundation for real progress. A modern economy is not necessarily fair in its distribution of opportunities and benefits. Perhaps because it is difficult to conceive of an efficient and democratic economy which would not make full use in all its components of contemporary technologies, and modes of organisation, there has been a tendency to view modernisation as a simple and clear-cut path to progress and to disregard the relevance of traditional ways of living, social structures and institutions. There is frequent failure to integrate the culture of peoples as a component of the discourse on development and as an element in projects for improvement in economic and social conditions. And yet, in affluent as in poor societies there is the continuous presence of traditions in the modernisation process. Only a superficial look at the reality of

90

social relations and institutions, including markets in diverse forms, can lead to the conclusion that modernisation implies a clear break with traditional ways of thinking and being. A linear perception of the evolution of societies and of progress is not realistic.

For example, the turning from an informal to a formal economy has the two main advantages of giving people more protection from exploitation and generating revenues for the state to promote the public good. But there are various forms of formalisation, and key is the meaning given to the concept of economic modernisation. Although large corporations and powerful financial centres are currently setting the tone in the world economy, economic modernisation should not be entirely identified with this situation. Small enterprises, small retail shops, and small farms can be modernised without loosing their identity and advantages for the people concerned. Some modern affluent societies have indeed managed to avoid excessive concentration of capital, other assets, and work opportunities. It is critical to separate "informal" from small and humane and "modern" from big and impersonal. A modern economy can be made of sectors and activities with very different sizes, types of technologies, styles of organisation, and degrees of integration into local, national, regional and international markets.

The example of the African culture illustrates both the necessity and difficulty of developing different types of modernity. Through colonisation and imported concepts of modernisation, Africa has lost a number of its time honoured values and traditions. In education, for example, the ethical basis of life provided by the teaching of societies' elders has apparently been lost. That teaching had been about personal and social responsibility vis-á-vis the immediate family, the extended family, and the entire society including enemies. Also, a leader was a person who could be trusted. If he was not performing well, he was replaced. Circumstances have, however, changed too dramatically to leave much hope that specific features of the traditional African village can be restored as they were. The trusted leader operated in stable and harmonious societies with few contradictions. The young people did not have to wonder whether it was appropriate or not for them to stay in the village. Options, real or fanciful, were not available. In general, the dream of looking back has to be challenged. Nostalgia, or the desire to live again a partly real and partly mythical past, acquires social and political significance in times of adversity or in times of spiritual vacuity. People mobilised by a sufficiently clear vision of the future, personal and collective, leave to nostalgia only small room in their hearts and activities. People who suffer without hope, or who do not find ideas, convictions and projects that give meaning to their actions and dreams find solace in the evocation of portions of a distant or recent past. When the artistic and political realms are permeated with longing for past harmonies, when the future is no longer the domain of dreams and ideals but is seen with fear or indifference, nostalgia becomes a political issue.

But there is a possible good use of an intimate knowledge of the past and of a sensitive and perceptive awareness of the attitudes, social mores and institutions that are challenged by the process of economic development. Many traditional ways of living do not need to be swept aside as they are actually compatible with economic development and positive social change.

Impatience, simplistic strategies and the lack of care for the fragile and the different are common failings of institutions in charge of developing and modernising. Some respect for the past and an active interest and love for peoples and their traditions and ideas would help to avoid mistakes perpetrated in the name of a simplistic notion of modernity.

Reconcile the Local and the Universal

There is a resurgence of interest in primordial ties stemming from community, language, gender, land and faith. These are powerful forces constructing cultural identities.

Localism is the urge of individuals and groups for a concrete and physically and psychologically limited expression of their interests, emotions and aspirations. It takes the form of attraction for the notion of community as applied to an area small enough for people to interact, or to an idea precise enough to generate a sense of common pursuit. The quest for roots is ubiquitous. For the better, because the capacity to live in harmony with oneself, others, and the world is strongly related to a sense of identity and security. And because languages, traditions, religions, arts and ways of relating to others and to the universe are precious expressions of the richness of humanity. Far from being obstacles to a sense of the universal and to a world view of the problems to be addressed, attachments are necessary building blocks for the emergence of shared values on a planetary scale. Fear and insecurity, rather than deep feelings of "belonging" lead to destructive surges of nationalism and racism. There is a positive link between localism and universalism through a sense of security.

The quest for roots is also for the worse, however, because what is primordial and fundamental can easily become nationalistic and chauvinistic. An emotional and political involvement with familiar local or national issues and horizons can lead to parochialism. There is no automatic passage from the local to the "global" village. One could foresee the emergence of a world fragmented into a multitude of communities of various sizes, more or less democratic and more or less affluent, with real economic and financial power being exercised by transnational corporations supported by governments and international organisations. Those believing in the virtues of a global democratic community have to develop counter forces. The concept of cultural diversity itself is not obviously compatible with a humanist perspective of history and society. Cultural diversity and the rights of women is a case in point. From an universalist point of view, and applying the principle that human beings have inalienable rights cutting across differences, there is no doubt that it is sometimes impossible to promote both human rights and cultural diversity. And, from the same perspective, there is no doubt either that the promotion and protection of fundamental human rights is an absolute value, an ethical imperative transcending all other personal, political, economic or cultural considerations.

Since cultural uniformity would impoverish humanity, it is necessary to reconcile various forms of universalism – from economic exchanges to the promotion of human rights – with respect for a large diversity of languages, ways of thinking and social mores that enable individuals and communities to maintain a sense of belonging to familiar psychological and physical roots.

The question of languages deserves a few more comments. There are currently in the world around 5000 languages that are alived and practised. This number is however rapidly declining and a global community should have the objective of protecting these languages. A lot of imagination and efforts are required to see the possibilities of combining the linguistic diversity that should be preserved with the meeting of the communication needs of the global community through a common language, which is currently English. To make this international language contribute to the construction of a peaceful world, a suggestion is that a team of people of various disciplines could work on a "Dictionary of the future international language". Together with the development of linguistic studies and the use of the modern technologies for translation, such an effort would be a critical contribution to the slow and difficult emergence of an international and global community. The 20th century has been a great polluter of languages. Concepts and words such as "equality", or "nation", or even "freedom" have been misused for reasons of deliberate manipulation of people. The current difficulties of political life and the lack of credibility of political institutions are partly explained by this pollution of the language. Also, it seems that only clear concepts and well formulated ideas can be easily translated in other languages. For example, "community" is translatable without difficulties, whereas "government" has no equivalent in many languages because the concept came late in the history of humanity and has different meanings in different cultures. By contrast, it can also be observed that in all languages there is a word, such as "the sacred king" that conveys the symbolic idea of the unity of a society. To a degree, the expression "world community" has currently this connotation. Another relevant observation is that the idea of a universal language – in a recent past the Esperanto – has been resolutely opposed by dictators and tyrants, including Stalin and Hitler. The existence of an international language is a strong antidote to despotism, particularly in an era of virtually universal possibilities for communications.

The development of a culture with a harmonious mix of universal, regional and local values is as necessary as it is difficult to conceptualise and implement. People have to be given a chance to reconcile affection for familiar mental and physical surroundings with attraction to new and distant undertakings. The United Nations, the UNESCO and other relevant organisations must deal with these issues with the same energy and commitment displayed by the IMF and the WTO when addressing structural adjustments and the removal of trade barriers. Undoubtedly, the tensions between internationalism cum globalisation and localisation cum marginalisation followed by alienation and violence are formidable challenges. When considering such issues, a mix of perspectives is necessary to provide for the tolerance and respect for the other without which cultural diversity can only be a source of conflicts. Intellectual curiosity, which promotes the desire to learn and expand one's horizons is critical for individual fulfilment and collective harmony. The cultural richness of the world will have a better chance to be enhanced when debates on development and social progress are slightly less diplomatic and more resolutely Socratic.

Develop Solidarity

Solidarity is a universal concept that should become a universal value. It has several dimensions.

Solidarity connotes protection and security. A family, a village, a tribe, a nation requires the solidarity of its members to survive, to secure its welfare. This implies specific forms of organisation, an allocation of responsibilities and a system of rewards and sanctions. Security of the individual and loyalty to the group are the two faces of the same social bond. In that elementary sense, solidarity is the most fundamental social requirement and there is no society without solidarity.

Solidarity also connotes the cohesion of a group of people sharing common conditions and common interests and cooperating to improve their position in society. This active form of solidarity, at the national and international levels, has been the vehicle for much progress in the human condition and for all movements towards more equality and social justice.

Solidarity within regions has taken very concrete and powerful forms during the last part of the 20th century. Its driving force was the conviction that a liberalisation of trade relations would bring economic and political benefits to the countries involved. By the mid 1990s, there were 62 regional trading arrangements, 40 having been set up in the 1990s and 11 in the 1980s; some of these were bilateral free trade arrangements between minor trading nations, while others, notably the European Union and the North American Free Trade Arrangement, accounted for preponderant shares of world trade. The contribution of constructive regionalism to a global democratic community is evoked later.

Solidarity with past and future generations has been a central value of most cultures and remains so for a few. It took the form of elaborate rituals for the cult of the ancestors, of respect for the experience of the elderly, and of care for the education of the young. The transmission to the new generation of both social mores and a hospitable physical milieu was a central preoccupation. This type of solidarity has been considerably eroded in the Western rationalist culture dominated by the utilitarian and the short term. This culture tends to hide death, to privilege innovation over experience and wisdom, and to idolise rather than teach youth. Lately, however, solidarity with future generations has been renewed by a growing consciousness of the damages inflicted to the environment.

Solidarity among groups and social classes with different levels of wealth and income is expressed in the payment of taxes, which is the main instrument for redistributing income from the affluent to those in need. Taxes have been, throughout history, a reason for revolt and a manifestation of civic virtue. Recently, in affluent societies, there has been a strong intellectual and political movement to denounce taxation as evidence of inefficient and malevolent government. There is an obvious correlation between this trend and the aggravation of inequalities. This issue is mentioned above in the context of the search for economic morality.

Solidarity is related to charity and fraternity. Charity has been much devalued in the modern psyche. For its detractors, charity provides satisfaction to the giver, only temporary relief to the plight of the receiver, as well as dependency and expected gratitude. It contributes to maintenance of the status-quo in social and political terms. Solidarity itself is being criticised as being too close to charity. Yet, charity should be, and often is, a disposition of the heart and mind, a capacity to love the other, rather than a political statement of superiority and an alibi for the perpetuation of inequalities. Charity is a virtue, not a policy. An act of love, not the fulfilment of a duty. In that sense charity provides a moral foundation for the search of justice and solidarity.

The Oxford Dictionary of Philosophy describes fraternity as the missing and forgotten aspiration. It suffered from the misuse of ideals and utopias that occurred during the 20th century. It was always difficult to reconcile fraternity with liberty. Even more difficult was the compatibility of the concept of fraternity with a culture of self-gratification. Fraternity was also set aside by social sciences. It was not a category that a narrowly utilitarian and quantitatively obsessed perception of economics could accept. And the sociological discourse preferred more "technical" concepts such as "social integration". Now that moral philosophy as a discipline and a dimension of the public discourse is regaining favour, and now that many societies are shaken by disintegrating forces, the concept of fraternity might be reopened. The emphasis on solidarity is a step in this direction.

At the international level, in its most commonly accepted meaning, solidarity expresses itself through gifts in money and in kind, notably in cases of natural or other disasters. One view is that on the international scene the concept of solidarity should be used only for this sort of occasional and specific assistance to people or countries in distress. Beyond this, international cooperation for development ought to be based on mutuality of interest, partnership, and fairness in the elaboration and implementation of the "rules of the game" for trade, investment and other types of exchange. For this school of thought solidarity evokes charity which is not an acceptable base for international relations. And also, why solidarity and not interdependence? In what way is solidarity a better concept than a true partnership? What about the ambivalent relationship between solidarity and old and new forms of conditionality?

Another view is that, indeed, solidarity cannot be a substitute for the struggle for fair economic arrangements and for economic justice, but that there is room for both. As in relations between social groups and classes in a national setting, even the best and most equitable world economic order would not eliminate situations requiring the expression of solidarity. Moreover, while there is indeed a contradiction between economic justice and solidarity, because solidarity implies inequalities, it can be a useful contradiction. To keep a tension between two poles of international cooperation for development enables the partners to find room for manoeuvre, negotiation and progress. Of course, this is possible only if a clear distinction is kept between these two modes of cooperation.

Having a strong emotional appeal, solidarity can be used as a mobilising force for a number of worthwhile causes, and can also be distorted and perverted. Young people have a particular capacity to experience solidarity, which expresses the joy of giving and the satisfaction of being human with other humans. But there is also solidarity in a gang and in organised crime. And authoritarian leaders call upon their people for discipline and solidarity.

Overall, while being a value in itself because no human being can live in isolation, solidarity has to be always seen in relation with its raison d'être and objectives. Its worth has to be assessed in relation with the attitude and behaviour of those who are, individually and collectively, partners in solidarity. Willingness to exchange, humility to accept criticism, ability for self evaluation, interest in the views and cultures of others, are, in addition to the capacity to give, necessary ingredients for a true culture of solidarity. It is because of these basic moral norms, valid for individuals as well as for institutions, that there is a continuum between various forms and expressions of solidarity. For example, there is a clear correlation between the willingness and capacity of a country to build solidarity among its citizens, and the interest of the same country to show solidarity at the international level. Ultimately the one – individual, group or nation – who gives, for whom solidarity has in traditional terms, a cost, is made richer – morally, intellectually and spiritually – by the very act of giving.

Make Self-interest Contribute to the Common Good

The existence of a continuum between the interests of individuals and the interest of the community is the central hypothesis of liberalism, in economics as in society. And the utilitarian philosophy has the same core. But both wonderful and horrendous things have been done on behalf of perceived self-interest by individuals, states, and other institutions. At one extreme, self-interest negates the existence of the other, pushes aside all obstacles to the satisfaction of needs and desires. At another extreme, self-interest leads to sanctity and to the identification of self-accomplishment with service to the community. More commonly, self-interest can be conceived narrowly or generously. For example, a person responsible for a private business might consider that self-interest means maximisation of profit within the law, but without particular care for the welfare of employees, the effects of production on the environment, and of products on consumers. Another person in the same position might go beyond the letter of the law. The challenge for individuals, society and the world community is to push the perception of self-interest as close as possible to the common good.

The Western persona, now dominating the world culture, was progressively freed from the tutelage of various authorities – including the church and the family – and told that self-accomplishment was a legitimate and worthy objective of life. Such liberation was and remains the source of much creativity and innovation. Today's scientific and economic development would not have been possible without the human mind having been freed from ancestral superstitions, taboos and other constraints. The same Western persona, however, was also told by parents, teachers and the shared wisdom of vox populi,

98

that there were duties to be accomplished and rules to be respected within the family, the community, and vis-à-vis humanity at large. As reason remained linked with conscience, freedom was not separated from responsibility. Acts of generosity and devotion to the common good were clearly not exceptional occurrences.

Is this Western ethos pandering to the easy, egoistic and ultimately most self-destructive instincts of the human psyche? The difference between "lower" and "higher" aspirations, the selfish and the generous, the noble and the mediocre, certainly needs to be taught and appreciated by both individuals and societies. During the 20th century, however, a number of influential intellectual currents have virtually negated the relevance of the distinction between the right and the wrong, the beautiful and the ugly, and the true and the false. And, yet, the search for the common good has to be a central feature of a new humanist culture.

A new global political project would require a strong ethical basis, clear moral orientations, and an enriched vision of the direction and components of progress for humanity. It would aim at compassionate states, humane markets and a decent world order. It would treat economic development as a means for human welfare. It would liberate public institutions from the embrace of pure capitalism and demonstrate that politics and ethics are compatible.

A new political project would have to be universal in its conception and ambition. The point of departure is the growing interdependence between countries and regions, and the globalisation of many techniques and institutions. Rejection of the globalisation of many facets of human activities and aspirations would be absurd and unwarranted. Ideas, social movements and eventually political forces will take shape in national settings and produce alternative visions of social progress, but the international and global dimensions of such undertakings are inescapable.

The same political project for a humanist world order will have to see development in its totality. Not only "do not harm", but positive policies are required by the magnitude and complexity of modern problems. States will have to develop institutions accountable to the people they serve. The current view that public goods, apart from the military, are not part of an efficient economy will have to be fundamentally revised. At the global level, the principle of the organisation of the provision of certain types of public goods was accepted well over a century ago when the first international regulatory agencies were established in postal communications, civil aviation, weather monitoring and labour standards. Now many other domains, ranging from the protection of the environment to the control of financial markets, and from the prevention of international competition over tax rates to the control of certain pandemics, are global public goods.

Those with the most power have also the greatest responsibility to serve humankind and promote the common good. For the governments of the most affluent and powerful countries, the exclusive pursuit of national interest is a dangerous anachronism. Similarly, the leaders of large corporations cannot be motivated only by the search for profit. As a minimum, they have to consider the welfare of their employees and the health of their consumers. Economic globalisation creates opportunities that are much emphasised. It also entails duties and responsibilities that have yet to be clearly formulated and understood. The same applies to the leaders of the media. The realm of power and politics can no longer be limited to professional politicians and elected representatives or presidents. And the responsibility for the common good can no longer be solely entrusted to the organisations of the United Nations system.

To fight for global democracy is to be convinced that a more inclusive political culture will greatly help to address the problems of the time. In modern history, great nations and civilisations were built by giving opportunities to a maximum number of people. Why should it be different for the construction of a harmonious world community, when there is so much richness in various cultures and so much human decency and goodwill waiting for a chance to make a contribution? In that context, global capitalism can represent a part of a mobilising democratic utopia. But that part will only be useful if subordinated to a political project embracing the spiritual and artistic dimensions of life as well as the material aspects of the human condition.

Call Upon Ideals and Utopias

For there is need for enriching ideals and mobilising utopias. Without a normative framework, public and private policies tend automatically to conser-

100

vatism. Norms are benchmarks that are necessary to assess a particular situation, for example the consequences of the merger of transnational corporations, and to delineate the contours of an intended policy, for example the reform of the international monetary and financial system. Human actions follow the dominant current, made of habits of the mind and heart, unless shaped by ideas stemming from dissatisfaction with the existing order. Along the course of human history, prophets, intellectuals and militants introduced in the political discourse norms and ideals, for instance of equality and dignity of all human beings. And a number of governments made radical changes in the distribution of resources and power among their citizens. Today, normative issues on the global scale are raised mostly by social movements, particularly through the United Nations. States are generally too exclusively concerned with economic issues and interests to exert properly their normative function. Perhaps partly because they have become managers of candidates at public functions rather than providers of ideals, political parties have limited influence on the spirit of the time. There is a loss of political space, related to a large expansion of "capital" space.

This secularisation of human dreams and institutions has liberated considerable energy for the improvement of the material aspects of the human condition. At the beginning of the process of secularisation, societies became extremely creative. Space for human freedom was used most productively if not always most peacefully. Many cultures had their Confucius, Erasmus, Thomas More, or Montaigne, their heroes of the advancement of the human spirit. Once achieved, however, secularisation brought an element of intellectual and moral disarray, as if spiritual richness required battles against oppressive powers. To find a renewed sense of purpose and at the same time to avoid nostalgia and reactionary schemes that put individual liberty in a straight-jacket, religious and scientific institutions and persons of good will should join politicians and public intellectuals in debates on common values and concepts that could nourish reflections on the future of humanity. The input of modern science in this intellectual and moral quest is essential. There is, for example, need to consider the principle of "entropy" according to which the universe was, from "the beginning", made to render possible the appearance of human beings. In this perspective, destruction of the human species, for instance through a nuclear holocaust would be absurd, even suicidal for the whole universe. By its scientific observations, humankind helps the universe to exist. Related is the view that terrible catastrophes are provoked by the sui-

101

cidal tendencies of civilisations ignoring the goal of self preservation. Excessive materialism may be a form of suicide, individually and collectively.

To ignore or reject as sentimental the quest for basic decency and generous idealism that exists in all human beings and all cultures is not a proof of realism. It is rather a convenient excuse for selfishness, cynicism, intellectual laziness and spiritual atrophy. Democracy, in that sense, is an active and organised expression of the faith in the capacity of all human being to be fully human, to do well, and to do good. Authoritarian or elitist regimes stem from a pessimistic view of the human capacity for rationality and virtue. Oligarchic or plutocratic regimes are based on the idea that those who have wealth also have a legitimate claim to power. Democracy rests on the conviction expressed in Article I of the Universal Declaration of Human Rights: "All human beings are born free and equal in dignity and rights. They are endowed with reason and conscience and should act towards one another in a spirit of brotherhood". The pertinence and applicability of such principles is not radically altered when attention moves from local to national and global democracy. Only practical arrangements raise, obviously, dramatically more difficult issues.

It is time to rehabilitate ideals and utopias. A look at utopian work, and particularly at the first produced by Thomas More at the beginning of the 16th century, shows that the important function of such endeavours is criticism of the established order. Thomas More's Utopia begins with a thorough and vigorous denunciation of the negative aspects of the English society of the time, including for instance the use of the death penalty to punish people forced to mendicancy and burglary by changes in economic laws and structures promoting the interests of the rich landowners. This type of criticism would not have been so pointed and so effective had not More, or for that matter Erasmus, or Karl Marx three centuries later, been stimulated by a clear perception of a desirable or ideal social order. Leaving aside alternative visions of Humanity and Society, reformism itself requires a coherent framework of assumptions and objectives so as to be more than an irrelevant commentary on the dominant order of the day. For example, not to have a precise view of an acceptable level of income inequalities is to condone the current excesses of wealth and poverty. After all, global capitalism is in fact a utopia – "prosperity and happiness for all" – often disguised into a natural phase in the evolution of the world economy.

Utopias, ideals and dreams are necessary ingredients in the individual psyche and in the culture of a society. It is often noted that young people need aspirations to fulfil, and ideals to serve. Including, and perhaps above all to help their fellow human beings in distress, men and women of different cultures need to share some convictions and beliefs in what ought to be done to improve the human condition. A message of material prosperity and entertainment through the modern techniques of communications is not sufficient. The building of democracy and social justice on a global scale should be a mobilising utopia relevant to the third millennium.

Measure Social Progress and Social Regress

Good statistics are as necessary as mobilising ideals to a new humanist political culture. Education and the dissemination of knowledge being critical conditions and expressions of democracy, statistics on the well-being of individuals and the functioning of society are indispensable ingredients of efficient government and informed citizenship. Reliable statistics produced by public agencies operating with a scientific ethos are unmistakable evidence that a society has reached a high level of overall development. The same applies to the international and global level. The ambitious objectives of the Social Summit, with regard to the elimination of absolute poverty, the promotion of full employment, and the fostering of social integration, would have a better chance of implementation if supported by accurate and comprehensive statistics and indicators.

This was recognised in the text adopted in Copenhagen in March 1995. In the Declaration, the commitment on the significant increase and efficient use of the resources allocated to social development includes the pledge by national governments to "ensure that reliable statistics and statistical indicators are used to develop and assess social policies and programmes so that economic and social resources are used efficiently and effectively". In the Programme of Action are references to the "development of methods to measure all forms of poverty"; to "strengthening international data collection and statistical systems to support countries in monitoring social development goals, and encouraging the expansion of international databases to incorporate socially beneficial activities that are not included in available data"; to "developing quantitative and qualitative indicators of social development, including, where possible, disaggregation by gender"; and, to strengthen "the United Nations system's capacity for gathering and analysing information and developing indicators of social development".

The current situation, in terms of availability of statistics and indicators on the various facets of the human condition, is far from satisfactory. Statistical concepts and techniques had progressed remarkably during the 19th century and the first part of the 20th century. By contrast, neither governments nor social scientists gave much attention to this fundamental aspect of "good governance" during the last decades. In many countries, statistical offices have little capacity to collect and analyse data. They are often "informed" by international agencies and publications of the conditions prevailing in their own societies, be it growth of national product or rate of infant mortality. And those agencies, having themselves very limited means, produced such data through extrapolations and educated guesses.

Reports and publications with statistics and indicators aiming at expressing the concerns of the international community, or having a normative approach to a particular problem, should reflect new concerns as rapidly and accurately as possible. From the perspective of the common good – regional or global and as defined by the organisations concerned – there is scope for defining and quantifying social progress and social regress and scope for bringing new issues to the attention of the public. During the last 50 years, there were two very important innovations in the domains of the protection of the environment and the question of gender equality. New data were collected and these major concerns of the time are progressively reflected in statistical compendiums and publications aiming at describing the current state of the world. In addition, new indexes were constructed to complement or challenge the GDP.

This is not sufficient to conclude that international statistics and indicators are reflecting the state of the art in various social sciences. In fact, statistics and related publications with a global reach and influence on the determination of the international agenda give an impression of excessive stability. Statistics on the functioning of the economy are still the most complete and the most visible. They continue to provide the sole indicators of the overall condition of a country. Data on the various facets of the globalisation process are missing, or if collected, not presented with traditional statistics on the world economy or on development. Data on the protection of human rights and, in general on political development and the functioning of public institutions are also missing or confined to specialised publications that do not influence the dominant discourse on human affairs. Statistics on issues of distribution remain of limited scope and exist only for a small number of countries. Data on economic participation are poor. They are even poorer to measure economic justice, and inexistent to assess economic morality and economic moderation. The notion of "regress", in economic or social terms does not seem to be part of the on going reflection on statistics and indicators. This overall state of affairs represents an obstacle to more democratic debates on the international agenda, its determination and the design of related policies.

In addition, there are problems of quality and reliability of internationally produced or compiled statistics and indicators. Fragile data, for example on poverty, even if initially presented with the proper qualifiers, tend to acquire a "political life" of their own and to be treated as verifiable truths. Statistics on phenomena open to different interpretations, for example the speed of urbanisation or the growth of "services" in the economy, are de facto presented as signs of development and progress. The legitimate desire to include in publications statistics from a large number of countries and the reluctance to admit that some situations are too radically different to be measured with the same concepts and data, lead to senseless comparisons, for example of rates of unemployment or levels of income. Statistics or indicators on different aspects of socio-economic conditions are presented sequentially and suggest correlation, or cause-effect relationship, or at least vague association between variables that may or may not be linked. A case in point is the juxtaposition of rates of economic growth and rates of infant mortality. Most frequently, the value-judgements that underlie the selected statistics and indicators are not made explicit. Even more damaging for the credibility of data and their producers, sometimes different international and regional organisations, different agencies of the United Nations Systems and even different departments or programmes of the same organisation publish divergent data on the same subject, or use different concepts and methods to capture statistically the same problem. Overall, and perhaps as an oversimplification, it could be argued that bad statistics and spurious indicators are disseminated with great energy and success, whereas serious data and analyses remain "confidential".

In sectoral domains such as trade, or health, or education, as well as in domains cutting across specific issues and pertaining to the foundations of societies, notably demography and economic activity, international organisations perform an essential public service in producing and disseminating, generally free of charge, statistics of general interest. This production is a critical component of information of the public, of teaching, of research work, and of debates at various levels. It has no normative intent, except to contribute to the enlightenment of those who care to read and use it. It has, by necessity, a conceptual framework which reflects ideas and values on what matters or not in human affairs and in particular domains of social life. For the authors of such statistics and related commentaries, "progress" is simply better quality of the product and hence greater contribution to knowledge. There is some evidence that a number of organisations have increasing difficulties in the discharge of this critical public service. Resources are scarce for an activity that is not spectacular, nor publicised, and for which there is no lobby. In the United Nations, only the regular budget is appropriate for the financing of this statistical work, and this budget is dwindling. Pressures are high for "commercialising" this activity and therefore setting prices that limit access to publications and data. To a large extent, the problems faced by organisations undertaking basic statistical work are comparable and linked to the situation of research institutions that are not attached to the private business sector, nor relevant to the military apparatus.

And yet there is no doubt that institutions that are public in their status and financing, but protected from government interference in their work, and shaped by a culture of objective search for the truth and service to the community, are the best suited to produce good statistics and good related reports. There are examples of such institutions in countries with long traditions of liberal democracy and public service. With adaptations due to technological developments and regional circumstances, a "model" is available. Problems of implementation of such a model are acute but not insurmountable. Apart from questions of resources and technical cooperation, are issues of independence and integrity in the context of the changing relationships between the public and private "sectors", the evolving notion of national sovereignty in relation to supranational organisations with a regional or global mandate, the increasing role of the media in the formation of judgements of people on their society and the world, and the challenge that various forms of fundamentalism – and therefore lack of respect for facts and data that contradict dogmas – pose to the quest for democracy.

To measure social progress and social regress, debate of their components and act accordingly nationally and internationally, social reports, taken in the broad sense of documents describing with the support of statistics and indicators the main aspects of living conditions and facets of the functioning of societies, should be encouraged. There are famous historical examples of reports and inquiries having had a strong and lasting influence on the spirit of the time and on policies. One might wish such reports on the process of globalisation, on the various forms of inequality and deprivation in the contemporary world, and on notions of "progress" and "regress" that would reflect local traditions, circumstances and aspirations while being compatible with universally accepted values and norms of behaviour. Locally as well as globally, democracy is best served by honest attempts at understanding and describing how people live and institutions function.

Chapter IV

Social Forces with a Global Agenda

Among the social groups that are influencing the current process of globalisation and giving its contours to the world community are the new world capitalist elite, the media with a global reach, the new idealists and world citizens, public servants, and social movements and non-governmental organisations. The continuation of the current "neo-realist" and cynical mood, or the emergence of a humanist political culture very much depend on their actions.

The New World Capitalist Elite

There are many examples, in countries of the North and South, of people recently gaining much wealth from "reforms" and global capitalism only to forget their obligations vis-à-vis their community, including the payment of taxes. The "nouveau riche" is a farcical personage and also a social nuisance when operating in a weak social fabric and in the midst of poverty. He/she uses the weakness of political regimes to pursue his self-interest, including through corruption. He/she conveys to his neighbours the impression that the market economy system has nothing to do with respect for ethical norms of behaviour and that democracy is simply the opening of opportunities to make money. Combined with pieces of information and impressions on the salaries of executives and on the rise of profit at time of high unemployment, this image of the unscrupulous arrivist suggests that global capitalism is simply the modern avatar of the age old propensity of human beings to exploit each other.

But nouveau riches, profiteers and speculators are only a fringe of a much larger new international social class of entrepreneurs, managers and financiers that has become more visible and powerful since various barriers to economic and financial transactions have been removed. These individuals belong to transnational corporations and international banks, or audit and consultant firms, but also to national private companies operating in an open economy. This is a class made of very powerful and affluent persons, and also of small entrepreneurs and innovators in a variety of domains aspiring to exert fully their creativity in a favourable environment. Beyond great differences in income and power, these people share a number of values, convictions and political orientations. They also share a common language, English, and a press with an international reach. As portrayed by the media, the role models emanating from this business world are ambitious and of quick intelligence and decisiveness. Very engaged, they take decisions of planetary consequences with great ease, and they move from one company to another, normally with substantial salary increases.

How relevant for such role models are a humanist political culture and the virtues of economic participation, economic justice, economic morality and economic moderation?

Through a mix of conviction that all human beings should have a chance to succeed, and of enlightened perception of self-interest, the global capitalist is generally hostile to blatant forms of exploitation. The new world elite believes that capitalism and political liberalism would be endangered by a sharp division within societies and globally between the "have" and the "have not". Members of this elite are convinced that talents are unevenly distributed and should be rewarded accordingly, but are very favourable to the concept of equality of opportunities which is at the core of the objective of economic participation. Yet, they do not hesitate to suppress jobs to reduce production costs, increase profits, or introduce "labour saving" techniques. And, for ideological reasons, they are hostile to employment in public services or public work.

The new world capitalist elite is wealthy and not overly preoccupied with economic justice, except as it relates to fair pecuniary rewards for entrepreneurship. It considers the concept of equality, particularly as it concerns income and wealth, as a vestige of past ideologies. This elite propagates an image and conception of success largely measured in terms of power and financial gains. These gains are often extremely rapid, related to merit and also to circumstances, clever exploitation of knowledge, influence or luck, as in the case of financial speculation. Truly enough, there is the great innovator who starts a

109

new business with a brilliant idea and gains fame and wealth. But even this sort of image, inherited from the "American dream", shines in a context of fast money, ruthless and predatory strategies, "downsizing" and "casino economics". Success in the capitalist world does not seem to require effort and patience. Perhaps because of the advent of the "virtual economy", and certainly in relation to the internationalisation of economic transactions and strategies, the today's successful capitalist appears to be indifferent to the condition of the "Common Man". Neither particularly exploitative, nor particularly humanistic, this successful entrepreneur is perceived to be "distant", belonging to a somewhat abstract world. With growing inequalities, "distance" between the fortunate and the excluded is one the causes of the emergence of dual economies and dual societies.

Though integrity is not a widely extolled virtue in the modern capitalist ethos, there is no evidence that the average behaviour of the economic actors is worse now than it was a century or twenty years ago. Corruption, involving business and politics, is widespread, but its healthy denunciation at the turn of the 21st century – particularly in Western Europe and Japan – is as much a sign of hope as a proof that the domination of money is eroding the very fabric of modern society. Members of the new elite do not seem to be motivated by the "Protestant Ethic" as described by Max Weber, partly because the process of capital accumulation does not require the same "bourgeois virtues" as in 19th century Europe. But while having their own "jets", they do not indulge too much in conspicuous consumption, and the image of the worldly businessman, or businesswoman, remains relatively "clean". The tabloid press has other heroes and other victims.

As regards economic moderation, many members of the new world elite are not necessarily pleased by the current wave of mergers and apparent concentration of economic and financial power, but they think that public regulations would be either ineffective or so constraining as to slash the spirit of free enterprise. They see competition as a fundamental feature of life and society. They often recognise that the current form of economic competition has negative social consequences, but they cannot imagine possible alternatives. The new world elite, and the very large middle class that share some of its values if not global outlook, is not insensitive to the danger of market economies turning into market societies. While believing in money as the most convenient, and the most democratic medium of exchange, modern entrepreneurs would like to preserve and expand other spheres of life, including families ties and athletic and artistic endeavours. But again, they do not trust the type of intellectual reflection and political action that could challenge the invasion of the modern culture by the capitalist logic and rationality.

However accurate or simplistic the above picture of the "average member of the world capitalist elite", there is nothing more necessary in practical political terms than a dialogue between this new class and those that have a different conception of the requirements of a democratic world order and of the desirable balance of power between public authorities and private forces. The two most obvious dividing lines between the enlightened capitalists and liberals and the also enlightened socialists and social democrats of various traditions and cultures, are indeed the question of economic and social equality and the question of the respective roles of "markets", in the sense of economic and financial powers, and "states", in the generic meaning of public authorities at all levels, including the international and global. There are currently power imbalances between these two political poles of reflection and action that impede the emergence of a meaningful dialogue on a planetary scale. But, of great importance for the construction of a democratic world order, is the recognition that a large part the new emerging world elite has a genuine interest in some of the basic principles of political democracy. Its ethos is based on the premise that freedom of initiative is a critical foundation to any viable society. It therefore needs political democracy. It is opposed to regimes that would subordinate economic activity to other goals such as national expansionism or the domination of a particular religious or secular ideology. World capitalists see themselves as the true liberals and the true cosmopolitans. The fact that this elite recruits in different regions and cultures is in itself favourable to global democracy.

The Media with a Global Reach

The role of the press and of the media in general is as important today as it has been in the past struggles for democracy. There is the same need as ever for freedom of the press and freedom of expression – a right that the International Covenant on Civil and Political Rights applies to "ideas of all kinds, regardless of frontiers", through "any media", and associates to "special duties and responsibilities".

In this regard, the Copenhagen Declaration and Programme of Action fully recognized the importance of communication media, on a par with educational systems, to promote the values that sustain social development, including tolerance, responsibility, non-violence and solidarity. It stated that an open political and economic system required access by all to education, knowledge and information. It also stated that, "consistent with freedom of expression", governments had the duty to encourage media to promote values enabling people to live in harmony with each other, and to "discourage the exhibition of pornography and the gratuitous depiction of explicit violence and cruelty" (Programme of Action, Chapter 1, para. 16 d).

The media with a global reach have an enormous political and cultural power. They are the main proponents of the values of global capitalism. Through advertising and through their reporting on economic and financial trends and events, they contribute powerfully to the shaping of attitudes, tastes, moral norms and aspirations. Not so long ago, Western democracies had public television programmes that were culturally enriching, publicly financed while respectful of different opinions, and unencumbered by advertising and commercialisation. Remnants of this sound system have now great difficulties to survive and cannot "compete" with channels financed by commercials and relying on the intellectual passivity of their viewers. At the same time, these media with a global reach are increasingly concentrated in a few hands. They respond with great competence to the demand they have themselves created for entertainment and "light" programs, and they disseminate a view of world affairs which is by definition monopolistic.

As a minimum, the construction of a global democratic community requires pluralism in the media with a global reach and the development of a public sector, notably in the United Nations system, interested in the enhancement of the knowledge and culture of its viewers. This is an issue that should figure prominently in national and international debates on a new political philosophy and project for the coming decades. Of particular importance is the teaching, through education and also the media, that respect for universal and shared values is entirely compatible with diversity of political views, customs, languages and ways of living.

New Idealists and World Proletariat

The new idealists are often intellectuals, members of social movements and religious organisations, and persons scattered in the academic, artistic and political circles, not to forget the "ordinary" citizenry. They are too dispersed, too diverse, and often too individualistic to constitute a group in political terms, or a *fortiori* a class in sociological terms. But when meeting, they recognise their common analyses, their capacity for indignation, and their willingness to work for a better world. Sensitive to the diversity of cultures and traditions, convinced of the common humanity of all peoples, keenly aware of the misery that plagues the world, feeling that a moral and "existential" malaise permeates the dominant modern psyche, the new idealist is attached to democracy first and foremost because of a repulsion for any doctrine or political posturing implying rejection or neglect of the fundamental equality of all human beings.

The new idealists would like to identify Truth with Beauty and Virtue. They believe that all human actions, and particularly those affecting other persons and societies, ought to be oriented and shaped by a normative and attractive vision of life and society. They see the dominant modern culture as too materialistic, as offering very few dreams to the young, and as destructive of the fragile harmonies linking individuals to themselves, others, and their environment. The new idealists are trying to establish a moral continuum between their convictions and their deeds.

Some new idealists are "public intellectuals" occasionally appearing in the media because of a book or a colloquium or on the occasion of a public debate on a major event. The public intellectual has antecedents – notably in the Russian tradition of the intelligentsia and in the French post-war role of the "intellectual engagé". It is sometimes deplored that, at present, many intellectuals, are highly specialised and sharing their knowledge with a limited audience. They should be encouraged to add their voice in the public debate and discourse on the problems and objectives of contemporary societies. Their role is to complicate the debate, to raise questions, and to offer interpretations. They should have an ethical discourse, with a language that refuses the protection of a jargon, and should work in a variety of institutions, including the mass media.

The new idealists and public intellectuals are in some sense a political force, especially when speaking and militating on behalf of the modern proletariat. This is a growing population of individuals and families who have been touched by modernity simply to loose their traditional livelihood, or who are the victims of economic forces or political events on which they have no control. The world proletariat is made of persons who are destitute in a context of mass advertising for consumption, deprived of access to knowledge while being told that skills and qualifications are necessary to survive, and powerless and without control over their lives in a world culture linking self esteem with income and influence. These people are in a constant psychological state of insecurity.

Composed of the excluded and of the poor in societies where destitution is still attributed to personal failure or lack of economic growth rather than to misguided modernisation, the proletariat of today does not have the means for class conscience. It has no organisations and practically no elected representatives in national and international institutions. It constitutes a social class in objective but not in political terms. At the time of the industrial revolution, exploited workers managed to develop unions and some soon powerful political parties fought on their behalf. At the end of this millennium, the very poor are alone. Only charitable and religious organisations have the desire and capacity to reach a few of them, and only some new idealists believe that their condition and fate matter, even though they do not currently represent a threat to the dominant order. This is obviously insufficient to transform the new world proletariat into an active force that could contribute to the establishment of a global democratic world order.

Towards the end of the 1990s one could see in international airports an advertisement for a magazine of the rich and powerful stating "Capitalists of the world, Unite". The mobilising myth to which this slogan seems to mockingly refer will have a chance to become again a source of hope for the destitute only if social movements, trade unions and political parties cease to be intimidated by "the end of history".

Citizens of the World

Associated with the new idealists is the notion of world citizenship, or citizenhood. Citizenship connotes the legal and political rights of a person who formally belong to a distinct entity, generally a country. Citizenhood has an active, positive and emotional connotation, as in the French word "citoyenneté". Obviously, there are no citizens of the world in a legal sense – the United Nations deliver "laissez-passer" and not "passports" to its civil servants – but there are throughout the world individuals who feel that their mental and emotional horizon is the planet. They interiorise universal values, especially human rights and fundamental freedoms, they have a sense of active solidarity with the achievements or problems and suffering of peoples of different regions and cultures, and they strongly believe in notions such as common heritage and common good of humankind. The new idealists are natural adepts of this cosmopolitan ethos. The elite evoked above has also a sense of world citizenship. Entrepreneurs and financiers with a global outlook see the world as a field to be conquered. They are democratic in their belief that markets can provide opportunities to all and universalist in their conviction that national borders are irrelevant obstacles to economic and financial transactions. Neo-liberals and capitalists of a globalised economy see nationalism as evidence of obscurantism.

At the same time, most citizens of the world, be they idealistic intellectuals and militants of social movements or entrepreneurs, see no contradiction between an attachment to a village or nation or region, and the sense of belonging to humanity as a whole. Local attachments tend to be sentimental and associated with periods of rest and retirement. National fidelities are more political and more intellectually cultural. At least a number of idealists are convinced that the nation-state remains the privileged space for modern citizenhood. They think that the highly desirable concept of world citizenhood will emerge only as an expansion of the practice of civic virtues at the local, national and regional levels. They know that attempts at creating world citizens on the basis of rejection of national citizenship are doomed to fail rapidly after an initial craze. They therefore oppose forms of globalism that weaken and eventually destroy national centres of political authority. They favour the emergence of a mix of supranational and global institutions. At the same time they are not afraid of a world government, which they see as a normal feature of a world society.

Believers in this internationalism mixed with supranationalism are of the view that a planetary citizenhood is being slowly created when dedicated individuals participate in great causes such as the management of the global commons,

115

the promotion of human rights, the alleviation of human misery, or the mastering of scientific and technological progress.

At an intermediary level, they also see the regulation of financial markets, the organisation of a democratic system of global security, or the reconstruction of a partnership for development and progress between affluent and poor countries, as steps in the formation of a political culture for a new and more equalitarian universalism. At this point of time, such forces animated by a global civic and democratic ideal have great difficulties not be swept out by strong adverse currents. But, cracks in the established order are rarely obvious to the contemporaries. It is both idealistic and realistic to develop an intellectual understanding of the contours of a future world citizenhood.

Public Servants

Servants of the political power have often been feared, sometimes admired or envied, and regularly mocked, but respected public servants are indispensable to national societies and international and global institutions for the management of a democratic world community. In some cultures, civil servants were near the apex of the social structure in terms of prestige if not income. They were the guardians of the public interest, those who insured continuity in spite of ups and downs in the quality of political leadership. When they colonised large parts of the world, the European powers transplanted their civil service systems. After decolonisation, those systems were widely considered as a useful legacy. The international civil service, starting with the United Nations, and to some extent the League of Nations after World War I, was built along the principles of the European tradition of public service. The notions of competence, integrity and neutrality were associated with security of employment and comfortable salaries set below those of the private sector in affluent societies. In this regard, the idea that salaries in the public service had to be "competitive" with those offered in the private sector in order to attract talented and ambitious people was not given much importance until the 1980s. Interest for public issues, prestige of the function and security of the tenure, were considered sufficient incentives.

For the international civil service, the second Secretary General of the United Nations, Dag Hammarskjoeld, enriched the notion of neutrality by subordinating it to the promotion of the basic moral principles embodied in the Charter of the Organisation. In so doing, he placed international civil servants at the service of humanity, beyond and above their deference to the Member States of the Organisation. To stay in the UN context, the two cracks in this system that appeared rapidly with serious long term consequences were the success of the Soviet Union to keep control over its nationals serving in the Secretariat, and the much briefer but symbolic success of the United States to censor the political views of its nationals serving in the same Secretariat as result of Senator MacCarthy's campaign against American citizens suspect of sympathy for Communism. Then was the collapse of the Soviet Union and the realisation that many civil servants of this regime had enjoyed great privileges and treated the res publica as their private property. Adding to this the difficulties in the development process in the South, attributed however wrongly to excessive interference from governments and "plethoric" bureaucracies, the stage was right for the offensive of the neo-liberals against public services and public servants.

There is no disputing the necessity for periodic critical review of the functioning of public services and the situation of civil servants, as the local, national as well as international levels. All public institutions should undertake such reviews. As circumstances and problems evolve, functions and allocation of resources and personnel have to be revisited. Conditions of service, including salaries, have also to be examined. Not only undue privileges but also overt or insidious forms of exploitation can easily creep in institutions, public or private. Because of their function, public institutions have a particular responsibility in correcting their deficiencies. And, in a good check and balance system, reviews, assessments, evaluations and other procedures for critical self examination of an institution and its personnel require encouragement from outside authorities. Institutional complacency and bureaucratic comfort mixed with indifference for objectives and arrogance in relations with the citizens, are not only subjects of satires. They are practices that can destroy a democracy.

The problem with the contemporary version of criticism towards public services and public servants is that since the beginning of the 1980s it has weakened rather than improved public institutions. There has been an intellectual and political offensive against "big government" and a valorisation of everything private. The emphasis was on less resources and less personnel. Civil servants were told they represented an obsolete culture and should retrain to acquire the values, attitudes and methods of work of their colleagues in the private sector. Large multinational companies of consultants were contracted to send their experts in national and international organisations to teach "management by objectives" and "competitive spirit". The most useful acquisition of new skills and new techniques, notably for the use of computers, was adorned with a set of prescriptions that amounted to a negation of the difference between serving the public interest and pursuing the search for profit, expansion and power. The objectives, rather than the virtues of the private sector's culture were imposed on the public service.

The results of this movement have been highly questionable. Public services and administrations have been reduced in countries where they offered the main source of employment and where the main issue was to improve their quality. In other countries, former public servants of central plans gained much wealth and kept their former privileges as they were given the ownership and management of "privatised" corporations and services. The much influential "structural adjustment programmes" and "market oriented reforms" at best ignored the necessity to develop strong, dedicated and respected public services, and at worse damaged those that were in place. And, both in national and international public institutions, the result of ideologically motivated reviews and reforms has been an aggravation of situations of privileges, excessive income differentials, and inequalities in status, power and prestige.

World campaigns against corruption in public and other institutions should not obscure the fact that inequalities of all types and the associated privileges of the most powerful are growing everywhere, including among national and international public servants. It would be an exaggeration but not an error to affirm that in many parts of the world, the upper level of the civil service is adopting the values and mentality of the new corporate international class, while the rest of this battered army is slipping towards the lower middle class of society. This evolution is in line with the progression of global capitalism. It represents an element of a world order based on the free interplay of economic actors with a global reach, facilitated and when absolutely necessary guided by international and global institutions. Is this trend of privatisation cum weakening of public and civil services, including education, compatible with the building of a humanist world political culture and global democracy?

This overall issue ought to generate a large number of more specific questions. For example: is the decline of the teaching profession and of public educational institutions announcing a political, moral and eventually economic decline of the societies particularly affected by this phenomenon? Is the privatisation of penitentiary institutions, already well advanced in some affluent societies, an extreme sign of abandonment by public authorities of their traditional functions? Will the United Nations and other international organisations with a comparable mandate be able to make a contribution to the search for the global common good if their functionaries are increasingly "seconded" from governments and private corporations?

Within the countries and organisations concerned, the process of privatisation and decline of public services followed a rather simple scenario. In the political and intellectual atmosphere of "victory" of "liberalism" over "communism", measures were taken which provoked sharp negative judgements from those with a tradition of public service. Then, after a few months and years, when remedies and alternatives are evoked, the movement against everything public has already achieved so much power that the burden of the proof falls upon its opponents. The "why not", for example "why not privatised jails"?, supersedes rapidly the "why"? As time passes, cause-effect relationships mentioned in the initial debates – for instance "a weakening of the UN Secretariat will lead to a weakening of international cooperation for development" – tend to be blurred into a complicated array of factors and positions and to loose its appeal. Thus, through innumerable small concessions, due partly to indifference and partly to the fascination that simplistic slogans exert when formulated by powerful individuals or institutions, ideas initially questionable become rapidly trends without alternatives. To oppose them is to be "unrealistic", "outdated", or simply "irrelevant". It is to be feared that the decline of the ethos of public service has probably become irreversible, at least until some reconstruction is imposed by obvious failures of a globalised but "monetised" world to address mounting common problems.

Social Movements and Non-Governmental Organisations

Advocates of social reform and changes in the dominant order are increasingly found in organisations of the civil society. In developing and developed economies, these organisations, known as "non-governmental organisations"

(NGOs) in the context of the United Nations, and increasingly as the "civil society", often hold public authorities accountable for their commitments to social progress, including the implementation of major international agreements.

The role of social movements in questioning the established order is not a new phenomenon. Suffice to recall the critical influence of trade unions since the end of the 19th century, and the efforts of dedicated individuals and groups, also since many decades, on major causes such as the abolition of slavery, the rights of women, the end of colonialism, the elimination of apartheid, and the protection of human rights and fundamental freedoms. But globalisation also has a civil society facet and more and more organisations are trying to convey global messages, to recruit global membership and to attract a global audience. The world conferences organised by the United Nations since the 1970s have contributed very significantly to this globalisation of the civil society. Some observers feel that this contribution was so important as to explain the hostility of major countries to the convening of new UN conferences. This interpretation would suggest that the advocacy role of non-governmental organisations is especially welcome to liberal democracies when it fits their agenda. At the international level in particular, governments are not overly anxious to be challenged by organisations that they support in principle as expressions of the civil society and often in practice as a demonstration of their democratic benevolence.

There are different types of organisations of the civil society. First are organisations often old and with religious and philosophical roots, but also sometimes recent, that have a strong ethical and spiritual orientation according to which success is defined as the increased well-being of others. The very act of giving is the inspiration and joy of persons who do not seek recognition and power. These are the traditional ideals of the charitable organisations that many governments had hoped to render obsolete by the promotion of economic and social justice. The fact that this has not happened is neither a condemnation of the welfare society nor simply a testimony to the resilience of religious and otherwise spiritually inspired movements. Societies which are not totalitarian are made of a large variety of institutions, initiatives, and ideas expressing the many facets of the human condition. And poverty, material, affective or spiritual, is both a problem to be addressed and an inherent dimension of the human condition. Those who are truly sharing the plight of the poor and trying to give them comfort and hope, know that poverty, when not a choice, is a Hydra to be repeatedly slain. To use a literary image, the devoted member of a charitable organisation is a happy and tireless Sisyphus.

The recent flourishing and visibility of the civil society is due to the second type of movements and organisations whose political behaviour is associated with the practice of lobbying and whose rise has coincided with the growing questioning of the relevance and effectiveness of political processes to solve the problems of contemporary societies. Questioning the dominant order – be it local, national or global – to improve it or transform it more or less radically, these organisations of the civil society have the potential to be actors for positive social change and to build global political alliances. To transform their values into actions useful to the construction of a global democratic community, they have to overcome obstacles partly inherent to all human endeavours and partly related to the current world ideological context. NGOs are not, by nature, immune from various forms of political or financial corruption and are not necessarily democratic in their structures and modes of operation.

There is a third breed of movements and organisations that rely on violence to expose its views and that have sometimes political, religious or ideological orientations that aim at limiting or rejecting altogether the basic tenets of the democratic doctrine. A recurrent dilemma of democratic regimes is to decide on the freedom of action that ought to be granted to organisations that intend to subvert them. Authoritarian regimes have a comparable dilemma in deciding to suppress, repress or tolerate dissenting individuals and groups, but democracies cannot use raw force against their internal adversaries without undermining their founding principles. This problem will become increasingly difficult as violence seems to be more and more frequently perceived as a legitimate alternative to persuasion in various spheres of life and society, including in the conduct of international relations.

A recognition of the diverse characteristics and quality of the organisations of the civil society does not alter the fact that they are indispensable components of the world social and political scene. Representatives of the civil society are often alone in raising their voices for the respect of human dignity and in denouncing abuses of all types plaguing the modern world. It is useful to ponder what would be the situation of basic human rights if private organisations had not been actively denouncing individual and collective violations of these rights. In many respects, organisations of the civil society represent the political conscience of society. They expose issues, campaign to mobilise support for their action, denounce the negligence or wrongdoing of public and private, national and international institutions and powers, and propose elements for solution. Without the voices of individuals, intellectuals, artists, religious persons and dissenters servicing various causes, there would be little hope for any kind of democracy in the world. All public and private institutions need to be monitored, checked, stimulated and sometimes pressured. There is no possible democracy if these institutions operate in secrecy and if scrutiny is either legally repressed or made impossible through intimidation or persecution. This applies in similar terms to national, regional and international institutions. Progress in international democracy, at this first level, means that a person or organisation for instance denouncing a mismanagement of atomic waste by a particular government has the possibility to appeal to a higher authority if that particular government is unresponsive of threatening. The right to petition to a superior authority to have one's rights respected in whichever place or situation is a fundamental element of an international democracy.

All efforts and sometimes sacrifices made by courageous individuals and dedicated organisations to expose problems and wrongdoing calling for regress are precious steps in the right direction. The questioning of dominant ideas and policies, the dissemination of information that public and private authorities would prefer to keep under their control, the formulation in public forums of proposals to address the problems of the time, and also the support to governments and international organisations that are in tune with the search for the common good are requirements of healthy democracy. Organisations of the civil society that keep their role of dissent and advocacy for good causes are sources of enrichment for democratic political regimes.

Ambiguity starts when social movements become highly organised lobbies having the means to dominate executive and legislative processes of decision, when organisations of the civil society are perceived as having more democratic legitimacy than elected representatives and civil servants. Signs of such problems in the balance of roles and responsibilities between the civil society and public authorities are already apparent on the international scene. To some extent, the rediscovery of the notion of "civil society" in the last quarter of the 20th century has coincided with the weakening of critical institutions of representative democracy, notably political parties and parliaments. For those who consider this as a problem, the solution is not so much to limit the influence of social movements as to improve or restore the image of politics and politicians. The continuing and most helpful mobilisation of a number of social movements for the cause of democracy on a global scale should be paralleled and fed by a reflection on the new concepts, procedures and perhaps institutions that should bring together traditional and new powers for a democratic and constructive dialogue on the world scene. Social movements and organisations pursuing objectives consequent with the common good should guard their separate identities and avoid assuming direct governmental responsibilities. They also should avoid adopting the values of the market economy and copying the ethos of private companies, including profitability or competitiveness. Of great importance is the language that they use to convey their message. Sometimes the desire to be heard and accepted leads to semantic concession that unavoidably erode the quality of the message. Charitable and other organisations of the civil society ought to be interested in peoples, not in "human resources", in working opportunities and not in "labour markets", or in working conditions, and not in "flexibility". If democratic societies are to be built on a "tripod" made of public institutions, market institutions and civil organisations – including the trade-unions – then each component has to hold on to its separate identity and responsibilities.

On the international and global scene, organisations of the civil society are just starting to gain access to the institutions they wish to influence. Although some organisations – such as Amnesty International, Médecins sans Frontières, or Greenpeace – are strong enough to have a global reach on their own, most need to use established intergovernmental fora to disseminate their messages. Some of these established institutions, notably the United Nations, have relatively long experience in relating to organisations of the civil society: the U.N. Committee on Non-Governmental Organisations was established in 1946 to examine the consultative relationship that the Economic and Social Council should have with international non-governmental organisations. Others, such as the World Bank and the World Trade Organisation, are only starting to define their relationships with the civil society.

The strengthening of the role of organisations of the civil society on the international scene should preferably stem from the development of these organisations in the different regions of the world. This means both an increased diversification in membership and leadership, and the creation of new organisations where they are currently absent, weak, or deprived of their dissenting role. Diversification of origin and culture is a quasi automatic enrichment. Questions on the agenda of international organisations are in essence political – notwithstanding the technical language in which they are sometimes presented – and of interest to the whole of humankind. Viewpoints of persons with different backgrounds always introduce nuances and beneficial disagreements.

Organisations of the civil society and social movements need resources to enhance their participation in international and regional debates. Money to travel and subsist in the cities hosting institutions and conferences is often an acute problem, especially for the NGOs of poor countries. In some cases, governments of affluent democratic countries contribute to the financing of their own NGOs and also provide financial assistance to NGOs of the least developed countries – currently 49 countries, essentially African, that are identified by the United Nations in light of their key economic indicators. The financing of organisations of the civil society by their own government is a priori in conflict with their status and a threat to their independence. There are, however, relatively successful examples in countries with a long democratic tradition and a high degree of consensus on essential matters of domestic and foreign policy. These conditions are difficult to replicate, but it is even more difficult to conceive of NGOs pursuing objectives contributing to the common good while being financed by the private corporate sector.

This point is important, not only because such financing is a frequent occurrence, but also in relation with the increasing confusion that seems to occur in national and international circles between organisations of the civil society with humanist goals (e.g the reduction of poverty, the status of women, the promotion of human rights or the protection of the environment) and lobbies working for the achievement of specific mercantile or power-seeking objectives. As to the financing of organisations of poor countries by governments of affluent countries, its potentially paternalistic, and manipulating aspects can be overcome when the intentions of the donor are benevolent. The motives for support and the source of the financing within a governmental structure, are useful indicators of its quality. Again, there are governments of affluent democratic countries whose financing of NGOs of poor countries constitutes a genuine transfer of resources and an honest attempt to strengthen the global civil society. In the United Nations context, this attitude was reflected in support to the participation of NGOs in the global conferences of the 1980s and 1990s. Some foundations play a comparable role. A permanent trust-fund within the United Nations to facilitate participation of duly accredited NGOs with limited financial means would be a laudable endeavour.

International organisations can do much to facilitate the contribution of the civil society in the elaboration of global norms and policies. But this task requires both attention to numerous procedural details of great practical importance and enthusiasm in constructing a new type of international democracy. The current extension of the participation of NGOs in the work of the General Assembly of the UN, or in the deliberations of a new institution such as the World Trade Organisation demand intellectual and political efforts to find appropriate criteria and mechanisms for accreditation as well as satisfactory arrangements for the exercise of the NGO's right to take the floor in debates and disseminate documents. The very significant increase in the number of organisations requesting NGO status is sufficient reason for building a more elaborate set of relationships between intergovernmental organisations and the civil society.

An all embracing political philosophy of equal participation for all in public decision making, without distinctions between purposes and sources of financing is bound to lead to a reinforcement of the prevalent distribution of power. Laissez-faire in access to political structures has the same pernicious effects as laissez-faire in the economic realm. When the very fruitful, utopian but achievable idea of convoking and then establishing within a modified United Nations framework a sort of "Global Peoples Assembly" is seriously considered, it will be critical to make a distinction between the civil society and the private business sector, and, within the civil society, between various types or organisations according to their goals. An unstructured Tower of Babel, or an assembly that convokes only the most powerful NGOs would undermine this critical aspect in the building of a global democratic community.

The enlarged role of the civil society in sparking the moral consciousness of humankind and the management of public affairs does not necessarily imply the creation and development of large permanent institutions. What often matters most from the perspective of the promotion of a cause is to link together the persons and groups involved through effective use of available modern communication technologies. The recent campaign against land-mines provides an example of a rather successful use of these technologies by individuals committed to the pursuit of a concrete objective requiring positive action from governments. This campaign had no permanent secretariat and no formal conference. There exist imaginative ways to bring issues to the global agenda of the international community.

In places where human suffering is widespread, the persons who give their time and energy to help others and to denounce abuses of various types and origins, do so as a gift to life and harmony in society. Their generosity is the essence of that part of civil society promoting solidarity in very concrete ways. They attend to problems that other individuals and established institutions tend to ignore. They do not think of reward, or promotion of their institution. Without them, the world would be a much worse place. But without organisations with the political and institutional power to promote the moral values of those heroes of the obscure day to day struggle for survival and dignity, the divide between the powerful an the powerless would have little chance of being lessened. Individuals working at the local level and institutions operating on the international scale are both necessary to build global democracy.

Chapter V
Institutions to Promote the Common Good

Institutions have a mixed reputation. In the etymology of the word there is "status", and it evokes conservatism, order, traditions and hierarchy, rules of behaviour and constraints on the freedom of the individual. For libertarians on the left and right of the political spectrum, institutions represent the enemy to be destroyed, be it the institution of marriage, the religious institutions, or the State administrations. For the neo-liberal political philosophy that is currently prevailing on the world scene, institutions tend to be identified with public institutions and therefore assailable. They are seen as unnecessary obstacles to the free interplay of market forces. To the argument that private corporations and markets themselves are after all institutions, the neo-liberal will retort that those are "natural" institutions made to facilitate the initiative and creativity of individuals. For the heirs of the Marxist doctrine, institutions are the suspect "superstructures" of the economic relations stemming from the bourgeois order. And, for the intellectuals of the South, institutions are typically expressing Western political and cultural dominance. In addition, on the international scene, the alleged heaviness of the existing institutions, notably the United Nations, is regularly criticized.

On the other hand, there is wide recognition that organised societies need structures and institutions, and that modernity is not simply the flourishing of individual freedom in a vacuum. "Institutional development" has been for a while a branch of the disciplines involved with the theory and practice of economic and social development. Some orientations on the role and functioning of institutions ought to be recalled before commenting on socialising institutions, the state, regional organisations, institutions to manage the global economy, and the United Nations system.

Institutional Diversity is a Condition for Democracy

The flourishing of a dense network of institutions, large and small, public and private, from the local to the international level, should be promoted. In a community, institutional richness is in itself an objective. Citizens of a nation and of the world cannot exert their civic spirit in a vacuum. Even a prudent functional approach to institutional development ought therefore to be open to ideas and initiatives from very different circles of society. For instance, an important development is the increasing internationalisation of higher education. A number of prestigious universities, notably in the United States, attract students from all parts of the world. There are numerous exchanges of students and academics in all regions. Such rise of multinational universities and transnational educational goals and programmes provide a basis for the pursuit of excellence in all domains of knowledge and for cultural richness. Truly international universities, established with the deliberate intention of forming world citizens can play a particularly useful role in this globalised world. Such universities should be supported by public and private funds, including in regions with limited resources. To improve the quality of education, competition and stimulation should be welcomed. There will never be too many good schools and universities in the world, and transfers of resources to give a chance for education to those who do not have it by their birth will never be a waste. For the creation of institutions clearly contributing to a better world, narrow cost benefit analyses are irrelevant.

It is erroneous to think in terms of a "zero sum game" when debating of such institutions. For example there is complementarity between national, regional and international organisations. States ought to remain in the foreseeable future the pillars of a well functioning world community. Only competent and legitimate governments can concede part of their sovereignty to regional or international organisations. There is also complementarity between well working political processes, in their traditional form, and strong organisations of the civil society playing an advocacy role. Unproductive trade-offs and zero sum games become unavoidable only when there is confusion of functions and objectives between institutions made to serve different purposes. And there is obvious complementarity between markets, which are themselves institutions, and governments and public administrations. Both sets of institutions correspond to basic needs of individuals and to fundamental requirements of social organisation. Discourses implying the desirability of destroying or drastically weakening either of the two types of institutions are misguided. Without markets, the only alternative would be a rationing of the production and distribution of goods and services by a totalitarian state. Without state institutions, other authorities would emerge. History has revealed few if any societies, however small, which have long tolerated anarchy.

Make Good Use of Existing Institutions

At the national level, a sure sign of underdevelopment or decline is the neglect of institutions such as schools, or hospitals, or administrations and courts, or agencies ensuring the maintenance of buildings and various facilities having often required sizeable investments. Some affluent countries have also a tendency to neglect their basic infrastructure because of wrong choices in allocation of resources and lack of funding for public agencies. Similarly, on the international scene, a number of institutions are neglected and sometimes misused. The United Nations is not given the means to follow up effectively the implementation of the decisions of the major conferences and summits it has been mandated to organise during this last part of the 20th century, or to monitor the respect by Member States of their obligations under the "International Bill of Human Rights". Influential member states often prefer to use the United Nations as a forum to score political points against other governments, rather than as an institution created to promote the betterment of the human condition. Explanations for this state of affairs include a prevalent narrow conception of national interest. It may also be that well established institutions have problems keeping the active interest of their members. Except in times of crisis, complacency and indifference are more common than creativity and commitment.

This is why the relationship between "good use" and "reform" deserves reflection. With perhaps a few exceptions, public institutions ought to evolve overtime, either to adjust their structures and modes of operation to a variety of changes in society, or to set a new tone and provoke such changes. There is normally a positive relationship between the relevance and effectiveness of a public institution and its openness to reform. In recent years, however, as already noted apropos public servants, the word "reform" has been used with prodigality, both as a programme and as a slogan covering initiatives and activities having little to do with an increase in the effectiveness of the insti-

129

tutions concerned. Pseudo reforms at odds with the mandate, or one might even say the soul of the institution concerned, are more destructive than a prudent status quo. Other types of reform stemming from the same "realism" are generally minor adjustments not commensurate with the gravity of the problems that are supposed to be addressed. For most public institutions in developing countries, in the former socialist countries, in the United Nations System, "reform" has meant reduction of resources, personnel and role. And the proponents of those "reforms" were usually hostile to the organisations they pretended to improve. In the perspective of effective use of institutions, the objectives of a reform are obviously of critical importance. There is ample evidence that original motivations largely determine the subsequent unfolding of the reform process, even when actors with different intentions enter into this process to rescue or reorient the operation.

In addition, a certain impatience in the dominant ethos of the time does not facilitate a positive relationship between respect for the culture of an institution and its reform. There is truth in the observation that institutions are as good as the political culture of their members. Initiatives to strengthen and democratise an institution that is clearly dominated by an adverse ideology would be doomed to fail or to be appropriated by hostile forces. For example, it could be argued that the political realists currently dominating the world diplomatic scene would transform the Economic Security Council mentioned below in the context of a strengthening of the United Nations into a body unable to perform the functions envisaged by its democratic and idealistic proponents. A counter argument is that institutional changes, even imperfect and potentially ambiguous, create a dynamic that is not necessarily controllable by the actors with a conservative agenda. And the political culture of the ruling elite can be modified during the process of reform. This view, however, has credibility only if there are significant forces within and outside the organisation that are promoting the democratic agenda. A dominant political culture can be challenged only by another political project.

Nurture Traditional Socializing Institutions

The decline in the Western world of institutions which have traditionally "socialized" and "civilised" individuals through the teaching of norms of behaviour and moral principles is a recognised and documented fact. It is clear that in the "developed" world, the school, the family, the religious institutions have lost a great part of their role and influence, perhaps because their primary function is not to promote individual freedom and material progress. Most citizens of these societies would argue, however that these institutions, as well as a variety of local organisations and associations, ought to provide young people with ideas and emotions that would shape their moral outlook in a positive manner. But the banality of this observation is matched only by the neglect of its practical implications. In many countries, educational institutions are in decline, for lack of funding from public sources and from great difficulties in reconciling the discipline and respect for the teacher inherent in learning, with the freedom and autonomy of the individual that characterises the modern culture.

The family remains in theory "the natural and fundamental group unit of society (...) entitled to protection by society and the State" evoked by the Universal Declaration of Human Rights. But in the type of modernity invented by the Western civilisation the rights of the individual are given more emphasis than the welfare and stability of the family unit. It is as if there was a "trend" written in the evolution of humanity that the extended and now nuclear family should progressively be replaced by a variety of arrangements based on the free determinations of individuals expressing their personal preferences. In this cultural context families are losing their role of giving security to the individual and transmitting values and social mores from one generation to the next. A balance ought to be found between the promotion of individual freedom and the protection of an institution critical to an organised society.

Still in the Western world, traditional dominant Christian religions are in a period of decline in terms of membership and influence on individual norms of behaviour and outlook on life and its meaning. Their emphasis on community values and on the responsibility of the person conflicts with the modern individualist hedonism of market societies. At the same time, a number of sects offering the comfort of simplistic and generally authoritarian recipe for happiness in this world and beyond are gaining a larger audience. The spiritual vacuity of societies focused on material gains is filled in a variety of ways, including extremist and racist political movements.

In other regions and cultures, the family remains the principal locus of the individual, schools and universities are still highly respected, and religion has

131

often maintained spiritual, moral and secular authority. But it is unclear whether these cultures will resist the formidable power of the prevalent conception of modernity, development and progress.

In the South and the North, the a-contrario evidence of the indispensable socialising role of institutions invented by all cultures since many centuries is provided by the situation of young people in many cities and suburbs. There, gangs provide the security and solidarity that is no longer given by broken families and inextistent or insufficient schools. Even places to meet and socialise in an attractive environment are badly missing in cities where the poor are segregated and "housed" in cheap and ugly dwellings. The focus of modernity on profit and the short term, and the type of urbanisation that has prevailed during the 20th century, have broken many of the social relations, family networks and local institutions that, if not always happily, maintained in individuals a sense of belonging to a community. Segregation, isolation and loneliness are frequent occurrences. Social scientists are looking at the notion of "social capital" to try to recapture and to protect elements of that "glue" that has made viable social fabrics and to prevent people from despair and alienation. In addition to political institutions that are slowly being put into place in countries trying to adopt a democratic market economy system, there are many initiatives throughout the world to reconstruct a community spirit. These initiatives should be encouraged, or at least not hampered by public authorities.

Set Clear and Ambitious Objectives

Clarity on objectives to be pursued is a prerequisite for launching new institutions. This means that a great amount of intellectual work is required before political negotiations get underway. This was obviously the case before the creation of the League of Nations, the United Nations, and more recently the WTO or the International Criminal Court. Hopefully, other initiatives will be taken in the academic and research community on the general and specific aspects of institutional development required for a world community. The reaching of political agreement on a new institution always entails reduction in the level of the ambition of the project as elaborated by its proponents. But if such preparatory work has not been done, or was of poor quality, the political process will offer few remedies and the desired institution will be rejected or established on fragile grounds. To have a functional and yet progressive approach is to favour intellectual work and debate on aspects of institutional development that are both at the centre and on the margin of the current international agenda. This sort of intellectual and political imagination is facilitated and, in a universal and democratic perspective, legitimised by a coherent set of moral principles and objectives on the features of a world community. Using the example of the Social Summit, new or strengthened institutions for social development at the international level would require much additional intellectual investment on issues such as the meaning and modalities of international cooperation for social progress on a global scale, or the articulation of the social and human rights perspectives in the promotion of goals such as the reduction of poverty and the promotion of solidarity. Likewise, the establishment of a World Peoples Assembly would also have to be the result of intensive work on its rationale and mode of operation.

It is difficult to imagine that the utilitarian approach to institutional development linked to a careful reformist political ideology would have the boldness to push for the ideas and organisations required to tame global capitalism, orient it to the service of the international community, and promote the common good. On the international scene, what is considered functional tends to correspond to the views of the politically most influential, or with what is imposed by spectacular events. The merits of this approach diminish when the problems at hand are "politically incorrect" or more insidious than highly visible. It is therefore necessary to be demanding of public institutions and international organisations, and of the new corporate and media powers shaping modernity.

Democracy means neither mediocrity nor sceptical acceptance of the limitations of human endeavours and institutions. It represents hope and refusal to yield to complacency. In the modern psyche there is a comfortable cynicism inhibiting political initiatives that might alleviate human misery and suffering. Politics of conviction carries an awareness of the danger of "routinisation" that affects human thinking and action. All institutions, public and private, national and international are inclined to confuse stability and self preservation with conformism and sclerosis. With routinisation of ideas and practices often comes an excessive simplification of analyses and policies. There is sometimes much arrogance in the manner difficult problems are given quick, neat, and painless "solutions". Expediency and opportunism denote lack of respect for democratic processes and institutions. To practice political and institutional imagination is to increase one's level of ambition in public endeavours.

At the same time, the building of a global democracy should not be identified with large representative assemblies and organisations. There is no reason to imagine the future on the model of the huge conglomerates that are dominating the current process of economic globalisation. Even a world government would not necessarily be a monstrous bureaucracy. To be handled in a manner beneficial to humanity as a whole, global issues do not automatically call for large structures and institutions. For example, science and technology is typically a global question. Yet, some decades ago a group of twenty to thirty scientists met regularly in Copenhagen around Niels Bohr and managed to develop forms of scientific cooperation and understanding on the organisation of science that would have been very difficult to achieve in a big and officially established institution. Today, some globalisation of scientific work is still done by such small groups. There exist simple informal structures of cooperation in space technologies. To be fruitful, truly globalised efforts do not necessarily require large numbers of people. Relations among small groups with a common outlook are important, including to prevent catastrophes.

Promote Humane and Effective States

Along human history the balance between the power of the public authority and the rights of the individual has been a contentious issue. All human rights have been gained against public power before being guaranteed by the same power. And abuses against the freedom and dignity of the individual have been and are perpetrated or condoned, or tolerated by the same apparatus. Parallel to this tragic history, has been a search for democratic forms of government and types of public intervention which would let human freedom and human initiative flourish while ensuring social justice, security and social cohesion.

When the industrial revolution gave mobility and power to capital, the struggle for social justice became associated with the quest for democracy. From the rise of socialist ideas by the end of the 19th century and the advent of the communist led revolution in 1917 in Russia, governments of the countries that were not replacing private capitalism by state collectivism were obliged to seek a balance between the respective interests of capital and labour. They did so through a variety of conservative, liberal, social-democratic and socialist political arrangements, with a search for the common good going beyond mere compromises between employers and workers. In a number of countries, the scope of governmental policies, placed in the framework of medium and long-term perspectives, was large. Different varieties of mixed economies were invented and a vast array of investments for the regulation and orientation of the economy were installed. Through decades of conflicts and political battles, the means to regulate capitalism and to ensure citizens with a fair share of the product of economic activity were progressively put in place. Such means included laws and regulations, for instance on working hours and minimum wages, and a diversified and constantly evolving set of distributive and redistributive measures. By the middle of this twentieth century some acceptable and accepted balance had been reached in a number of Western societies, through more or less explicit social contracts involving the social partners, and, invariably, public authorities. Labour regulations and later environmental regulations, as well as measures to protect consumers, were elements of such social contracts.

Efforts were made to transpose features of this "model" in the former colonies of the Western powers. The doctrine of development, as propagated by the United Nations in the 1960s, had the main characteristics of state intervention cum democratic structures to reconcile market dynamism with social justice. In the wake of gaining political independence, countries now considered "developing" were encouraged to adopt structures ensuring a strong role of the state in the management of the economic and social life of the nation. Mixed economies and negotiations between capital and labour were characteristic of the non-communist world. Together with strong public services, these composite systems made a significant contribution to growth and social welfare in different parts of the world.

Even before the resistible ascension of global capitalism, however, there were plenty of negative comments on the performance and validity of mixed economies of the planned, liberal and social-democrat types. It was said that it was difficult to have growth without inflation; that taxes and regulations were stifling entrepreneurship and hampering the functioning of the market; that redistributive policies were too costly and were edulcorating the responsibility and dignity of the recipient individuals and families; and that societies had become too bureaucratic, creating a great distance between citizens and the various central, regional and local administrations which were supposed to serve them. Also, the problems faced by a number of developing countries, notably in Africa, were attributed first to the sequels of colonialism, then to unfair economic and financial rules of the game on the international scene, and then – with a comparable militancy and lack of nuances – to bad "governance" and the wrong policies of governments and public services seen as corrupt and ineffective.

When the Soviet Union collapsed, and with it the idea of a control of the economy by public authorities, the intellectual and political climate was ripe for the rapid and pervasive dissemination of the neo-liberal ideology during the last quarter of the 20th century. A counter-revolution of global dimension altered dramatically the distribution of power between the public sector, guardian of the general interest, and the private sector, purveyor of goods and services. It was the triumph of the Anglo-Saxon liberal utilitarian political philosophy, seen as resuming its historical course after the interruption provoked by the Bolshevik revolution and Hitler's Nazi Germany. At least at the level of political rhetoric and propaganda relayed by the press and the media with a global reach, any form of state intervention and mixed economy was identified with the totalitarian monster that had been vanquished by the liberal democratic forces.

The ideas of Friedrich von Hayek on the prosperity to be obtained through the free interplay of market forces were revived, and the democratically elected leaders and governments of the United States and the United Kingdom made a powerful contribution to the spreading of the idea that everything public was tainted with inefficiency and irrelevance while everything stemming from the private business ethos was beneficial to the individual and the Nation. Numerous well established states sold public assets and public entreprises willingly and democratically – that is with the formal or tacit agreement of elected representatives – and deprived themselves of the instruments they used to regulate financial and economic activities. Obviously of critical importance was the decision taken by the main economic and financial powers to remove all obstacles to the free circulation of capital across borders. In the well known context of enormous technological progress taking place in the crucial domains of information and communications, free circulation of capital became the main instrument and manifestation of the dominance of this contemporary form of alliance between State and corporate power. Globally, the governments of the affluent countries grouped in the OECD lent their power to the service of the corporate sector seen as capable to bring prosperity to all those individuals, countries and regions able to seize the opportunities offered by markets.

Countries from the former Soviet block were declared "in transition" and their march toward the "Market Economy" was presented with the eschatological quality of a paradise to be easily attained through immediate privatisation, deregulation and liberalisation of economic and financial transactions. A decade later, the fallacy of this "shock therapy" has been amply exposed. Those countries which had reasonably well functioning institutions and elements of a democratic culture allowing for a responsible use of private initiative and capitalist development have done reasonably well in economic and political terms. Those that did not have such institutions and democratic culture have failed and their citizens are worse off than before the "reforms" in terms of living standards and security.

Developing countries were also advised and often heavily pressured to reduce their public expenditure, privatise and deregulate. "Structural adjustments" were undertaken according to a rigid set of perscriptions. Little consideration was given to the fact that many developing countries had weak governments and administrations in terms of their capacity to provide a secure framework to the free interplay of market forces.

Overall, institutions of the private sector whose function is the production and trade of goods and services have gained much power during the last part of the 20th century. Owners and managers of private corporations have largely supplanted trade unions. In terms of the traditional dichotomy between capital and labour, the distribution of power is now comparable to the situation that prevailed at the beginning of the industrial revolution in Europe and North America. Many circumstances are indeed different, but the person from a poor country and family seeking employment in the plant of a transnational company established in an "export zone" has no more bargaining power than had the North American or French peasant hired by a textile mill during the 19th century. And, in both poor and affluent countries, workers and employees with short term contracts have very little personal autonomy and security. Their fate is determined by forces they can neither reach nor influence. "States" were treated as a generic abstraction, neglecting the enormous differences among the actual public institutions throughout the world. At the end of the cold war the opportunity for a sober assessment of the complementary virtues of liberalism and socialism for affluent and poor countries, was missed.

And yet it is all too obvious that humane societies require humane states, not minimalist governments whose main function would be to facilitate the operation and expansion of markets. Harmonious societies need institutions responsible for the general interest and the security and welfare of all citizens. Public institutions and civic spirit are necessary to organised societies. Market economies are efficient and geared to participation and justice only when governed by effective public laws and regulations. The extension, particularly in Europe after World War II, and then throughout the world, of the responsibility of the state for the welfare and economic security of individuals and families, represented progress. The withdrawal of the state from such distribution and redistribution of welfare is regression. The escape from taxation by the affluent, corruption and abuse of privileges in public and private sectors, use of public office for self enrichment or self indulging behaviour, are all tendencies destructive of the social fabric. Humane markets require humane states oriented towards the freedom and security of their citizens and the promotion of the common good.

Many governments are too weak in their structures and policy-making and administrative capacity to formulate and implement measures beneficial to their citizens. Economic stagnation and high incidence of poverty in a number countries can be largely attributed to deficiencies and failures of public institutions. Weak states are often corrupt and predatory. If the police and the army are used to maintain the state apparatus rather than protect the citizens and enforce the rule of law, economic transactions are themselves hampered. Markets cannot flourish in situations of anarchy, arbitrariness and fear. These are fertile grounds only for black markets and criminal activities. In fact, and in spite of the deregulation movement, in the well established national market economies private enterprises constitute an integral part of the social fabric and are subjected to a large number of laws and regulations pertaining to their establishment, functioning, inheritance rules and dismantling in case of bankruptcy. Most important also are laws in respect of taxation, working conditions, wages and benefits, and dismissal of employees.

Humane states have imaginative approaches to the development of institutions needed for people to have access to markets and productive activities. Humane states have room for market exchanges, for altruism, for the nurturing of traditions, for innovative forms of social organisation and for all those multiple forms of life in society that constitute a culture. Simple intermediate institutions such as local councils or cooperatives are often very efficient. They provide people with a measure of empowerment that is both liberating for the individual and positive for the community. There are many examples of successful development efforts at the local level, of changes for the better with the support of public authorities. Efficient administrations and financial institutions with proper regulations and legal systems on property rights and other requirements for economic transactions, are indispensable foundations for equitable economic growth and development. The same applies to the need for an adequate infrastructure which, even if financed by private investment, cannot be put into place without the intervention of public authorities.

It is not the size of the state that matters most, but the way public institutions and public officials handle their responsibilities. The public sector, restricting itself to administrative functions or actively involved in the economic realm, ought to strive for excellence in terms of integrity and efficiency as well as quality of the services it provides to the collectivity. The fact that such standards are not always respected does not provide a rational for condemning the public sector as inherently incompetent and inefficient. Similarly, "downsizing" for more profit or the dumping of harmful products on unprotected markets are not practices justifying an overall moral condemnation of the private sector.

Governments have to recognise that their function is to govern and that this implies assuming responsibility for the regulation of the economy and process of globalisation. They cannot protect themselves behind the "market" and justify absenteeism by the virtues of a laissez faire philosophy. Various forms of mixed economies ought to be rehabilitated, or reinvented, depending on national circumstances. It is desirable and possible to make governments work better. Key notions remain legitimacy, accountability, transparency and openness to debates. A central requirement is the ability to balance leadership and the capacity to listen to the vox populi. A pre-condition for good government is the recognition by society that politics is an art and a profession deserving respect and requiring total dedication.

The frontiers between the public and the private spheres are moving and such change ought to be oriented by some basic principles. The sharing of responsibilities implies distinct roles and a reasonably clear division of labour. The state and markets cannot be substitutes for each other but must complement each other. This relationship cannot be specified once and for all. The two institutions must adapt to one another in a cooperative manner over time, while keeping their specificity.

Thus, a viable world community requires effective, competent and humane national states. This is not in contradiction with the need for states to cede some of their sovereignty to regional and international organisations. Social progress on a world scale implies that the promotion of some shared principles and values be given a superior status, in legal, moral and political terms, to national sovereignty. But this has to be achieved in an orderly and progressive manner. The subordination of the legitimate government of a poor country to the interests and dictates of a transnational corporation or financial international organisation is not a sound and secure path to a peaceful and prosperous world community.

Make Regional Organisations the Building Blocks of a Global Community

Regional organisations with the task of promoting cooperation between their sovereign members have multiplied during the second part of this century. To a large extent they have replaced the alliances and coalitions that marked international relations of nations and empires. In line with the spirit of the time and the priorities of political action, regional groupings are primarily concerned with promoting economic cooperation and eventually economic integration between their members. Or, when the main objective is political rapprochement and the elimination of the recurrence of military conflict, the creation of close economic relations is the principal means to that end. At this point, the European Union is by far the most ambitious and most advanced regional organisation.

Partly because of the achievements of the European Union and partly because regional arrangements have an aura of proximity and reasonableness, the notion of "constructive regionalism" has gained some favour. Regionalisation is considered a good antidote to the dangers and excesses of globalisation. From the perspective of taming the process of economic globalisation, the interplay and competition between different types of market economy systems – American, Asian with variations within the region, European, Latin America, Middle Eastern, and hopefully in the near future Russian and African – could become a form of global cooperation preventing the "clash of civilisations", as a protection against the economic imperialism of a few powerful actors, and as a laboratory for fruitful analyses of comparative political cultures, notably for the relations between states and markets.

Here is a region with pro-business rather than pro-market policies; there a region with close relationships between elites in the public and private sectors; and, elsewhere a region with powerful middle classes benefiting from universal education and undertaking capitalist activities in a protective context of personal security. Such diversity nurtured by regional loyalties and institutions might contribute to the working of a global community. It has obvious connections with the objective of cultural diversity and with the view that only countries with confidence in their identity and effective public institutions can meaningfully cooperate in a larger setting.

Regional cooperation is an effective school for international cooperation. Quite clearly, however, if not controlled and oriented towards the welfare of humanity as a whole, regionalism can lead to fragmentation, unchecked competition, trade wars and even cultural and political conflicts. Constructive regional institutions can always slide into siege mentality if economic achievements are in question and if pressures from outside are perceived as threatening the group. In parallel, again in local, national and international settings, the best guarantee against such slippage resides in check and balances, in procedures for decisions that are irritatingly slow and cumbersome in happy times but precious when the main objective is to control political emotions and passions, and in organised cooperation with other regions through international organisations. Hopefully, "regionalism" will not have in next century the same loaded and tragic meaning that "nationalism" acquired during the 20th century. Neither economic nor cultural wars between regions and civilisations should be regarded as catastrophic but unavoidable steps towards an organised world community.

Manage the Global World Economy

Effective public institutions are necessary to enhance and disseminate the positive aspects of the globalisation process and to control and remedy its excesses and deficiencies. Such institutions are required not only in national and regional settings, but also at the global level.

Global capitalism is not spreading in a totally anarchic manner. It has the active support of the public authorities and agencies of the dominant country and power, the United States of America, and of a number of other governments. Transnational corporations have their own strategies, often elaborated and implemented in conjunction with the same governments. The most powerful international organisations – the International Monetary Fund, the World Bank and the World Trade Organisations – are both promoting and, to a limited extent, regulating global capitalism. So is the less public but most critical Bank for International Settlements, acting in symbiosis with the most prominent national central banks and financial institutions. And, active in the same realm are a number of partly private partly public "hybrid" institutions such as the International Standards Organisation, the International Securities Markets Association, the International Organisation of Securities Commissions, or the International Association of Insurance Supervisors, and a few others that elaborate and monitor the enforcement of the norms that are necessary for the developing of global markets.

Thus, when perceived as necessary by the ruling powers, institutions are strengthened or established. Apart from the WTO, the European Central Bank is a recent prominent example. And, problems revealed in the financial crises that effected Asia and other parts of the world at the end of the 1990s prompted leaders of the world economy to consider reforming the "architecture" of the world financial institutions. In 1999, finance ministers of the major industrialised countries discussed the establishment of a Financial Stability Forum that would aim at enhancing international supervision and surveillance of financial flows. Experts in this domain who do not have an ideological bias against international regulatory institutions predict that in a few years, probably in the aftermath of one or several severe crises, a new World Financial Authority will be set up, with effective power to control instability and thwart collapse of the financial system.

In the related domain of ensuring that economic growth will remain sustainable, in the wake of the UN Conference on Environment and Development that took place in Rio de Janeiro in 1992, the world was able to set up a few new institutions to boost the struggle against the deterioration of the environment. The United Nations Framework Convention on Climate Change, that entered into force in March 1994, held its third conference in Kyoto in December 1997 and adopted a number of targets for the reduction of emissions of "greenhouse gases". The 1985 Vienna Convention for the Protection of the Ozone Layer and the 1987 Montreal Protocol on Substances that Deplete the Ozone Layer also contribute to the protection of the global commons by promoting and to some extent financing measures against the production and consumption of ozone depleting substances. The Ozone Secretariat is part of the United Nations Environment Program, located in Nairobi. These efforts, which also include initiatives at various levels of ambition and success on desertification, fresh water management, the protection of forests, or the development of Consumer Protection Guidelines for Sustainable Con-sumption by the UN Economic and Social Council, demonstrate the dramatically important intellectual change in the dominant western culture that has shaped the modern agenda on development and social progress. This change was prompted by a recognition from governments and other powers that the warnings formulated by a few individuals and organisations, starting in the 1960s essentially in the United States and the Nordic Countries, were valid.

Yet, overall, the management of the globalised part of the world economy is either private and secretive through institutions such as transnational corporations and central banks, or openly undemocratic as in the case of the annual meetings of the Group of Seven Most Industrialised Countries. The meetings organised annually by a private organisation in Davos, Switzerland, and bringing together leaders of the political, economic and financial world to debate of matters of common interest, symbolise the running of world affairs by a small group of persons and institutions. National Parliaments are by and large left out of the governmental decisions that, for instance, open the doors to private foreign investment or to the absorption of domestic firms by transnational companies. Regional organisations, as the European Union, are only at the beginning of a questioning of their own technocratic culture. At the international level, neither the United Nations nor the ILO are recognised by the main powers as fully legitimate actors in the process of economic globalisation. They are only occasionally used to smoothen some sharp angles and develop proclamations and agreements without immediate practical conse-quences. The global conferences organised by the United Nations, notably the Social Summit, provided occasional forums for large debates on development matters, but their follow-up has little bearing on the management of the world economy. The "core labour standards" that the ILO strives to imple-ment are extremely important to the avoidance of various forms of exploita-tion, but they do not address the question of a new historical compromise between the powerful and the weak, the successful and the marginalized.

The main shortcoming of the current version of global capitalism is indeed that it seems to exclude a reasonably consensual sharing of economic power and economic benefits, both among social classes and among countries. Unopposed intellectually and politically, global capitalism shows no interest for a new social contract that could secure its role in the context of econom-ic and political democracy at the world level. Through deregulation, laterali-sation and privatisation, capital has been freed to act in ways that escape the controls and fences painfully put in place to ensure some acceptable and fair distribution of income, assets, and power. From a perspective of democracy and social justice, of creating conditions making possible new agreements between capital and labour, or between a few powerful individuals and groups and the masses of world citizens, there is a need to recapture a sense of polit-ical control over the raw economic forces that are moving the process of eco-nomic globalisation. New social contracts are necessary at the international and global level.

It may seem futile to advocate global regulations and agreements on the func-tioning of the world economy when deregulation at the national level is still on the agenda. But the need to promote effective and humane states evoked above will not disappear, and the fact that a number of issues are too global to be addressed solely by individual governments will not disappear either. The only rationale for rejecting a more transparent and more democratic management of the world economy is the belief that current arrangements work well and are in any event the only ones compatible with the free market philosophy and practice. Confrontation of this view and belief with the nor-mative and interventionist approach evoked here should precisely be at the heart of debates on the features of a global democratic community.

Are new institutions needed to manage and regulate the globalised part of the world economy in a manner that would balance and check the power of its main actors? The question of the strengthening of the United Nations is discussed below. It is certain that the responsibility and democratic accountability of corporations and financial institutions operating with considerable freedom across borders and having planetary influence in a variety of domains, including the culture of millions of people, will be an intensely debated subject in the coming years. New institutions might emerge, hopefully from the United Nations system. For such debate, a few markers are in order.

Critical is a clarification of the principles and objectives of a democratic control of corporations with a global reach. In a universalist perspective, the common good of humanity is the most important objective of political action. Framed by basic moral values derived from the concept of human nature which transcends all differences, the common good needs nevertheless to be continuously defined. This should be done through a democratic process, that involves a maximum number of the actors concerned, and by authorities that have the mandate to propose an agenda and the capacity to monitor the implementation of the relevant decisions. Private corporations need to be consulted in all steps of the process. But, ultimately, it is the legitimate political authority that has to make decisions and control their implementation. In this regard, international democracy is not different from national democracy.

Critical also is public knowledge of the current relationships between private corporations and international authorities. The issue is not new, but has taken on a different dimension and urgency since the rise of global capitalism. In addition to the ILO conventions and the relevant provisions of the International Bill of Human Rights, there are regulations in a few other domains including the protection of the environment and property rights. Obvious gaps are in the areas of taxation, investment and anti-trust legislation. A modern Candide would be astonished to discover that mergers and acquisitions of huge companies employing thousands of persons are done without public scrutiny, and that it is often legal for a corporation to avoid taxes by moving its official headquarter to a tax haven. Questions for analysis and debate include the functioning of the institutions in charge of monitoring agreed policies, for example the ILO conventions; cases of guidelines without procedures and means to enforce them; and the dissemination of the

145

information available to international organisations on the activities of global corporations. There is little possibility of democratic debate without a large amount of shared knowledge and equal access to the sources of information. Enormous progress in global democracy would already be made if there were a forum in which private and public corporations and banks could explain their strategies and report on their observance of international laws and guidelines. At this point, neither the General Assembly nor the Economic and Social Council play this role. There is need for more conceptual work to better comprehend the characteristics and roles of transnational corporations currently operating in a large variety of domains. Political science and theories on international relations have recently added a global dimension to their concepts and should be increasingly able to consider not only the interplay of states but also the power of these new actors.

Equally critical for the management of the global world economy is the recognition that fair rules of the game need to be established and regularly updated. At present, a number of countries and social groups, not to mention the immense majority of people throughout the world who are struggling for survival, feel powerless and marginalised. Existing rules and institutional arrangements are widely seen as reflecting the interests of the most powerful countries and other major actors, and as biased in their favour. For example the multilateral regimes for trade in services and for trade-related investment rules and property rights are seen as asymmetrical, as they promote a liberalisation of trade and capital flows while remaining restrictive for technology and labour. If the world economy is to be more democratic in its management and the distribution of its fruits, new arrangements have to be made at the international level to ensure the effective participation of all countries and social groups. There is need for multilateral processes to give a voice to developing countries and all small partners in order to reach a shared understanding of global issues. This requires, inter alia, a strengthening of the negotiating capacity of developing countries. Partnership implies equality and a sense of ownership of processes and institutions. There is also a need for stronger pressure in favour of the poor and the vulnerable, people and countries. Often, to be fair and equitable, the "rules of the game" ought to be biased in favour of the weakest. As some national democracies try to redress inequalities through "affirmative action", global democracy requires deliberately established biases to protect those that cannot "play on an even field". This is a never achieved task, as circumstances and conditions evolved. The essential, on the part of

146

those with the greatest power, is an attitude of care and respect for those who happen to be less fortunate, or simply less vocal and demanding.

Economic relationships between people have always two elements: common interests and differences. Adversarial discussions and processes are therefore unavoidable. Everything should be done, however, to prevent such processes from turning into conflicts. To do so, it is critical to understand and even value differences, to agree on facts, to avoid any casting of blame, and to build themes which are unifying. Partners have to be convinced that debates and negotiations offer opportunities to learn and to be enriched. Antinomic to this attitude, is a narrow and impatient conception of efficiency and self-interest.

Lastly, a managed global world economy requires clarification of the social responsibility of the private sector. Corruption in the public and private sectors is on the agenda of the United Nations and the OECD has developed comprehensive guidelines to prevent corrupt practices. Most governments declare their intention to combat corruption. In itself, this moralising movement is positive. It is particularly beneficial for societies and for the international community when embracing both private morality – for instance the refusal of a bribe or proper conduct of a superior vis-a-vis subordinates – and public morality, such as rigorous testing of new products or the avoidance of misleading or manipulating advertisements. Further progress will be achieved when the social responsibility of those who have significant economic and financial power is extended to issues of employment and distribution of opportunities, income and wealth. The increasingly negative image conveyed by the reduction of the number of jobs to save labour costs and to increase profits should pave political grounds for an international debate on the current characteristics of global competition. On opportunities for work and private initiative, significant progress has been made in the elimination of various forms of discrimination, including gender, race, or religion. This is an important contribution to the construction of a global democratic community, and where most successful, it was at least initially imposed by legislation: a reminder that public morality often requires a mix of hard law and personal virtue.

By their nature, private corporations do not have the responsibility to redistribute income and wealth. Through the products and services they offer, the image they convey of what constitutes a successful life and a prosperous soci-

147

ety, the salaries of their executives, their systems of incentives and rewards, their treatment of employees with the lowest skill, the use of their profits, the distribution of their investments between poor and affluent regions, all elements of their ethical behaviour, not to mention respect for labour rights, they have nevertheless a powerful demonstration effect. In many ways, these new powers influence the minds of people and the dominant culture as have religious institutions in times and places of unquestioned faith. In that sense their social responsibility is immense.

Strengthen the United Nations System

The various institutions of the United Nations system, from the General Assembly to technical organisations dealing with telecommunications or property rights, can be seen as elements of the management of world affairs. They have been created to address problems and facilitate the functioning of this world, normally through cooperation of states and other actors, and exceptionally through coercion, as when the provisions of chapter VII of the Charter of the United Nations are used to force a Member State to behave according to international law. It is a system which has the International Court of Justice and hopefully soon an International Criminal Court, if the decision taken in 1998 in Rome by a majority of Member States to establish such court is followed by ratifications. Although they are not part of it in strictly legal terms, the World Bank, the International Monetary Fund and the World Trade Organisation can be legitimately added to this system. This is enough to alarm those who are hostile to the emergence of a world government, or to give hope to those who are seeking an organised world society.

From the perspective of the construction of a global democratic community, and before commenting on the United Nations itself, the role and evolution of this system of organisations raise questions of coherence, gaps, and accountability. Assuming that over the span of almost a century that separates the creation of the ILO from the establishment of the WTO, the constitutions and mandates of the various organisations have been established in accordance with a reasonable division of labour, a first level of coherence is achieved if these organisations do properly what they are suppose to accomplish. Subjective and sweeping as it may be, the judgement can be made that this is indeed the case. The second level of coherence stems from the coordination required to avoid duplications and create complementarities among programmes and activities. Much has been written and said on this question of coordination among UN entities, usually with a critical streak. In what is called the "field", that is the delivery of various forms of assistance to countries in need, progress is underway with regard to the determination of the various agencies and programmes to talk to each other and also to listen to the recipients.

On global issues, coordination is only an aspect of the third level of coherence which is the consistency of the political orientations and objectives of the organisations concerned. To a degree, these organisations share a universalist ethos. None of them would openly challenge the political philosophy expressed in the Charter of the United Nations and the Universal Declaration for Human Rights. They are all in favour of "development" and "progress". While reflecting in their structures and modes of operation the unequal distribution of power among their members, they all try to compensate for these inequalities because they exist to distribute tangible and intangible benefits to all the people of the world. In that sense, they are both international and transnational institutions. Such commonality is far from being negligible. At the same time, however, it would be somewhat daring to affirm that the organisations of the United Nations system are working in unison for the advent of a global democratic community. Their conceptions of the common good may not be dramatically different, but their strategies and policies vary greatly.

Are there issues of global relevance which are not covered by the existing network of institutions of the United Nations system? The identification of such gaps depends of course on the philosophical and political perspective of the observer. Apart from the management of the global economy, mentioned above, a case could be made for the regrouping in a new specialised agency of all the various programmes pertaining to the protection of the environment. It would seem that when a domain is scientifically important and active, and politically very visible, time has come for the creation of an entity with enough prestige and weight to make a breakthrough. Issues currently neglected, like fisheries, would perhaps have a better chance to be addressed. A counter argument is that, particularly through the notion of sustainable development, the protection of the environment has become a dimension of the work of the various parts of the system, including the World Bank and the United Nations itself. Could such integration continue to flourish if an agency was created with a sort of monopoly over the issues?

The same interrogation applies, mutatis mutandi, to the institutional location of objectives such as the equality of women and men and social development as comprehensively defined by the Social Summit. A seemingly correct division of labour implies, for instance, that employment is treated by the ILO and culture and education by the UNESCO, and that the United Nations and the World Bank, or the WHO, simply incorporate the work of these agencies into their own work, when relevant. But a recognition of the critical importance of the same issues for all the facets of the system dealing with broad global problems means that specialisation cannot be fully respected. Overall, however, there is a positive relationship between the institutional visibility of an issue and the seriousness and scope of the actions taken to address it. Science and technology, and their role in the shaping of the globalisation process and the unfolding universal culture, is a prominent a-contrario example. In spite of the useful work of UNESCO, there is in this domain a gap that should not be ignored.

The secretariats of the various institutions of the UN system are accountable to their governing bodies, generally composed of representatives of Member States, with a few exceptions like the tripartite structure of the ILO. The organisations themselves are not accountable to the citizens of the world. There is no World Parliament. The General Assembly of the United Nations, and the Economic and Social Council, have from the Charter the power to exert some leadership and coordinating role over the system. A revival of this role will require political forces that are not yet on the horizon.

Accountability partly depends on the circulation of information and the transparency of the work of the institutions of the United Nations system. This system does not have its television network or newspaper. The international media with a global reach provide some information on events and crises involving the parts of the system dealing with peace-keeping, trade, finance and humanitarian assistance. The internet might give to a large public the possibility to get acquainted with other aspects of the work of the United Nations and the specialised agencies. The increasing involvement of non-governmental organisations in this work is in itself a step towards a greater democratisation of the UN system. NGOs are very efficient channels for dissemination of information.

The United Nations itself is the political core of the system. It is the only organisation with quasi universal membership and the mandate for political debates on the ways humanity intends to address its problems and construct its future. As the principal world forum, including on universal moral issues and international law, the United Nations has the mandate for providing policy orientations to all international programmes, specialised agencies, and financial and trade institutions. It ought to set the tone of international and global cooperation for a democratic world order. A stronger United Nations would seek to improve the character and benefits of cooperation among countries and between countries, and to direct more harmoniously the forces that are currently fueling the process of globalisation.

Such strengthening should be undertaken through a variety of means.

The United Nations needs more financial resources. There is no effective global community without resources commensurate to address global problems. It should continue to be financed primarily by assessed contributions based on the wealth of its members and conceived as a progressive income tax. These contributions should be supplemented by resources coming from international taxation of various global transactions, for example along the lines suggested by the "Tobin Tax". Voluntary contributions from private donors – corporations, foundations or individuals – should be placed in a Trust Fund and their use should be subjected to the same guidelines and control as the resources from the regular budget. Priorities established through a process that seeks to be transparent and democratic should not be distorted by the preferences of private contributors. In a related domain, official development assistance through bilateral and multilateral channels should be increased as a first step in the development of a redistributive system at the world level. The global social contracts evoked above would require such financing.

In the process of reform and expansion of the Security Council, that should include a reflection on the concept of security for countries and people at this particular historical juncture, room should be made for a parallel discussion on the establishment of an Economic and Social Security Council. The links between peace and development and social progress are such, and the process of globalisation has so many ramifications with the security of nations and people that there would be some logic in merging this new body and the existing Security Council. It could be a Council on Security and Progress. A few years ago, in 1995, the Commission on Global Governance, in its report *Our Global Neighbourhood*, proposed the establishment of a separate and independent Economic Security Council whose tasks would be to assess the overall state of the world economy, provide a long term policy framework for sustainable development, secure consistency between the policy goals of the major international organisations, and give political leadership on international economic issues. Whether this road, or the more ambitious evoked above is taken, the essential at this point is that some initiative put the United Nations into a position of political leadership on matters of common interest to all countries and human beings. The easier road, for example, a progressive enlargement of the Group of Seven Most Industrialised Countries to other smaller powers and countries of the South would mean a further marginalisation of the United Nations. There are no reasons to believe that such course of action would be a contribution to the common good and the building of a viable and fair democratic world community.

The strengthening of the United Nations will also require the progressive integration in its fora and councils of the forces which, is addition to states and their governments and representatives, are shaping societies and the world, and are expressing a variety of interests and views. These forces include the private corporate sector, trade-unions and social movements, the media, as well as the scientific, artistic and religious communities. The non-governmental organisations, present in the United Nations since its birth, and which have expanded their role with the world conferences of the 1980s and 1990s, are paving the way for such enrichment of the world body. It is essential for the United Nations to remain an international organisation, made of Member States that should themselves be more and more democratic and therefore more and more representative of their citizens. A world democratic community cannot be build only around a few dominant countries, corporations, and some global social movements representing "the people". But it is equally essential for the United Nations to attract and welcome those forces that have a power of their own and those movements and institutions that have something to say on the meaning of a good life and a good society, or/and that care about those people who, for whatever reason, have no voice and no power. In such perspective, attention should be given to the possible convening of a World Peoples Assembly, and to the transformation of the Economic and Social Council, or the Trusteeship Council into a permanent body bringing together with a consultative role the social forces mentioned above.

The strengthening of the United Nations might be considered utopian in the present configuration of political trends and forces. It is true that most major public institutions have been created after crises of planetary magnitude. But lesser albeit significant events such as failures in the functioning of the international system should provide strong incentives for institutional reform and development. There is little courage in the attitude of waiting for historical events, generally tragic, to force the advent of desirable changes. Political imagination involves a creative use not only of crises but also of times of relative tranquillity. To have political power is both to react and to guide. And there are always people who are suffering and nations that need the helping hand of the more fortunate. The search for stability, in institutions as in other aspects of world affairs ought not to be an excuse for prolonging unfairness and injustice.

For the difficult task of building, strengthening, or maintaining institutions that have a role in the promotion of the common good, an obstacle is the evidence of anti-democratic tendencies in the world despite the spreading of some modern techniques of communications and institutions drawn on the Western liberal democratic model. The lack of official concern for the growth of inequalities, and the apparent concentration of economic and social power are signs that democracy is far from progressing on all fronts.

Another obstacle is the domination of international organisations by a few governments, that do not attach priority to the level and type of cooperation, including between rich and poor countries, required by a well-functioning world community. The emphasis on privatisation and the role of market forces to address issues of development had negative effects on the concept and practice of international cooperation.

These obstacles are reason for action. And there are strong sources of hope.

Forces favouring democratisation of international and global relations gained visibility at the turn of the 21st century. They are still scattered, however, and their visions of the future have yet to coalesce into an overall political project that could challenge the neo-liberal doctrine. Considerable intellectual and political work is needed to establish the foundations of a democratic world community. Dedicated individuals and organisations have to work to that end while calling attention on the many more urgent problems that continue to plague the world, from poverty to violence.

At least compared with the situation twenty years ago, there is a change in ideas, shared to some extent by those who have the power to influence the world state of affairs. Market fundamentalism is regressing and a more balanced view of the role of public authorities, corporations, and organisations of the civil society is emerging.

It is easy to underestimate the potential power of individuals, groups and institutions aspiring to a different, richer, and more just world order. This is not so much an allusion to a "silent majority" as recognition that in all societies and all groups are individuals of goodwill and good spirit. A manicheist vision of the world would be dangerous and false.

It is also easy to underestimate the power of the call for an ideal. There is in the world a strong demand for stimulating projects, not only as a reaction against the malaise that seems to permeate the modern ethos, but also because of the natural propensity of human beings to work for causes that require political imagination and generosity of the spirit.

Most importantly, in spite of either poverty or consumerism, human beings have not lost appetite for information and knowledge. This is a major reason for hope, because the capacity for intellectual rigour, the desire to search for the truth, and the ability to question accepted views are sine qua non conditions for good government and democracy. When rooted in a rich intellectual and moral soil, pragmatism can go a long way towards the realisation of the vision of the idealists.

Additional Contributions

Realizing the Copenhagen Vision: The Political Imperative

Richard Falk
Professor, Princeton University, Princeton, USA

Aspiration and Action

Five years after Copenhagen the challenge of making progress in relation to aspirations for a more socially accountable global political economy remains mostly unmet. And yet there are encouraging signs that the political climate is more receptive to social and ethical claims than it was in 1995. The Asian Financial Crisis and The Battle of Seattle disclosed severe limitations of mainstream thinking about globalization both at the level of policymaking and with respect to the previously unsuspected suspicions and outright opposition to prevailing modes of globalization by a broadband of the citizenry in leading democratic societies. Such tensions are relevant politically, suggesting that those in positions of dominance now have a clear incentive to accommodate and compromise with the critics of globalization that seemed absent in the early 1990s when the neo-liberal consensus about public policy seemed virtually unchallengable. As the 21st century begins, the space for debate and opportunities for mainstream media access have widened, making it far more plausible than a few years earlier to consider approaches to global problems that question to varying degrees postures of deference to market forces.

Such a change of circumstances could even soon generate a feasible political project that reconciles the continuing growth and integration of the world economy with a firm commitment to the humanization of globalization. This reconciliation is essential if all peoples in the world are to reap the benefits of growth and innovation, while at the same time becoming better insulated against the worst fallout effects of economic marginalization.

It would seem to me that a validation of the Copenhagen seminar process arises from the depth of its commitment to the viability of comprehensive global reform designed to achieved a far greater degree of social equity than currently exists. The seminar deliberations laid some of the essential intellectual groundwork, including exchanges of ideas and concerns expressing widely differing ethnic, civilizational, and developmental perspectives. Despite globalization, it is more apparent than ever before, that effective social initiative of regional and global scope must become sensitive to these primordial diversities that have been responsible for generating most of the world's violent conflicts in the period since the fall of the Berlin Wall.

Assessing Globalization

Much of this ongoing, intensifying debate about globalization is admittedly fuzzy. Partisans and antagonists focus on different parts of the elephant, and often dogmatically confuse what they experience as the whole animal. Such fragmentary ways of knowing generate polarized debates that exaggerate both the benefits and detriments attributed to globalization, and thereby distort its more contradictory reality. The tendency to situate globalization exclusively to the events of the past decade also contributes to misunderstanding. The abrupt and one-sided ending of the cold war encouraged ideological interpretations of the drift of history that produced two major impacts on the climate of opinion and belief. It discredited socialist values and thinking, along with a more generalized repudiation of any visionary ideas about political change. The latter was stigmatized by being linked to the failed utopianism of the Marx/Lenin experiment in the Soviet Union. The cumulative effect of these influences was to shutdown the moral and political imagination, and pave the way for the uncritical adoption of such "neo-liberal" priorities as deregulation, minimizing governmental interventions in the market, entrusting social concerns to the market as abetted by charity, lowering tax rates, and privatization. Gone from arenas of discussion and advocacy were socialist alternatives, and all perspectives with explicit normative proposals designed to improve the human condition by means other than the market were tarred with a socialist brush. Such a mood of ethical disillusionment was reinforced by the related abandonment of redistributive demands emanating from the ex-colonial Third World.

157

There was a generalized acceptance by elites throughout the world of this view that it was only the American ideological package of "market-oriented constitutionalism", that opened a hopeful path to the future. It was "the only game in town", as Henrique Fernando Cardoso famously summed up the situation a decade ago. Because of this dual collapse of socialist and Third World challenges, there appeared a kind of inevitability to the manner in which the world economy was evolving. This dynamic was theorized in a memorable, if absurd, manner by Francis Fukuyama, who contended that the human species had actually reached "the end of history". This disappearance of the socialist "other", tended also to push capitalist thinking to its amoral extreme. It recalls the ideological atmosphere that prevailed during the predatory phases of the first stages of the industrial revolution in Europe, despite the more guarded endorsements of early capitalist methods and morals by such formative thinkers as Adam Smith. This ideological mood of closure preceded the emergence of a labor movement and the articulation by Marx and others of a radical socialist alternative to capitalism. These latter developments shook the foundations of capitalist complacency, scaring elites by the emergence of what Immanuel Wallerstein has usefully identified as "the dangerous classes". It was this fear of class war that induced a spirit of compromise in many sectors of the established order even before the traumatizing experience of the Russian Revolution in the wake of World War I.

The relative humanization of capitalism that followed was prompted by this incentive to restore social peace. It depended on meeting this challenge halfway, giving workers a stake in the stability of the existing order and introducing by stage welfare policies to protect the weak and vulnerable, while in exchange keeping control over production and profits mainly in private sector hands. What the first years of the era of globalization in the last decade of the 20th century disclosed was a second predatory cycle of capitalism, but this time on a regional and global scale, abetted by volatile currency trading and free for all financial markets.

In standing against what had seemed like a hurricane of affirmation, the early critics of globalization appeared mainly as isolated romantic figures, victimized by an unwelcome nostalgia for the good old days of welfare capitalism, or worse, rightist populists who were playing on the fears of society associated with all that was "foreign". Most of these critics could not bring themselves to admit either the analytic and political failures of the old left or the constraining limitations of territorial nationalism and sovereignty. They often additionally seemed foolishly unwilling to acknowledge the fantastic emancipatory potential of emergent globalizing technologies. Their repudiation of global capitalism was thus easily dismissed as little more than residual leftism, or at best part of a wider deconstructionist cultural mood that was undermining the legitimacy of all existing institutions without having the wit or wisdom to posit preferable alternatives. In some extreme instances, the anti-globalization attacks seemed even to embrace a philosophical outlook that denied the possibility of a coherent alternative way of organizing the political economy of the world.

This sort of embittered rejection of globalization made it all too easy for the market-oriented establishment and media to disregard such negativity, being continuously exhilarated and vindicated by the ascent of world stock market indicators to record levels. It needs to be understood that the main mode of wealth creation in this period seemed to be speculative, "casino capitalism", as dubbed years ago by Susan Strange. Thus it was natural to perceive the world through the lens of venture capitalists and financial wizards, especially realizing that the global media and its advertising network was itself both a manifestation and a constant source of celebration of this mode of globalization. Of course, we now realize how simplistic and partial was this world picture of the new capitalism. The giants of Silicon Valley were reconstructing a new capitalism along the post-industrial lines of an emergent Information Age, a process that is already having a transformative impact on the way we work, live, communicate, and do business.

As a consequence of these shortcomings in assessment, no relevant political space has yet been cleared. The main set of protagonists proclaimed the multiple benefits of globalization loud and clear, while their scattered antagonists, far less vocal and affluent, decried the harm often in the nasty rhetoric of chauvinistic nationalism. A constructive orientation for the critics of globalization depends on having a capacity for a more nuanced opposition that does not trap itself into an allegience with largely outmoded ideas about national self-reliance and territorial sovereignty. There is no doubt that an extraordinary array of revolutionary effects are arising from recent applications of the hardware and software of the Internet to the human condition, generating wealth and income in unprecedented quantities, creating opportunities and spreading benefits to many previously impoverished societies, particularly in

Asia. If globalization is conceived non-ideologically as a series of technological innovations that have eased the burdens of life, enabled free communications on a global basis, and given many peoples access to a storehouse of information, then there are no intrinsic adverse consequences for social policy. It is also evident that the market, with its way of rewarding risk-takers with money, has injected a dynamic force into the world economy that domestically driven territorial ambitions and large bureaucracies under the control of sovereign states, were no longer able to do on their own. These acknowledgements do not at all imply an ideology of deference to the global discipline of capitalism. It does not mean an acceptance of a race to the bottom resulting from the struggle to maintain "competitiveness" in an unregulated market that takes full advantage of uneven conditions, especially bearing on cheap labor and loose regulation.

In other words, the agenda of the Copenhagen Social Summit never had a chance of meaningful implementation so long as the neo-liberal consensus held uninhibited sway, which precluded the pursuit of normative concerns associated with public sector efforts to mitigate human suffering arising from joblessless, poverty, and societal insecurities. But this consensus was *always* artificial. It rested on a successful hijacking of "globalization", that is, insinuating a set of economistic ideas as if they were organically embedded in globalization. But it has become increasingly clear in the last part of the 1990s that insisting on such an ideological view of globalization was not even persuasive economically, and was no longer acceptable for significant constituencies in democratic societies. The neo-liberal honeymoon of the early 1990s seems definitely over. First came the Asian Financial Crisis of 1997, and the inadequacy of IMF-led neo-liberal responses, which inflicted great suffering on the more vulnerable parts of the population beneath the banner of fiscal austerity and banking reform. This crisis also exposed the shortcomings of minimally regulated financial and currency markets that could be rapidly destabilized by speculators who were themselves extreme embodiments of asocial market logic. Then came the street protests directed at the ministerial meeting of the WTO held in Seattle late in 1999, which cast a long shadow over the political legitimacy of the procedures and substance of economic globalization. And most recently, in the early months of the 21st century, a return of high energy costs are sweeping away the former complacency of the ideologues of globalization who gather each year at World Economic Forum in Davos.

Re-framing Globalization

There is no good purpose served by attempting an escape from the prevailing terminology. "Globalization" as a description of the historical originality of the present world is here to stay, at least for some years, if not decades. But our perception of globalization needs to be clarified, and freed from certain unexamined and highly contingent assumptions. To begin with, it is important to leave intellectual space for "globalization with a human face" or "compassionate globalization". Even the World Economic Forum in 1999 used as its theme the awkward phrase "responsible globality" to signal its sudden openness to critical perspectives and social concerns. Of course, such co-opting language proves nothing by itself, aside from some sense that the earlier ideological complacency of the celebratory phase of neo-liberal globalization is no longer acceptable. But the prospect of turning this more receptive political language into some embodiment of "compassionate globalization" needs to be assessed at the policymaking and behavioral levels, and so far, the adjustments that have been made seem overwhelmingly cosmetic. It is the postulate of this essay that the realization of compassionate globalization awaits the enactment of a political project that is capable of mobilizing effective agents of social change. At least we have advanced since 1995 to the point where the contours of such project can now be discerned, and will be depicted in the final section of this essay.

The other part of the re-framing process is a recognition of the plural nature of globalization. The earlier reductive framing of globalization tended automatically to situate critics of neo-liberalism as the basis of world economic policy in an "anti-globalization" camp. This had the consequence, earlier discussed, of making it easy to reject criticism because it was either expressive of one or another nostalgia: for a pre-industrial pastoral ideal that never existed or for a statist delimitation of community and market that also never truly existed. A re-framing of globalization takes account of the extent to which those who oppose neo-liberalism, as embodied in IMF thinking about "structural adjustment programs", are properly located within an enlarged tent of globalization, rather than being forced to be without looking in. That is, a re-framing of globalization allows ample space for the espousal of cosmopolitan values and human solidarity.

To foster this more plural understanding of globalization, it seems helpful to propose an initial convenient division between "globalization-from-above" (GFA)

It is also the case that the main expressions of the anti-globalization movement have become more sophisticated. There is a greater effort to refrain from attacks that either express neo-Luddite dispositions to thrash the innovative achievements of the Information Age or the ravings of right wing populism that blames immigrants and transnational labor mobility for the declining living standards and the loss of nationalist coherence.

Admittedly, there were many policy crosscurrents among the protesters in the streets and in the meeting halls at Seattle, including some contradictory policy positions. Despite this cacaphony of voices, there was a common call for a more democratically guided world economy that gave greater attention to issues of social justice, and to the priorities of the countries of the South. Even such notable rivals as China and India closed ranks after Seattle to assert a common front dedicated to achieving more leverage for the South in future operations of the WTO.

There are then two major conclusions to be drawn and considered. First of all, "globalization" as a dominant motif of current international relations needs to be reformulated in such a way that it does not automatically incorporate the ideological presuppositions of neo-liberal economics. The appropriate economic enactment of the globalizing technologies that are altering our lives and blurring the significance of territorial boundaries is itself what needs to be discussed in a framework that includes adequate representation for and participation by all the peoples of the world. And secondly, opponents of neo-liberalism must learn not to direct their assault at globalization as such, but rather work toward the formulation and embrace of positive forms of globalization that enhance the material, moral, and spiritual well-being of people and take especial account of those who appear most disadvantaged by current trends in the world economy. Also relevant for opponents is a greater stress on the guardianship of global common interests, both as conceived in relation to the sustainability of the environment and the life prospects of future generations. For such an undertaking we require a sensitive and balanced critical discourse on globalization rather than a collision of polar discourses that veer between the extremes of unconditional enthusiasm and uncompromising diatribes.

and "globalization-from-below" (GFB). GFA essentially represents those capital-oriented perspectives that measure global economic performance by aggregate growth, productivity trends, and returns on capital. In contrast, GFB is people-oriented, assessing economic performance by reference to quality of life indicators, emphasizing impacts on poverty, employment, life expectancy, education, health, social security, human rights, and access to information and communication resources. The dualism between these two orientations toward globalization draws too bright a line in certain respects. It tends to overlook the spectrum of outlooks on either side of the divide, and to ignore diagonal line-crossing orientations, as when a socially oriented government also tries to join the WTO or to use World Bank loans for a pro-poor approach to development.

Despite this qualification, there do seem to be these two fundamental orientations toward globalization that made the encounters in Seattle during the WTO meetings seem so significant. GFB were basically blocking the streets of the city and interfering with access by the delegates to the inter-governmental meeting halls. Adherents to GFA were within the buildings, wearing conservative suits and ties, representing the governmental elites who were in turn representing large transnational corporations and banks. In these inner precincts there were also secondary tensions between the North and South as to the degree to which the structures and arenas of GFA should be as dominated by the governments of the rich and powerful countries of the North as is currently the case. As well, there were some coalitions between those within the buildings and those in the streets, as well as some hostility between militant advocates of GFB from the North and their counterparts in the South on such matters as the application of international labor and environmental standards to the circumstances of the most economically disadvantaged societies.

It is important to realize that most adherents of GFB, whether from the North or South, are ready to acknowledge the important positive effects of recent patterns of technological innovation, while working to overcome the negative effects. A transnational identity and sense of solidarity, which encompasses the whole of the global village, shape their viewpoint. Just as the forces of GFA have generated institutions to facilitate their transnational goals, the forces of GFB are now both seeking meaningful participation in these institutions, especially the leading international financial institutions and working toward the establishment of a parallel set of institutions that adopt a people-oriented planetary perspective.

Toward a Political Project: Compassionate Globalization

It is my view that the predominant creative energy for compassionate globalization under present world conditions derives mainly, although not exclusively, from GFB. There are encouraging resonances from elements aligned with GFA that it is important to acknowledge and nurture. Such emblematic figures of GFA as George Soros and James Wolfensohn issue their own strident warnings about dangers of neo-liberal globalization, calling for democratizing steps and advocating attention to social factors when making an assessment of economic policy options and approaches. Also, the governments of Nordic countries are continuing to promote, in a decidedly non-neo-liberal spirit, carefully targeted development assistance programs designed to alleviate the suffering of the most severely disadvantaged peoples in world society. In a like manner, the Foreign Minister of Canada, Lloyd Axworthy, has been setting forth a conception of "human security" that is deliberately intended to adopt a people-first perspective that is generally missing from traditional efforts by GFA collaborators to promote their "national security" or to conceive of global policy in economistic terms.

Kofi Annan, as Secretary General of the United Nations, has been articulating various ideas over the last several years that appear designed to bridge the gap between GFA and GFB, as well as to put compassionate globalization on the policy agenda. In this vein, Annan has proposed partnership relationships between the United Nations System and the private sector on one side, and between the UN and global civil society on the other. In effect, such an idea would both redefine GFA in less statist terms, as well as open the arenas of the UN to participation by GFB. In a like vein, Annan proposed a one-time millennial assembly of NGO representatives to put forward a more people-oriented view of the global policy agenda. Also, in 1999 at Davos he called upon the mega-capitalists in attendance to implement on a voluntary basis standards of well-being relating to human rights, labor practices, and environmental protects, and to do so even in the absence of governmental pressure by the territorial state to do so. Such moves, if behaviorally registered, would begin to overcome "the normative deficit" associated with GFA in its neo-liberal phase, and make the ideals of global citizenship seem politically relevant.

The more energetic, unambiguous initiatives are being shaped by the networks and linkages associated with GFB. There is an increasing conviction that the mobilized power of transnational social forces can meaningfully challenge GFA, and modify its most objectionable tendencies. One expression of this potency was undoubtedly the show of force in Seattle that overshadowed the formal WTO meetings, and contributed to the inter-governmental sense of frustration and failure. Another is the sense that transnational boycotts can be very effective in confronting specific corporations and banks whose policies are perceived as detrimental to human well-being. The campaigns against Shell, Nike, Exxon, and others have turned these companies into proponents of compassionate globalization, presenting themselves as responsible and caring global citizens in relation to human rights and environmental protection. Whether this turn toward stakeholder capitalism signals a deeper turning away from a market-driven view of rational economic behavior is difficult to say. What seems evident is the increasing conviction that if GFA is to sustain its legitimacy and win widespread acceptance, then it must meet the minimal ethical demands being put forward by the main proponents of GFB.

Additionally, there is evident in several settings, a new type of collaborative politics that might be aptly called "the new internationalism". It brings together alliances of NGOs with governments that seek to pursue goals that are not endorsed by the geopolitical leaders of the world system. The Anti-Personnel Landmines Treaty and the Rome Treaty establishing an International Criminal Court are excellent examples of this new internationalism. In each instance, lawmaking treaties opposed by leading states were agreed upon that would probably never have been brought to such an advanced stage without the commitment and pressures generated by hundreds of transnational NGOs joined in the effort.

Also relevant, and encouraging, are spontaneous political formations and proposals that seem to be gaining more attention, and building momentum for moves in the general direction of global democratization. One such initiative was the Hague Peace Assembly in 1999 that gathered activists from throughout the world for several days of deliberation, and established a process of interaction and localization that seeks to build grassroots awareness and support for the priorities of GFB. Along the same lines is the idea of an institutional innovation, adding a Global Peoples Assembly to the United Nations System, thereby giving voice, and eventual authority, to the perspectives of greatest concern to the constituencies that compose GFB. As the experience of the European Parliament suggests, a legislative organ that defines political community on a non-statist basis, can gain authority and respect over time even if it is derided as impotent in its institutional infancy. For the political project associated with compassionate globalization to move ahead, it is necessary to support such institutional experiments that embody the spirit of global democracy even if their establishment seems visionary from the outlook of the present. Fashioning compassionate globalization requires changing perceptions of "the political" in relation to the accepted meaning of "the art of the possible". Perhaps, at this stage GFB must be willing to go further, and embrace a more transformative view of politics as "the art of the impossible"!

It is understood that not all tendencies in the world today are favorable to the promotion of this particular global project. There has been a statist/geopolitical backlash against the sort of global conferences of which the Social Summit at Copenhagen was a signal example. The pretext is fiscal downsizing at a time of budgetary pressure, but the political explanation is that such global conferences were becoming too receptive as arenas for GFB, and gave some substantive inkling of the sort of struggles likely to occur if global democracy were to become a reality. Without such a struggle there is little likelihood that the reform of GFA will get very far, and certainly without generating countervailing power it will not be capable of embodying compassionate globalization in the structures of world order.

Conclusion

We enter a new century at a moment of decisive importance for the human future. The next several years will provide a preliminary indication as to whether the efforts by GFB to mount a movement to bring legitimacy and influence to global civil society have been successful. The main idea is to include the constituencies seeking international justice with democracy within the gates of globalization. A critical test of whether this political project is moving forward will be whether the vision and program of Copenhagen begins to be seriously implemented. This would require some substantial evidence of concrete benefits to those regions, countries, and social segments that have been so far most marginalized by the impacts of globalisation from above.

Reflections on Development, Growth, and Well-being

Peter Marris
Professor, Yale University, New Haven, USA

The Copenhagen Seminars explored a dilemma so profound and far-reaching, that the way we resolve it, or fail to resolve it, will determine the history of the 21st century. All our hopes for ending the poverty and inequalities which afflict the world are pinned on economic growth: and the pattern of growth to which we are committed has, in the past fifty years, brought prosperity to many poor countries and raised the standard of living of much of the world's population. At the same time, this growth has also been enormously disruptive, deepening inequalities, creating new forms of poverty, exhausting resources it does not replenish, and destroying the environment with its wastes and heedless exploitation. It is, in its present form, so disruptive of both human societies and the natural environment that it undermines its own foundation. Yet no viable alternative to this pattern of global capitalism presently exists.

The self-destructiveness of growth is most obvious in the exploitation of natural resources. A simple calculation shows that to endow the rest of the world with the diet, cars, houses and amenities enjoyed by most people in the United States and Western Europe would be impossible. The earth does not possess the water, soil, or fuel to achieve that; and the attempt would involve a level of pollution so degrading, that health and quality of life would fall steeply everywhere, most likely with devastating consequences for the world's climates. For China to follow the path of industrialization taken by Japan, South Korea, and Taiwan would place an overwhelming claim in the world's resources of grain, and exhaust China's already over-exploited reserves of water.

The participants to the Copenhagen Seminars acknowledged this, but concentrated their discussions more on social and institutional aspects of the dilemma, whose potential for undermining the benefits of growth are just as profound, if not quite so obvious.

As capitalist enterprise penetrates every corner of the globe, integrating an unbounded market, it disrupts familiar patterns of livelihood and social obligation, and so threatens to overwhelm the sense of identity on which each of us depends to find our place in an intelligible world. When people no longer know where they belong, they become vulnerable to extreme ethnic and religious movements. Such allegiances offer a moral community transcending the daunting, often humiliating circumstances of everyday life. These idealized communities do not depend on reciprocity, but the certainties of faith – in a religious doctrine, a political dogma, or ethnic mysticism. And because this faith is a defense against a hostile and chaotic world, it is necessarily rigid, exclusive, and contemptuous of pragmatic self-interest. It encourages martyrdom and holy war: violent conflict is one of the most powerful of all organizing principles of social cohesion. Hence a world which is economically integrated, overwhelming cultural and political boundaries, but socially divided at every level by ethnic and religious differences and growing inequality, risks being torn apart.

Global capitalism willingly equips these self-destructive impulses with an abundant supply of small arms and sophisticated weapons. Defense industries in the United States and Europe, with the encouragement of their governments, market their products to the world, with little regard for where they may end up. The United States government, for instance, requisitions weapons, which it acknowledges it does not need, to subsidize the export potential of American weapon makers. This represents the third aspect of the dilemma which the Seminars explored: that governments are being subverted by and subordinated to the interests of global capitalism, to protect and enhance the competitiveness of their national economies, and so give up their ability to contain or reform its self-destructive tendencies. The rich nations of the world have set up an international economic structure, through the World Bank, the International Monetary Fund, trade agreements and the World Trade Organization, designed to eliminate government interference in the free flow of world trade and investment. And through its structural adjustment programs, this regime has virtually dictated the economic policies of many poorer nations, with devastating social consequences. At the same time, this subservience of government alienates its electorate, discourages political participation, and, especially perhaps in America, leaves politicians ever more dependent on their corporate sponsors.

Thus, in its relentless search to accumulate new wealth, global capitalism progressively destroys the natural environment on which it ultimately depends; disrupts the social stability of the societies in which it seeks to invest, sell or produce; and co-opts the government institutions which might contain and reform its self-destructiveness. In the face of this dilemma, the Seminars asked three questions. How can we distribute the benefits of economic growth more fairly, both within and between countries? How can we make a competitive market economy more humane? And how can we enable the institutions of government, nationally and internationally, and of civil society, to reassert social, as opposed to pure economic values? A fourth, more elusive question underlay them: how much does economic growth contribute to human happiness? In tying development so closely to measures of productivity, are we ignoring, even disparaging, our need for love, belonging, dignity, spiritual awareness, giving?

In answering these questions, the consensus of the discussions emphasized, above all, the need to reassert democratic governance of the global economy. Market economies should not become market societies, guided by the Panglossian conviction that everything will be for the best, if only an untrammeled market is left free to work out its inexorable logic. Without cooperation and distributive justice, a viable political and social context for a market economy cannot be sustained. To achieve this, the most powerful international institutions, such as the World Bank, the International Monetary Fund, and the World Trade Organization, need to become more open and accountable; and the growing role of non governmental organizations should be encouraged, provided that they too are open and accountable. Technocratic authoritarianism breeds corruption and alienation. At the same time, the thrust of global economic integration needs to be slowed, to give time for new rules, new systems of governance, and new cultures of social restraint. The criteria for measuring economic development should emphasize its contribution to creating jobs, reducing inequalities and relieving poverty, rather than the gross per capita increase in production. And corporate culture itself must become more responsive to the social and environmental impact of its overweening power.

Essentially, these answers reiterated the question in prescriptive form: how do we reassert government? By reasserting government – and so on. The discussion tended to be circular, although the issues became enriched by example and added complexity in the process. The critique of global capitalism throughout the discussions is more incisive than the strategies for its reform. It is not surprising that a group of people drawn from all over the world, from politics, international bureaucracies, universities, charitable organizations, journalism, should find it easier to agree on broad principles than specifics. Diplomats and political leaders devote months, sometimes years of patient negotiation to the intricate task of translating mutually accepted principles into mutually acceptable actions. But beyond the diversity of perspective, the participants were inhibited by the nature of the dilemma they confronted. For all their criticisms of global capitalism, they did not intend to deny its benefits, or exclude its access to any part of the world. Hence the consensus of the discussions covers an underlying ambivalence, which surfaces again and again, about every issue from environmental regulation to the spread of democracy.

For instance, the participants repudiated any attempt to restrict less developed countries' access to technology and growth, regardless of the environmental consequences. They attacked the greediness of the capitalist market, but warned against nostalgia for pre-industrial economies, or romanticizing informal economies that provided, at best, a meager subsistence. They urged democratic accountability, but acknowledged that democratic openness could entangle decisive action on crucial international issues. They wanted to introduce values explicitly into development debates, but recognized how divisive that could be, upsetting the delicate balance of international commercial give and take. The dilemma is real: to exclude anyone from what the global economy has to offer – a better job, a new technique, livelier entertainment, new ideas – seems both presumptuous and immoral. But the attempt to include everyone seems to threaten environmental catastrophe and social disintegration. The participants in the Copenhagen seminars insistently probed the dilemma, searching constantly for institutional, cultural, and technological innovations that could help to resolve it.

The Seminars also wrestled with a less obvious dilemma. The neo-classical theory, which informs the prevailing ideology of development, assumes that people act rationally to maximize their self-interest. Or, as exuberant apologists like Milton Friedman put it, greed is a wonderful thing, creating out of selfishness the abundance of the marketplace. Crude as it is, the assumption has the great virtue of being readily usable to predict behavior, in any situation where advantage is calculable. The whole elegant structure of economic laws is built upon it. The participants in the seminars unanimously rejected this reductionist view of human nature. Again and again, they emphasized the spiritual, nurturing, non-material yearnings of people's lives. But they had great difficulty in articulating these impulses, so as to lay out a logic of human behavior coherent enough to challenge the neo-classical model. Democracy and community spirit may set the framework, economists seem to say, love and trust may oil the works, but greed is still the mainspring, which keeps the whole mechanism ticking along. If it is not greed, what is it?

Part of the difficulty lay in the participants' sensitivity to the threat of Western cultural domination. Democracy as an ideal may represent universal aspirations, but democracy in practice stems from a European political tradition shaped by both specifically Protestant notions of personal spiritual autonomy, and a philosophical equation of citizenship with property rights. Both of these are foreign to most other cultures. Women everywhere may want equal rights and equal respect, but still resent the presumption of European or American feminists who seem insensitive to their culture. And so with environmental responsibility, human rights, social justice, freedom: the principles have their counterpart in many cultures, but they are embedded in different traditions and different practices, and so have different implications for behavior. Hence a normative approach to development has great difficulty in prescribing, in practice, how it should operate. As soon as it becomes specific, cultural anomalies and perverse consequences begin to surface. At the same time, the rhetoric of political idealism has so often been abused in the service of tyranny, petty partisanship and corrupt practice, that a simple, morally unassuming concept like rational self-interest begins to seem not only more workable, but more benign.

Yet the Seminars' participants were, I believe, right to see that any alternative conception of development had to challenge the basic premises of global capitalism. Especially because they did not challenge the potential of a global market economy to enhance the quality of life, they needed to justify the framework of social regulation they argued should contain that market. The justification was crucial to the framework, which in turn was crucial to finding a way out of the dilemmas of growth. Their difficulty arose partly because they tried to find that justification in a cross-cultural ethical synthesis, rather than by tackling directly neo-classical assumptions about human nature.

Where would an alternative account of human nature begin? I suggest that meaning is crucial. Our lives have to make sense to us. When everything seems meaningless, we no longer want to live. The preservation of meaning is more fundamental than biological survival, because a meaningless existence is unmotivated, a kind of living death. This is why those who have experienced a traumatic bereavement, which seems to rob their lives of meaning, suffer such acute anxiety, pain, and despair, as they work through their grief. Meanings organize experience so as to enable us to identify what matters to us, relate it to previous experiences and determine how to respond. They classify events, order purposes and articulate emotions. We would not be able to survive for any length of time without them. Unless experience can be perceived as patterns that repeat, we cannot learn or predict anything. And this applies as much to our patterns of feeling and purpose as to the events around us.

The first and most fundamental relationship through which human beings learn to organize meaning is the attachment of an infant to its parenting figures. Since an infant's well-being depends on securing the protection of its attachment figures, that relationship is our central concern throughout childhood, and its unresolved insecurities linger into adult life. It is the starting point for everything we learn about love, order, control, reward and punishment, and out of it grows our ability to become attached as adults to a sexual partner and our own children, and to conceive the meaning of these relationships. As we grow up, too, we learn what it means to be a member of our social group, to be admired and respected, and what we can contribute that will earn respect and admiration. The meaning of our lives evolves as a constantly elaborated structure of purposes and attachments, seeking to make good sense of whatever happens to us, for better or worse. Our well-being is grounded in the richness and resilience of these meanings. Hence what matters most to us are our primary attachments, the people we love; and the work that we do, which brings respect and a sense of self-worth. For the most part, these structure the everyday purposes and understandings, which govern our lives and make them meaningful. Beyond that, we need to embed these purposes in some larger context of meaning, less ephemeral than our span of life, such as a religion, patriotism, an intellectual tradition, a sense of family enduring from generation to generation, or a cause.

Such an account is compatible with many patterns of attachment and distinctive cultures. The attachment relationships which mean most to people have a different emphasis in a traditionally polygynous, patrilineal African society than in modern middle class American suburbia. But attachment itself, the unique bonds to specific people – mother, son, lover, sister, spouse, is always central to the patterns of feeling and purpose which inform our lives, and make them meaningful. So, too, the kinds of behavior which earn us respect and reassure us of our own worth differ, even within a society, from group to group. But we all need respect and a sense of worth that only a stable connection to some social group can provide.

Like the economists' conception of rational self-interest, this is a very simplified and abstracted sketch of basic human nature. But unlike the economists' disembodied calculator, it seems to me to be recognizably human. Love, respect, feeling that we have a meaningful place in the world, are surely what matter to us. And if so, the relationship of economic development to human well-being is radically different from the economists' model. This is not to say that their model is inappropriate to the artificial theoretical structure which constitutes economics. But applied to the realities of development it becomes perverse.

Firstly, the economic model emphasizes consumption – the business of buying and selling in the marketplace – and everything, in these terms, becomes a commodity, including human labor. But we find the meaning of our lives in the part we play as producers, not consumers; and the work we do is not a thing, but a relationship through which we are connected, with dignity or in humiliating squalor, to the rest of society. Of course, we have basic needs for food, water, shelter, medicine, that are a precondition of well-being. But well being itself lies, not in satisfying these needs, but in what we are able to do once we have satisfied them – nurture our children, be sociable, make something worthwhile. So a pattern of development which promises an abundance of cheap goods, at the cost of undermining secure employment, relegating production to sweat shops and factories in which work is degraded and exploited, is not, on balance, contributing to human well-being. People need secure employment where they are treated with respect much more than they need more, cheaper things. Advocates of development may argue that even demeaning work is better than no work at all: but why should that be the only choice?

Secondly, as the meaning of our lives becomes embedded in a web of unique attachments and relationships of mutual respect, uprooting becomes traumatic. The economic emphasis on consumption implies that if someone is plucked from one setting to another, and so is enabled to buy more, that person must be better off. But if he or she is lonely, bereft of the company of those they love, disoriented, no longer sure of themselves, they are clearly worse off. And the loss may be as great for those they leave behind. People can, and often must, adapt to change. But that does not justify rapid, involuntary social disruption, on a worldwide scale, in the interests of competitive production for the benefit of consumers in the richest nations.

Ideally, then, development would create a world in which everyone could make a respected contribution, in a social setting stable enough for them to sustain deeply meaningful attachments and purposes, with enough to ensure their essential needs. The grimmer advocates of global capitalism may argue that this is wishful thinking, at least in the short run. Disruption and squalor are the price we have to pay, if we are ever to generate an increase in world production, enough to provide for another three billion people in the next half century. But this argument is based on two false assumptions: that there are no other viable ways of raising productivity; and that any government interference in the flow of capital only does harm.

It may be true that there are no alternatives to corporate capitalism in the efficient production of automobiles, for instance, or electronic appliances. But food and clothes, shelter and tools, entertainment and crafts can be produced in many different ways – at home, through cooperatives, as part of a pattern of subsistence, in small businesses. And the productivity of these small organizations is not necessarily any more static than capitalistic manufacture. Micro development is given much less attention than the macro development of global corporatism, but as much can be achieved by small loans to women farmers working traditional plots as by attracting international agribusiness. Cooperative small holder production can manage the harvesting and processing of export crops as well as large plantations. These alternative forms of production characteristically generate more employment, and are far less socially disruptive.

But these alternatives will not survive without policies that protect and invest in them. The claim that social intervention only stultifies the market rests on the assumption that a competitive economy implies a competitive society. But, in practice, all societies intervene to restrain market forces from gross distortions, anarchic competition and speculative disasters. Pure competition creates a pervasive uncertainty, whose effects the most powerful contrive to hand down to the weaker, until a crushing burden falls on those with the fewest opportunities to evade or transpose it – the poorest and most marginal. The organization of much global production follows this pattern, as work is subcontracted to factories where labor is cheapest and workers most ruthlessly exploited. But the idea that governments cannot, or should not, intervene to protect their workers, for fear of undermining their development, is contradicted by all historical experience. Markets, since they are after all the work of people, do not function well unless they are contained within a framework of cooperation and reciprocity.

This recapitulation articulates, with a sociologist's bias, the central argument that I see running through the Copenhagen seminars. It is also, I believe, the argument which underlay the diverse and sometimes incoherent protests in Seattle against the World Trade Organization. Those who condemned the protesters as mere Luddites, standing in the path of progress, fundamentally misunderstood what they were protesting about. The protesters were not attacking trade, as such, or seeking to deny poor countries opportunities of development. Like the Copenhagen participants, they were trying to reinsert the real needs of real people into a dauntingly inhuman economic equation.

Toward a Global Community of Solution

Saad Nagi
Professor Emeritus, Sociology Department, Ohio State University;
and Research Professor, Social Research Center,
American University in Cairo.

By articulating visions in which human needs and aspirations are optimally fulfilled, utopian views, ideational by definition, serve the important function of inspiring refinement in goals, means, and action, on the part of individuals and collectives. They provide guide posts for the road to progress. In a utopian world, there would be peace and security, sustainable and shared prosperity, openness and equality of opportunity, a rule of fair law impartially applied, sanctity of human life, respect for human dignity and rights, not only tolerance but appreciation of diversity and pluralism, civility and compassion in interaction, and a healthy balance in emphasis on private and public goods. Clearly, current conditions in the real world are quite different: continuous armed conflicts within and/or between states, millions of casualties and refugees, oppressive regimes in the majority of countries, rampant corruption and exploitation, deeply seated prejudices openly expressed in various forms of discrimination, great divides in knowledge and resources, and inequitable distribution of power and income. These conditions are reflected in poverty, illiteracy, hunger, and poor health. The propositions advanced in this statement are that: (a) as dismal and intractable as these problems may seem, the real world today is far better than it was half a century or a century ago – there has been improvement; (b) progress in human affairs is largely powered by the forces of modernization; (c) these forces are also propelling a fast trend toward globalization in many aspects of life; and (d) the global level, becoming the "community of solution" for many newly emerging and previously unattended problems, will need to develop institutions appropriate for managing these responsibilities.

Forces of Modernization

Historians describe the evolution and awesome significance of the modernization process as follows:

"The change in human affairs now taking place is of the scope and intensity that mankind has experienced on only two previous occasions, and its significance cannot be appreciated except in the context of the entire course of world history. The first revolutionary transformation was the emergence of human beings, about a million years ago, after many thousands of years of evolution from primate life...

The second great revolutionary transformation in human affairs was that from primitive to civilized societies, culminating seven thousand years ago in the three locations, the Valleys of the Tigris and Euphrates (Mesopotamia), the Valley of the Nile, and the Valley of the Indus... Three (civilizations) – the Mesopotamian, the Egyptian, and the Cretan – have transmitted their knowledge and institutions to later societies...

The process of change in the modern era is of the same order of magnitude as that from prehuman life and from primitive to civilized societies; it is the most dynamic of the great revolutionary transformations in the conduct of human affairs. What is distinctive about the modern era is the phenomenal growth of knowledge since the scientific revolution and the unprecedented effort at adaptation to this knowledge that has come to be demanded of the whole of mankind....

Since the challenge ... in the societies that modernized earlier was primarily internal, the processes of transformation took place generally over several centuries. In the later modernizing societies this challenge has been increasingly external, hence more rapid and even abrupt"[1].

For some countries, the change is crisis-ridden, traumatic, and feared. For others, it has become anticipated, routinized and welcomed. And, indeed, nothing short of unprecedented effort is needed for adapting current institutions, organizations, and citizens in traditional and transitional societies to this transformation. "At the most fundamental level", success in such an effort is dependent on the ability of leaders "to keep the delicate balance required for

177

survival between the maintenance of the traditional pattern of values that serves as the basis of cohesion and adaptation to new knowledge that requires a revision of the traditional value system"[2]. Responsibility here is not limited to political leaders, but extends to intellectual, educational, and informal leadership at all levels. However, centuries of colonialism and exploitation have left the populations of many, if not most, developing societies highly suspicious of trends that originate in the West, and susceptible to mobilization around nationalistic sentiments of various kinds. This tendency is often used by many political and intellectual leaders, whose words and actions shape the public opinion, in ways that hinder the course of development in these countries. For them, modernization is equated with the popular culture of the West, the spread of which is condemned as a form of "cultural invasion", and as a threat to the moral and nationalistic fabric of the society.

However, driven by ever expanding production, diffusion, and application of knowledge, the inescapable conclusion is that the course of human history and the progress of nations are tied to modernization and to the change it brings about. It should be noted that the transformation continues to evolve in the developed world. While entailing some negative side effects, it has produced spectacular improvement in the various aspects of life. Yet, the results are far from being equitably distributed among and within nations. For the most part, the lack of access of large proportions of the world population to the fruits of change is due to institutional weaknesses and dislocations, at the national and global levels.

A Global Community of Solution

Modernization has helped to unleash a powerful synergetic trend toward globalization. Advancement in communication and transportation has enormously facilitated the flow of information and people across national boundaries. Other technological breakthroughs are changing the face of business by expanding the global reach of enterprises, and expediting the movement of capital, production, and goods (although not as yet labor). Leading at times, and following at others, national governments have become more heavily involved in attempts to promote peace and stability, and to protect the interests of their countries and citizens. In short, the global community is rapidly becoming the level for resolving many important and complex concerns.

Community has been defined by geographic boundaries, political jurisdiction, as market or service centers, and/or in terms of social interaction and identification. Useful to this statement is the concept of "community of solution", which refers to boundaries within which "a problem can be defined, dealt with, and solved"[3]. This community can be local for certain problems, regional within a country for others, and national still for others. Some international problems are effectively addressed at the level of regions of the world, while others require global management.

As has already been mentioned, trends toward globalization mean an increasing number and variety of issues will need to be resolved at this level. Equally important, is that the vertical pattern of relationships among communities *should* render the influence of policies and actions at the international level highly pervasive. However, much is yet to be done to achieve "a more perfect global union". Essential, and urgent, is to bridge the lag in building institutions with the capacity to handle the problems calling for solutions at this level. An *institution* means a complex of values, norms, and organization that coalesce around a set of community needs and functions, e.g. political, economic, legal, educational, health, and others. Crosscutting the relatively specialized values and norms that cohere around these functions, are moral values and ethical norms that influence behavior within all institutional contexts – fairness, tolerance, civility, compassion, helpfulness, public good, among others. The strength of commitment to these more universal values and norms can greatly influence communal cooperation and cohesion.

The Challenges

At this juncture in history, as indicated by the current world conditions described earlier, the capacities of global institutions are too limited for handling the needs and functions to be addressed at this level. Of the many important challenges, on the road to their development, we briefly review a select few. *First,* is dissonance in values held in different parts of the world. Modernization and increased cross-cultural communication and interaction have been, and continue to be, strong influences toward homogenization of certain values and norms. This is particularly the case in institutions heavily influenced by science and technology, such as those of economics, education, and health. And, as mentioned above, there are moral values and ethical norms that are widely shared. Nevertheless, there are considerable differences and tensions among value systems within, and across, nations. The challenge at the global level is defining common grounds sufficiently important to elevate the consideration of issues beyond narrow nationalism.

Second, are the roles played by national governments which are responsible for multiple difficulties. To begin with, global organizations vested with authority are basically inter-governmental; that authority is expanded or limited by decisions of national governments. The tendency is that when governance at higher levels of aggregation is established, power seeps away from the intermediate levels in both directions – to the higher and to the lower level authorities. Historically, this has been the case in the United States and is beginning to take place in Europe. It is to be expected that the development of global institutions would be generally subject to reluctance if not outright hostility by national governments. And, it is not surprising to see the nationalist sentiments of citizens often stirred up for partisan gains. Unfortunately, this is frequently the case for many advanced countries that have considerable influence, and should be providing leadership, in these matters. Thus, the pursuit of "national interests", and "power politics" continue to dominate the scene of international relations, with little attention, if any, to the global public good. It should be noted in this respect, that exclusive attention to the interests of individual units would tear apart the fabric of a community, and exclusive emphasis on public interests would stifle the initiatives of the units. This applies to a community of nations as it does to a community of people. Balancing these interests would help maintain cohesion while liberating energies – both crucial conditions for progress.

The problems brought about by the governments of developing societies are quite complex. Most represent weak national institutions that depend primarily upon the use, or threat, of violence against citizens, and the backing of loyal and beneficiary military and technocratic establishments, to maintain their power. Lacking public support and legitimacy at home, these ruling groups claim the sovereignty of nations to promote their collective interests. The policy choices they have made, and continue to make, in their respective countries have produced prevalent and intense poverty, extreme inequities and polarization in the distribution of resources, high rates of illiteracy, poor health conditions, and inefficient and corrupt public administration. A recent study of the Less Developed Countries (LCD) concludes that "a stable political order and protecting basic political rights is critical to reducing hunger"[4]. It is no longer sufficient to view these conditions as strictly "internal" matters that should be left to the citizens of the respective countries who, in fact, have been stripped of all means to effect change. Because of the potentially destabilizing effects that can spill over beyond borders, these problems are percolating up to the global agenda. The challenges are: how can democratic institutions be developed at the global level while most constituents are authoritarian governments? And, how can a global community, and its institutions, promote responsive and accountable national governance while being responsible themselves to governments abusive of these principles?

Third are challenges stemming from institutional hegemony or dominance[5]. One of the guiding principles of the Copenhagen Seminars: "Market Economy, Yes; Market Society, No" accurately sums up the issue. In different societies, and in the same ones over time, the values and norms of certain institutions have overpowered those of others. This can be seen in the dominance of "religion" throughout the world for centuries, and its continuation in many parts. Consider also the dominance of family and kinship values and norms in numerous societies manifested in nepotism and ascription in organizations that need to be built on merit and achievement. This pattern underlies the reference to systems of public administration in these countries as "familial bureaucracies". This can also be witnessed in the "crony capitalism" that led to economic meltdown in certain parts of the world. Concern here is with the sweeping trend of dominance of "economic" values and norms over those of other institutions. Thus, "corruption" of the political and administrative systems is called "cost of doing business"; and the violation of professional norms in health care and education as well as the neglect of other human needs are justified as "cost containment". This ethos "encourages an exaggerated emphasis on monetary achievements while devaluing alternative criteria of success, it promotes a preoccupation with the realization of goals while deemphasizing the importance of the ways in which these goals are pursued ... [that is] "by any means necessary"[6]. The dominance of economic institutions is also evident at the global level as indicated by the influence of the IMF and the World Bank in comparison to other international organizations. The challenge is to enhance the specialization of institutions in order to protect the integrity of each. This is not to negate the close interdependence among all of them, but to call for careful articulation of the relationships based on clear differentiation in functions and structures. In this context, it would be remiss not to bring up

181

the role of "multinational corporations". Effective competition in a global economy requires a large inflow of international capital and advanced technology. Governments in most developing countries are in no position to provide the capital necessary for large scale enterprise development. Neither can the required capital come from the private sector which, by international standards, is comprised predominantly of small to middle size enterprises, with modest organizational and managerial skills, and perversion of incentives. Multinational corporations are the one remaining source of inflow of large capital and transfer of technology at the scale needed, as well as imbeddedness in the global markets. These giant enterprises are being courted by advanced and developing societies alike. It is no secret that these corporations are business, not welfare organizations; the interests they serve are primarily those of their owners, stockholders, managers, and workers. Their concerns are for the quality, efficiency, and costs of production as well as in markets. These concerns should neither be ignored nor exaggerated; they should be part of a regulatory framework that balances them with those of the country's workers and consumers. The ultimate goal of economic development is to improve people's material well-being and living conditions, through productive endeavors. Close attention is needed to ensure equity in the distribution of gains and pains associated with macro-economic change. In fact, a recent longitudinal study shows that economic growth is actually hindered by income inequality[7]. At the global level, the challenge is to institutionalize rules and enforcement mechanisms that would universally outlaw bribery, unfair labor practices, environmental degradation, and provide consumer protection.

Fourth, and finally, is the performance of agencies of international organizations at the national level. At issue here is development assistance rather than the many other functions these organizations perform. A number of problems need to be addressed in this respect. To begin with, the lack of enforcement mechanisms renders resolutions practically non-binding – the organizations are free to formulate them, and the countries are free to ignore them. At the country level, coordination among agencies is too weak to generate cumulative results; in fact, competition is the more common pattern. The processes of project initiation and administration do not provide for serious assessments of results. Members of missions carrying out negotiations often find themselves under pressure from both sides – their agencies and the respective authorities in the national governments – to reach agreement. Furthermore, accountability for outcomes of programs is almost non-existence. The challenge is to reform approaches to development assistance to refocus it on the ultimate objective of effecting positive change in the conditions of people, and to institute a system of accountability tied to this criterion (more to be said about that at a later point).

The Leverages

At whatever level of problem solving, local to global, it is essential to remain mindful that the primary objectives of development are to improve the living standards and well-being of people in a sustainable manner. It is needless to say that the processes involved are too complex to clearly distinguish between causes and effects. Of the multitude of dimensions of development, and the influences that shape its course, we briefly highlight a few believed to form strong foundations.

First is *education,* which has profound significance to the various dimensions of development, at both the individual and societal levels, needs no elaboration. The knowledge, skills, ethics, and aesthetics of citizens are key to enhancing the capacities of institutions and organizations. In fact, in contemporary societies, education has been shown to be the most common avenue for individuals and households to climb out of poverty[8]. Four issues, concerning education, are consequential to development: access, quality, attainment, and relation to the labor market. There is a pressing need, especially in developing societies, to advance along all of these dimensions, for in this lies the future of nations. As has been mentioned, scientific knowledge and technological application have been the primary forces behind the transformation of societies with spectacular results in all fields. Breakthroughs have not been limited to hardware technologies; they also include systems of management, administration, education, institutionalization, and other aspects of organization. To be noted is that knowledge and skills cannot be equated simply with the proliferation of educational institutions or by the prevalence of degrees or other forms of licensure in a population. These indicators neither assure the quality of knowledge and skills nor their assimilation into the national character.

Second is *justice,* to be understood and practiced in a broad and encompassing manner. It includes a constitutional structure and modes of governance that guarantee fundamental human rights and freedoms, assure people security in thought and property, provide effective avenues for political participation, and promote a sense of belonging and commitment. It includes the checks and balances necessary to channel authority and the use of discretion away from self-serving arbitrariness and toward the public good. It means impartiality in other aspects of the law – civil and criminal – and universal application that instills self-discipline and respect for the law and legal institutions. It calls for equity in the system of rewards so that people's earnings and gains are proportional to the quality and amount of preparation and effort they put into their work, and sanctions proportional to violations. It entails redistributive measures to meet the needs of the unfortunate and dependent while preserving the motivation of the capable and talented. Equally important to these legal expressions, justice also means people's fairness and civility to each other in daily interaction.

Third is *accountability.* Literature, observation, and common-sense, all point to three forces that motivate and shape human behavior. The first two are reward and punishment, whether in material or psychic forms, or a combination of both. The third is building the desired behavior into the individual's own value commitments and internalized norms. Families are expected to do their part through early socialization, and schools through education and professional preparation. Obviously, a mix of the three is necessary to maintain behavior that meets defined standards. Shortcomings in institutions and organizations can be traced, in large part, to failure to enforce these simple but powerful principles. A system of public accountability, if implemented effectively, can go a long way in bringing discipline to governance, markets, and other areas of human affairs, and to refocusing them on serving the public. An effective framework should include several elements: (a) clearly identified and understood *objectives;* (b) meaningful and measurable *criteria* with indicators of both quality and quantity; (c) a system of *information* to gather, analyze, and present data based on the performance criteria; (d) *targets* that hold authority and responsibility at all levels; (e) *consequences* derived from a fair and effective system of incentives and sanctions; and (f) certain initial *conditions* in place to enable responsible decision makers to carry out their duties. The integrity of information is crucial, to the effectiveness of accountability as a whole. Data should be gathered directly from people "in contact", as well as the public at large. Following the metaphor "sunshine is the best disinfectant", it is important that results be made public. Finally, it must be stressed that this framework should not be viewed as a cafeteria from which politically expedient items are selected and the less popular are disregarded. The elements are inter-dependent and mutually reinforcing.

A reminder is necessary in regard to accountability at international assistance organizations as well. Officials who negotiate with national agencies and con-clude agreements that commit funds for particular programs should be held accountable for the performance of these programs. The merit of these offi-cials should not be measured by the numbers of programs they negotiate, and the size of resources they commit, but by how well the programs achieve their objectives. Actually, accountability of the negotiating officials, and those to whom they report in the central offices, can be important leverages in nego-tiating and monitoring programs. And, officials on the ground would be more likely to have the needed backing and support of their superiors in ensuring appropriate conditions for the success of programs. Once funds are commit-ted, the assistance organizations nearly, or totally, lose their leverages. Projects can be delayed, poorly managed, not maintained, or not followed through in terms of replication and generalization to other parts of the country[9]. A relat-ed issue concerns the notion of "ownership" which has gained wide currency in the verbal and written communication of international assistance organiza-tions. The idea is that when officials in a recipient country feel they "own" a concept underlying a project, they would become committed to it, they would work hard to implement it, and there will be a successful outcome. This is not necessarily true. Considerable risks are entailed in each link of this chain, the explanation of which is beyond the purposes of this statement. Furthermore, this notion of ownership lifts accountability, for the failure of programs, off the shoulders of representatives of the assistance programs. A reassessment of the concept is necessary. Assistance programs can neither finance ongoing government operations nor administer them. What they are best positioned to do is to provide funds and expertise to mount demonstra-tions and develop prototypes for desired change. An effective presence needs to be maintained by donors throughout the duration of the projects.

Fourth are *non-governmental organizations.* They are built around common interests of categories of people who form "interest groups" such as labor unions, trade associations, business alliances, professional and scientific soci-eties, political parties, philanthropic organizations, civic and communal groups, and others. These voluntary organizations countervail the powers of each other as well as those of a governmental nature, and become part of a system of checks and balances. Many are concerned with the interests of their members, others with advocacy for certain causes, and still others with providing various services to individuals, families, and communities. They operate at different levels varying from local to transnational. In developing societies, a strong impetus was given to the proliferation of these organizations by international donors. The intention is to seek alternatives to inefficient government agencies for channeling developmental resources and efforts. The NGOs are also viewed as avenues for encouraging volunteerism and enhancing opportunities for participation at the grass roots level.

The efforts of many international NGOs can provide leverages for reform and development, as in the case of those concerned with human rights, transparency, the environment, population, and other issues. However, the function of checks and balances is far from being fulfilled by these organizations. At the international level, the structure of authority allows them only limited means and opportunities to influence inter-governmental organizations. In most developing countries, with some notable exceptions, the movement has been a top-down process, and frequently attracted exploitative leadership. The benefits they seek include finances and privileges, the prestige and influence associated with visibility, and/or access to those in positions of power and authority. Beneficiaries are usually members and kin of the elite who have knowledge about the process, sufficient influence to sail through the bureaucratic hurdles (e.g. government permits required in many countries), and the networking to facilitate funding which is largely from international donors. The importance of non-governmental organizations cannot be overstated; their formation should be encouraged and their activities facilitated. On the other hand, self-serving entities can be wasteful if not outright harmful to the causes they espouse. The obvious answer to the dilemma is in the application of the requirements of public accountability and transparency, outlined above, to these organizations.

The *fifth* element to take up is *information*. Abundant, timely, and accurate information is indispensable to the identification of problems, the effectiveness of policies and programs, and to the preparation of informed citizenry capable of contributing to development. As explained earlier, it is also necessary for monitoring and for accountability. Information may turn out to be one of the most significant contributions of international organizations. Unfortunately, for many developing societies, there are various restrictions on the production and dissemination of information because of shortsighted and self-defeating policies. The need is not only for sources of data and information other than those generated by government agencies, but also for a multiplicity of these independent sources. In this age of fast communication, the flow of information through print and mass media, and especially the internet, may emerge as one of the most influential leverages for development.

Sixth, and finally, is *access* to affiliation with regional and global communities and to the economic and political benefits such relationships may bring about. International communities need to be fair, clear, and firm on standards of participation. The European Community's standards on democratic institutions, for example, have influenced change in certain countries before admission.

A Prognosis

The hazards of prediction are always intimidating, especially of such complex phenomena as societal and global change. This is rendered more difficult since the time horizon for such change is measurable in generations and centuries. As explained earlier the world is beset by many difficult problems that may proliferate and increase in intensity in the short-term. However, with frequent setbacks and even reversals, the long-term trend is toward more effective institutions at the various communal levels, and better human conditions. This prognosis is rooted in the influence of the growing interdependence and globalization of interests, and the continuously expanding forces of knowledge and education. As the transformation unfolds, more and more issues and problems will need to be addressed at the transnational communal level.

Notes

1. Black, C. E. 1966. *The Dynamics of Modernization.* New York: Harper & Row, pp.1-8
2. Ibid, p.4
3. National Commission on Community Health, 1966. *Health is a Community Affair.* Cambridge, Mass: Harvard University Press
4. Jenkins, J. Craig and Stephen Scanlan 2000. *Improving Food Security in Less Developed Countries: A Longitudinal Analysis of Food Supply and Child hunger in Less Developed Countries,* 1970-1990. Under review for publication.
5. For further discussion of the concept, see: Williams, Robin M Jr. [1955] 1970. *American Society: A Sociological Interpretation (3rd ed).* New York: Alfred A. Knopf; Houseknecht, Sharon K. 2000. "Social Change in Egypt: The Roles of Religion and Family". In Sharon K. Houseknwcht and Jerry G. Pankhurst *Family, Religion, and Social Change in Diverse Societies.* New York: Oxford University Press.
6. Mssner, Steven F. and Richard Rosenfeld 1997. *Crime and the American Dream.* Belmont CA: Wadsworth Publishing Company, pp.4,10
7. Kenworthy, Lane 1999. "Inequality and Growth", Under Review for Publication in *Journal of Sociology.*
8. Nagi, Saad Z. 2000. "Poverty in Egypt: Human Needs and Institutional Capacities". Book Under Review for Publication.
9. Nagi, Saad Z. 1997. "Basic Education in Egypt: A Framework for Accountability", Report to The World Bank, Mimeograph.

Globalisation and Development: A Historical Perspective

Deepak Nayyar
Professor, Jawaharlal Nehru University, New Delhi, India

There is a common presumption that the present conjuncture, when globalisation is changing the character of the world economy, is altogether new and represents a fundamental departure from the past. But this presumption is not correct. Globalisation is not new. Indeed, there was a similar phase of globalisation which began a century earlier, *circa* 1870, and gathered momentum until 1914 when it came to an abrupt end. This recognition is essential for an understanding. And there is much that we can learn from history, for there is the past in our present. The object of this short essay is to outline the contours of globalisation in our times and situate it in historical perspective through a comparison with the late nineteenth century, to explore its implications for development then and now.

I

Globalisation means different things to different people. And, the word *globalisation* is used in two ways, which is a source of some confusion. It is used in a *positive* sense to *describe* a process of increasing integration into the world economy. It is used in a *normative* sense to *prescribe* a strategy of development based on a rapid integration with the world economy.

Even its characterisation, however, is by no means uniform. It can be described, simply, as the expansion of economic activities across national boundaries. In this elementary sense, the world economy has experienced a progressive international economic integration since 1950. However, there has been a marked acceleration in this process of globalisation during the last quarter of the twentieth century. There are three manifestations of this phe-

189

nomenon – international trade, international investment and international finance – which also constitute its cutting edge. But there is much more to globalisation.

It refers to the expansion of economic transactions and the organisation of economic activities across political boundaries of nation states. More precisely, it can be defined as a process associated with increasing economic openness, growing economic interdependence and deepening economic integration in the world economy.

Economic *openness* is not simply confined to trade flows, investment flows and financial flows. It also extends to flows of services, technology, information and ideas across national boundaries. But the cross-border movement of people is closely regulated and highly restricted. Economic *interdependence* is asymmetrical. There is a high degree of interdependence among countries in the North. There is considerable dependence of the South on the North. There is much less interdependence among countries in the South. It is important to note that a situation of interdependence is one where the benefits of linking and costs of de-linking are about the same for both partners; where such benefits and costs are unequal between partners, it implies a situation of dependence. Economic *integration* straddles national boundaries as liberalisation has diluted the significance of borders in economic transactions. It is, in part, an integration of markets (for goods, services, technology, financial assets and even money) on the demand side, and, in part, an integration of production (horizontal and vertical) on the supply side.

The gathering momentum of globalisation has brought about profound changes in the world economy. It is worth highlighting the characteristics of these changes:

- An increasing proportion of world output is entering into world trade, while an increasing proportion of *world trade* is made up of intra-firm trade (across national boundaries but between affiliates of the same firm). Between the early 1970s and the mid-1990s, the share of world exports in world GDP rose from 12 percent to 18 percent[1], while the share of intra-firm trade in world trade rose from one-fifth to one-third[2].
- There is also a surge in *international investment* flows. Between 1980 and 1996, the stock of direct foreign investment in the world as a proportion

of world output rose from less than 5 percent to more than 10 percent, while world direct foreign investment flows as a proportion of world gross fixed capital formation rose from 2 percent to almost 6 percent[3].

- The growth in *international finance* has been explosive. So much so that, in terms of magnitudes, trade and investment are now dwarfed by finance[4]. The expansion of international banking is phenomenal. The international market for financial assets has experienced a similar growth. And there is a growing international market for government bonds. The size of international foreign exchange markets is staggering. Global foreign exchange transactions have soared from $ 60 billion per day in 1983 to $ 1500 billion per day in 1997[5]. By comparison, in 1997, world GDP was $ 82 billion per day and world exports were $ 16 billion per day, while the foreign exchange reserves of all central banks put together were $ 1550 billion[6].

Globalisation needs to be analysed in terms of the economic factors underlying the process and the political conjuncture which has enabled it to gather momentum. The economic factors which have made globalisation possible are[7]:

- The *dismantling of barriers* to international economic transactions. Globalisation has followed the sequence of deregulation in the world economy. Trade liberalisation came first. The liberalisation of regimes for foreign investment came next. Financial liberalisation – the deregulation of the domestic financial sector and the introduction of convertibility on capital account in the balance of payments – came last.

- The development of *enabling technologies*. The technological revolution in transport and communications – jet aircrafts, computers and satellites – has pushed aside geographical barriers. The time needed is a tiny fraction of what it was earlier. The cost incurred has come down just as sharply. Information technology, remarkable in both reach and speed, is bound to accelerate the process further.

- New *forms of industrial organisation*. The emerging flexible production systems are exercising a strong influence on the strategy and behaviour of firms in the process of globalisation. The nature of technical progress, the declining share of wages in production costs, or the increasing importance of proximity between producers and consumers, are constantly forcing firms to choose between trade and investment in their drive to expand activities across borders.

191

The politics of hegemony or dominance is conducive to the economics of globalisation. The process of globalisation beginning in the early 1970s has coincided with the political dominance of the United States as the superpower. This political dominance has grown stronger with the collapse of communism and the triumph of capitalism. And the political conjuncture has transformed the concept of globalisation into a "virtual ideology" of our times. Dominance in the realm of politics, however, is not enough. It has to be combined with an important attribute in the sphere of economics. For globalisation requires a dominant economic power with a national currency which is accepted as the equivalent of international money: as a unit of account, a medium of exchange and a store of value. This role is being performed by the US dollar.

II

A century earlier, this role was performed by the pound sterling. The period from 1870 to 1914 was also the age of *laissez-faire*. The movement of goods, capital and labour across national boundaries was almost unhindered. Government intervention in economic activity was minimal. It was believed that the virtuous circle of rapid economic growth and the process of international economic integration in this era were closely related.

In many ways, the world economy in the late twentieth century resembles the world economy in the late nineteenth century[8]. The parallels between the two periods are striking.

- The integration of the world economy through *international trade* at the turn of the last century was about the same as it is towards the end of this century. For sixteen major industrialised countries, now in the OECD, the share of exports in GDP rose from 18.2 percent in 1900 to 21.2 percent in 1913, even though tariffs were much higher then[9].
- The story was about the same for international investment. In 1913, the stock of direct foreign investment in the world economy was 9 percent of world output[10]. At constant prices, total foreign investment in the world economy in 1914 was four-fifth of what it was in 1980[11]. What is more, the stock of foreign investment in developing countries was probably equal to about one-fourth their GDP at the turn of the century. And, at constant prices, in 1914, this stock was almost double what it was in 1980[12].

- The integration of markets for *international finance* was also comparable. The cross national ownership of securities including government bonds, reached very high levels[13]. International bank lending was substantial. And, in relative terms, net international capital flows were much bigger than now. The only missing dimension was international transactions in foreign exchange (given the regime of fixed exchange rates under the gold standard).

There are striking similarities in the underlying factors which made globalisation possible then and now[14]:

- There were almost no restrictions on the movement of goods, capital and labour across national boundaries, so that there was no need for dismantling barriers or liberalising regimes for international economic transactions.
- The advent of the steamship, the railway and the telegraph brought about a revolution in transport and communications[15]. This led to an enormous reduction in the time needed, as also the cost incurred, in traversing geographical distances.
- Emerging forms of industrial organisation performed a critical role. Mass production realised economies of scale and led to huge cost reductions compared with craft manufacturing[16].
- Apart from dominance in the realm of politics, *Pax Britannica* provided a reserve currency, the pound sterling, which was the equivalent of international money. For this was "the age of empire" when Britain more or less ruled the world[17].

But there is a fundamental difference between the two phases of globalisation. It is in the sphere of labour flows. In the late nineteenth century, there were no restrictions on the mobility of people across national boundaries. Passports were seldom needed. Immigrants were granted citizenship with ease.

Between 1870 and 1914, international labour migration was enormous. During this period, about 50 million people left Europe, of whom two-thirds went to the United States while the remaining one-third went to Canada, Australia, New Zealand, South Africa, Argentina and Brazil[18]. This mass emigration from Europe amounted to one-eighth of its population in 1900. But that was not all. Beginning somewhat earlier, following the abolition of slavery in the British empire, about 50 million people left India and China to work as indentured labour on mines, plantations and construction in Latin America, the Caribbean, Southern Africa, South East Asia and other distant lands[19]. The destinations were mostly British, Dutch, French and German colonies. In the second half of the twentieth century, there was a limited amount of international labour migration from the developing countries to the industrialised world during the period 1950-1970. Since then, however, international migration has been reduced to a trickle because of draconian immigration laws and restrictive consular practices. The present phase of globalisation has found substitutes for labour mobility in the form of trade flows and investment flows. For one, industrialised countries now import manufactured goods that embody scarce labour. For another, industrialised countries export capital which employs scarce labour abroad to provide such goods.

III

The ideologues believe that globalisation led to rapid industrialisation and economic convergence in the world economy during the late nineteenth century. In their view, the promise of the emerging global capitalist system was wasted for more than half a century, to begin with by three decades of conflict and autarchy that followed the first world war and subsequently, for another three decades, by the socialist path and a statist world view. The return of globalisation in the late twentieth century is thus seen as the road to salvation, particularly for the developing countries and the former communist countries where governments are being urged or pushed into adopting a comprehensive agenda of privatisation (to minimize the role of the state) and liberalisation (of trade flows, capital flows and financial flows). The conclusion drawn is that globalisation now, as much as then, promises economic prosperity for countries that join the system and economic deprivation for countries that do not[20]. It needs to be stressed that this normative and prescriptive view of globalisation is driven in part by ideology and in part by hope. It is not borne out by history. For those who recall development experience in the late nineteenth century, it should be obvious that the process of globalisation will not reproduce or replicate the United States everywhere just as it did not reproduce Britain everywhere a century earlier. It was associated with an uneven development then. It is bound to produce uneven development now, not only between countries but also within countries.

This is a lesson that emerges from history. The economic consequences of globalisation in the late nineteenth century were, to say the least, asymmetrical. Most of the gains from international economic integration of this era accrued to the imperial countries which exported capital and imported commodities. There were a few countries like the United States and Canada – new lands with temperate climates and white settlers – which also derived some benefits. In these countries, the pre-conditions for industrialisation were already being created and international economic integration strengthened this process. Direct foreign investment in manufacturing activities stimulated by rising tariff barriers, combined with technological and managerial flows, reinforced the process. The outcome was industrialisation and development. But this did not happen everywhere. Development was uneven in the industrial world. Much of southern and eastern Europe lagged behind. This meant divergence rather than convergence in terms of industrialisation and growth[21]. There was, in fact, an increase in economic inequalities between countries and within countries. The income gap between the richest and the poorest countries, for instance, which was just 3:1 in 1820, more than doubled to 7:1 in 1870 and increased further to 11:1 in 1913[22]. Countries in Asia, Africa and Latin America, particularly the colonised, which were also a part of this process of globalisation, were even less fortunate. Indeed, during the same period of rapid international economic integration, some of the most open economies in this phase of globalisation – India, China and Indonesia – experienced de-industrialisation and underdevelopment.

We need to remind ourselves that, in the period from 1870 to 1914, these three countries practised free trade as much as the United Kingdom and the Netherlands, where average tariff levels were close to negligible 4 (3-5 percent); in contrast, tariff levels in Germany, Japan and France were significantly higher (12-14 per cent) whereas tariff levels in the United States were very much higher (33 per cent)[23]. What is more, these three countries were also among the largest recipients of foreign investment[24]. But their globalisation did not lead to development. The outcome was similar elsewhere: in Asia, Africa and Latin America. So much so, between 1860 and 1913, the share of developing countries in world manufacturing output declined from over one-third to under one-tenth[25]. Export-oriented production in mines, plantations and cash-crop agriculture created enclaves in these economies which were integrated with the world economy in a vertical division of labour. But there were almost no backward linkages. Productivity levels outside the export enclaves stagnated at low levels. They simply created dualistic economic structures where the benefits of globalisation accrued mostly to the outside world and in small part to the local elites.

The growing inequalities between and within countries, particularly in the industrial world, were perhaps a significant factor underlying the retreat from globalisation after 1914. The following passage, written by John Maynard Keynes in 1919, vividly highlights the benefits of globalisation for some people and some countries, those included, but also recognises how economic and political conflicts associated with the process stopped what had seemed irreversible at the time.

"What an extraordinary episode in the economic progress of man that age was which came to an end in August 1914. The greater part of the population, it is true, worked hard and lived at a low standard of comfort, yet were, to all appearances, reasonably contented with this lot. But escape was possible, for any man of capacity or character at all exceeding the average, into the middle and upper classes, for whom life offered, at a low cost and with the least trouble, conveniences, comforts, and amenities beyond the compass of the richest and most powerful monarchs of other ages. The inhabitant of London could order by telephone, sipping his morning tea in bed, the various products of the whole earth, in such quantity as he may see fit, and reasonably expect their early delivery upon his doorstep; he could at the same moment and by the same means adventure his wealth in the natural resources and new enterprises of any quarter of the world, and share, without exertion or trouble, in their prospective fruits and advantages; or he could decide to couple the security of his fortunes with the good faith of the townspeople of any substantial municipality in any continent that fancy or information might recommend. He could secure forthwith, if he wished it, cheap and comfortable means of transit to any country or climate without any passport or other formality, could despatch his servants to the neighbouring office of a bank for such supply of the precious metals as might seem convenient, and could then proceed to foreign quarters, without knowledge of their religion, language or customs, bearing coined wealth upon his person, and could consider himself greatly aggrieved and much surprise at least interference. But most important of all, he regarded this state of affairs as normal, certain, and permanent, except in the direction of further improvement, and any deviation from it as aberrant, scandalous and avoidable. The projects and politics of militarism and imperialism, of racial and cultural rivalries, of monopolies, restrictions and exclusions, which were to play the serpent to this paradise, were little more than amusement of his daily newspaper, and appeared to exercise almost no influence at all on the ordinary course of social and economic life, the internationalisation of which was nearly complete in practice"[26].

IV

The process of globalization has led to uneven development, now as much as then. The reality that has unfolded so far, clearly belies the expectations of the ideologues. From the early 1970s to the late 1990s, the world economy has experienced a divergence, rather than convergence, in levels of income between countries and between people. Economic inequalities have increased during the last quarter of a century as the income gap between rich and poor countries, between rich and poor people within countries, as also between the rich and the poor in the world's population, has widened[27]. And income distribution has worsened almost everywhere in the world. The incidence of poverty has increased in many parts of the developing world and in most transitional economies. Over the same period, the rate of growth in the world economy has also registered a discernible slowdown. And the slower growth has been combined with greater instability.

It is obviously not possible to attribute cause-and-effect simply to the coincidence in time. But it is possible to think of mechanisms through which globalisation may have accentuated inequalities. Trade liberalisation has led to a growing wage inequality between skilled and unskilled workers not only in industrialised countries but also in developing countries. As a consequence of privatisation and deregulation, capital has gained at the expense of labour, almost everywhere, for profit shares have risen while wage shares have fallen[28]. Structural reforms, which have cut tax rates and brought flexibility to labour markets, have reinforced this trend. The mobility of capital combined with the immobility of labour has changed the nature of the employment relationship and has reduced the bargaining power of trade unions. The object of managing inflation has been transformed into a near-obsession by the sensitivity of international financial markets, so that governments have been forced to adopt deflationary macroeconomic policies which have squeezed both growth and employment. The excess supply of labour has repressed real wages. Financial liberalisation, which has meant a rapid expansion of public as well as private debt, has been associated with the emergence of a new rentier class. And the inevitable concentration in the ownership of financial assets has probably contributed to a worsening of income distribution. Global competition has driven large international firms to consolidate market power through mergers and acquisitions which has made market structures more oligopolistic than competitive. The competition for export markets and foreign investment, between countries, has intensified, in what is termed "a race to the bottom", leading to an unequal distribution of gains from trade and investment.

Globalisation has, indeed, created opportunities for some people and some countries that were not even dreamed of three decades ago. But it has also introduced new risks, if not threats, for many others. It has been associated with a deepening of poverty and an accentuation of inequalities. The distribution of benefits and costs is unequal. There are some winners. There are many losers. If we think of people, asset-owners, profit-earners, rentiers, the educated, the mobile and those with professional, managerial or technical skills are the winners, whereas asset-less, wage-earners, debtors, the uneducated, the immobile and the semi-skilled or the unskilled are the losers. If we think of economies, capital-exporters, technology-exporters, net lenders, those with a strong physical and human infrastructure, and those endowed with structural flexibilities are the winners, whereas capital-importers, technology-importers, net borrowers, those with a weak physical and human infrastructure, and those characterised by structural rigidities are the losers. It needs to be said that this classification is suggestive rather than definitive, for it paints a broad-brush picture of a more nuanced situation. But it does convey the simultaneous, yet asymmetrical, inclusion and exclusion that characterises the process of globalisation. It is not surprising, then, that the spread of globalisation is uneven and limited both among people and across countries.

The exclusion of people and of countries is a fact of life. In 1997, a quarter century after the present phase of globalisation gathered momentum, the share of the richest 20 per cent of the world's people, living in high income countries, in world GDP was 86 per cent, while that of the poorest 20 per cent of the world's people, living in low income countries, was a mere 1 per cent[29]. The income gap between the richest 20 per cent widened from 32:1 in 1970 to 45:1 in 1980, 60:1 in 1990 and 74:1 in 1997. This sharp divide between rich and poor countries is no surprise. But the spread of globalisation is just as uneven within the developing world. There are no more than a dozen developing countries which are an integral part of the process of globalisation: Argentina, Brazil, Chile and Mexico in Latin America, and the Republic of

Korea, Hong Kong, Singapore, Taiwan, China, Malaysia, Thailand and, to some extent, Indonesia in Asia. These countries account for 70 per cent of exports from the developing world, absorb almost 80 per cent of investment flows to the developing world and receive more than 90 per cent of portfolio investment flows to the developing world[30]. Sub-Saharan Africa, West Asia, Central Asia and South Asia are simply not in the picture, apart from many countries in Latin America, Asia and the Pacific which are left out altogether.

Joan Robinson once said: "There is only one thing that is worse than being exploited by capitalists. And that is not being exploited by capitalists". Much the same can be said about globalisation, which may not ensure prosperity for everyone but may, in fact, exclude a significant proportion of people[31].

Globalisation has introduced a new dimension to the exclusion of people from development. Exclusion is no longer simply about the inability to satisfy basic human needs in terms of food, clothing, shelter, health care and education for large numbers of people. It is much more complicated. For the consumption patterns and lifestyles of the rich associated with globalisation have powerful demonstration effects. People everywhere, even the poor and the excluded, are exposed to these consumption possibility frontiers because the electronic media have spread the consumerist message far and wide. This creates both expectations and aspirations. But the simple fact of life is that those who do not have the incomes cannot buy goods and services in the market. Thus, when the paradise of consumerism is unattainable, which is the case for common people, it only creates frustration or alienation. The reaction of people who experience such exclusion differs. Some seek short cuts to the consumerist paradise through drugs, crime or violence. Some seek refuge in ethnic identities, cultural chauvinism or religious fundamentalism. Such assertion of traditional or indigenous values is often the only thing that poor people can assert for it brings an identity and meaning to their lives. Outcomes do not always take these extreme forms. But globalisation inevitably tends to erode social stability[32]. Thus, economic integration with the world outside may accentuate social tensions or provoke social fragmentation within countries. It is clear that markets and globalisation have a logic of their own, which leads to inclusion for some and exclusion for others, or affluence for some and poverty for others. Such outcomes of market driven processes in the economy, we know from experience, can continue only if they are acceptable to polity and society. History may not repeat itself. But it would be wise to learn from

199

history. The process of globalisation is sustainable only if it is democratised, so that it includes a much larger number of countries and a much higher proportion of people. The concern for efficiency must be balanced by a concern for equity, just as the concern for economic growth must be balanced by a concern for social progress. The fundamental objective should be to ensure decent living conditions for people, ordinary people, as the welfare of humankind is the essence of development. This needs to be combined with the quest for a more equal distribution of income, wealth and power between countries. And, ultimately, a global democracy must provide much more freedom for the movement of people.

Globalisation has made it so much easier to move goods, services, capital, finance and technology across borders. But explicit immigration laws and implicit consular practices have made it far more difficult for people to move across borders. Indeed, as we enter the twentyfirst century, the asymmetry between the free movement of capital and the unfree movement of labour lies at the heart of the inequality in the rules of the game for globalisation. It is, then, reasonable to argue that if there is almost complete freedom for capital mobility across national boundaries, the draconian restrictions on labour mobility across national boundaries should at least be reduced even if they cannot be removed. Similarly, it is plausible to suggest that any provisions for commercial presence of corporate entities (capital) should correspond to provisions for temporary migration of workers (labour), just as the right-to-establishment for corporate entities (capital) has an analogue in the right-of-residence for persons (labour). And, if the freedom of movement within countries is a basic human right, in an ideal world, there is no reason why it should not extend across countries. This rights-based argument is not, at least for the present, in the realm of the feasible. But more freedom for the cross-border movement of people is both feasible and desirable in this age of globalisation. It would have to be an integral part of any attempt to move from the world economy to a world community.

Notes

1. The export-GDP ratios in this paragraph are calculated from data on exports in UNCTAD, *Handbook of International Trade and Development Statistics* and United Nations, *Yearbook of National Account Statistics,* various issues.
2. UNCTAD (1994), p. 143.
3. UNCTAD (1998), p. 385 and p. 399.
4. For evidence on the magnitudes, see Nayyar (1995) and Nayyar (1997).
5. Bank for International Settlements, *Survey of Foreign Exchange Market Activity,* Basle, various issues.
6. The value of world GDP and world exports in 1996, reported by the United Nations, has been converted into an average daily figure for the purpose of comparison. The figure on foreign exchange reserves of central banks is obtained from the IMF *Annual Report 1998.*
7. This outline of the underlying factors draws upon earlier work of the author. For a more detailed discussion, see Nayyar (1995).
8. This historical parallel was the theme of my Presidential Address to the Indian Economic Association in December 1995. For an analysis, see Nayyar (1995).
9. Cf. Bairoch (1982) and Maddison (1989).
10. This estimate is reported in UNCTAD (1994), p. 130.
11. At 1980 prices, total foreign investment in the world economy in 1914 was $347 billion (Maddison, 1989) compared with the actual stock of direct foreign investment in the world economy in 1980 at $448 billion (UNCTAD, 1994).
12. For sources of evidence and method of estimation, see Nayyar (1997).

13. In 1913, for example, foreign securities constituted 59 per cent of all securities traded in London. Similarly, in 1908, the corresponding proportion was 53 per cent in Paris. See Morgenstern (1959).

14. For a discussion of these underlying factors, see Nayyar (1995).

15. For example, the substitution of steam for sails, and of iron for wooden hulls in ships, reduced ocean freight by two-thirds between 1870 and 1900 (Lewis, 1977).

16. The production of perfectly interchangeable parts, the introduction of the moving assembly line developed by Ford, and methods of management evolved by Taylor, provided the foundations for this new form of industrial organisation. See Oman (1994).

17. Cf. Hobsbawm (1987).

18. Cf. Lewis (1978).

19. See Tinker (1974) and Lewis (1977).

20. See, for example, Sachs and Warner (1995), who provide the clearest articulation of this view.

21. See Bairoch and Kozul-Wright (1996), who show how globalisation in the period 1870-1913 led to uneven development in the world economy, not simply between the colonisers and the colonised but also within Europe.

22. Maddison (1995).

23. See Maddison (1989) and Bairoch (1982).

24. Cf. Maddison (1989).

25. Cf. Bairoch (1982).

26. Keynes (1919), pp. 9-10.

27. For supporting evidence, see UNCTAD (1997) and UNDP (1999).

28. Some evidence on the increase in profit shares in industrialised countries and the decrease in wage shares in developing countries is reported in UNCTAD (1997).

29. The evidence cited here is from UNDP (1999). See also UNCTAD (1997) for comparisons over time.

30. Cf. Nayyar (1995) and UNCTAD (1998).

31. For a detailed discussion on globalisation, development and exclusion, see Nayyar (2000).

32. The hypothesis that there are actual or potential sources of tension between global markets and social stability is developed, at some length, by Rodrik (1997).

References

Bairoch, P. (1982), "International Industrialization Levels from 1750 to 1980", *Journal of European Economic History,* Vol. 11, pp. 269-310.

Bairoch, P. and Kozul-Wright, R. (1996), "Globalisation Myths: Some Historical Reflections on Integration, Industrialisation and Growth in the World Economy", *Discussion Papers,* No. 13, Geneva: UNCTAD.

Hobsbawn, E. (1987), *The Age of Empire,* London: Weidenfeld and Nicolson.

Keynes, J.M. (1919), *The Economic Consequences of the Peace,* London: Macmillan.

Lewis, W.A. (1977), *The Evolution of the International Economic Order,* Princeton: Princeton University Press.

Lewis, W.A. (1978), *Growth and Fluctuations:* 1870-1913, London: Allen and Unwin.

Maddison, A. (1989), *The World Economy in the Twentieth Century,* Paris: OECD Development Centre.

Maddison, A. (1995), *Monitoring the World Economy:* 1820-1992, Paris: OECD Development Centre.

Morgenstern, O. (1959), *International Financial Transactions and Business Cycles,* Princeton: Princeton University Press.

Nayyar, D. (1995), "Globalisation: The Past in Our Present", Presidential Address to the Indian Economic Association, Chandigarh, 28 December, reprinted in *Indian Economic Journal,* January, pp.1-18.

Nayyar, D. (1997), "Globalization: the Game, the Players and the Rules", in S.D. Gupta *ed. The Political Economy of Globalization,* Dordrecht: Kluwer Academic Publishers.

Nayyar, D. (2000), "Globalisation and Development Strategies", paper for *High-Level Round Table on Trade and Development* at UNCTAD X, TD (X)/RT.1/4, Geneva: United Nations.

Oman, C. (1994), *Globalisation and Regionalisation: The Challenge for Developing Countries,* Paris: OECD Development Centre.

Rodrik, D. (1997), *Has Globalization Gone Too Far?,* Washington DC: Institute for International Economics.

Sachs, J. and Warner, A. (1995), "Economic Reform and the Process of Global Integration", *Brookings Papers on Economic Activity,* No.1.

Tinker, H. (1974), *A New System of Slavery: The Export of Indian Labour Overseas:* 1830-1920, Oxford: Oxford University Press.

UNCTAD (1994), *World Investment Report 1994,* New York: United Nations.

UNCTAD (1997), *Trade and Development Report 1997,* New York: United Nations.

UNCTAD (1998), *World Investment Report 1998,* New York: United Nations.

UNDP (1999), *Human Development Report 1999,* New York: Oxford University Press.

Economic Growth and Social Progress Reconsidered: The Realm of Politics

Ignacy Sachs
Professor, Ecole des Hautes Etudes en Sciences Sociales, Paris, France

The twentieth century ended in frustration, leaving behind unprecedented global prosperity marred by a preposterous maldistribution of assets and incomes (between nations and within nations), daunting social and humanitarian problems, the horrendous record of wars and genocides[1] and an international system too weak to promote lasting peace, equity and genuine development.

The changes occurred during the century were phenomenal indeed, in spite of two murderous and terribly destroying world wars.

The population increased from 1.7 to 6 billion people and the normal life span in industrial countries grew from 45 to 75. The progress was even more spectacular in poor countries: from 25 years in 1900 to 63 in 1985. Woman's risk of death by childbirth declined by 40 times since 1940. At the beginning of the century 9 out of 10 people lived in the countryside; we are nearing the moment when rural and urban populations will balance out[2].

Thanks to the increase in productivity of labour[3], the global GNP was multiplied by 17.5, allowing for an almost fivefold increase of GNP per capita. An egalitarian distribution of the global GNP would entitle each inhabitant of our planet to five thousand dollars, enough to meet comfortably all his needs. Instead, we are witnessing at a continuous worsening of the income distribution. According to Paul Bairoch, in 1900 the income per capita of the future industrialized countries was three times greater than in of the future third world countries. The gap rose to 1 to 7 in the 1990s. The share in global income of the richest fifth of the world's population is today 74 times that of the poorest fifth[4].

The dismal social and humanitarian condition of our planet is only too well-known. Let us just recall here that nearly 1.3 billion people live on less than a dollar a day, about 800 million people are malnourished and a full thirty per cent of the world workforce is unemployed or severely underemployed, while more than 250 million children are working as child labourers.

Even the most industrialized countries experience serious social problems and face massive social exclusion. One does not need to go as far as to suggest that there exists a positive correlation between wealth and anomie. But some symptoms of the social malaise are troubling enough, be it the inability of the Western European countries to return to a situation of almost full employment or that of the United States to cope with violence and racial discrimination to the point of keeping almost 2 million people in prisons[5].

Growth is Necessary but by No Means Sufficient

On the one hand, unprecedented economic growth and technical transformation, on the other, the dramatic social condition of so many people whose lifes are being irrevocably wasted; an obvious conclusion flows from this contrasted picture: growth as such does not bring automatically development, or for that, happiness. The *trickle-down* theory is contradicted by historical evidence. At best, it has some weak positive effects on the condition of the people at the bottom of the social pyramid when growth rates are very high.

But a much more common situation is that of *growth through inequality with perverse social effects:* the accumulation of wealth in the hand of a minority with a simultaneous production of massive poverty and deterioration of living conditions. In extreme cases, we are in presence of *growth with dedevelopment.*

The problem, however, is that implicitly the trickle-down doctrine continues to dominate the mainstream economic thinking. We did not free ourselves as yet from the economic reductionism, which prevailed during the cold war on both sides of the iron curtain[6] and still permeates the neoliberal doctrine.

On the other hand, the fact that development is not subsumed in economic growth should not be interpreted in terms of an opposition between growth and development[7]. Economic growth, conveniently redesigned in order to

206

minimize the negative environmental impacts and put to socially desirable goals, is still a necessary condition of development. As a matter of fact, we need higher rates of economic growth to speed up the social rehabilitation, as it is easier to operate on the increments of the GNP, rather than to redistribute assets and incomes in a stagnant economy.

We must therefore learn to distinguish between different kinds of growth. A frequent but unacceptable variety is the *savage* growth with unbearably high social and environmental costs.

During the golden age of capitalism, as a result of full employment coupled with fordist income policies, Western Europe experienced a *socially-benign* growth; however, it generated, at the same time, considerable environmental disruption.

Some attempts at greening the present patterns of growth may end up by producing an *environmentally-benign,* yet socially disruptive variety because of its inability to deal with chronic unemployment and underemployment.

Important as may be in this context the social security-nets, financed by the redistribution of a parcel of GNP, they do not constitute a lasting solution, because they address the symptoms and not the roots of the problem. At best, they alleviate the effects of deprivation and social exclusion without succeeding to include people back in the productive process. One is reminded of Joan Robinson's *boutad:* worse than being exploited, is not to be exploited.

We know today that *market-led growth* will not reestablish by itself a satisfactory situation on the labour market, not speaking of the danger of offsetting some of the most significant advances of the Welfare State under the pretext of seeking greater labour flexibility. It is very difficult, indeed, to translate in policies the formula: *yes to market economy, no to market society.* That is why it is so urgent to center again the debate on full employment and its equivalents (self-employment particularly important in developing countries, where family-farms and petty businesses have still a major role to play) addressing more specifically to the *employment-led growth strategies*[8].

At the same time, a much larger place ought to be reserved for the *need-oriented* component of the development strategies (as distinct from the market

207

imposed components)[9] in the form of provision of social services, particularly health-care and basic education, without waiting for dramatic increases in per capita levels of real income. As stressed by A. Sen, such services *are very labour-intensive and thus are relatively inexpensive in poor – and low wage – economies. A poor economy may have less money to spend on health care and education, but it also needs less money to spend to provide the same services, which would cost much more in the richer countries"[10]*.

Benign varieties are better than savage growth. But genuine development requires *three-win solutions,* socially-responsive, environmentally-prudent and economically viable, offering everybody an opportunity to earn a decent livelihood, by wage employment, production for self-consumption or a mix of both. Genuine development must obey to the double ethical imperative of synchronic solidarity with the present generation and the diachronic solidarity with future generations and rest on a democratically established *social contract* complemented by a *natural contract.*

In a recent, brilliant and polemical essay, the Indian novelist Arundhati Roy argued persuasively that development is about human lives. Breaking up the economics from the politics, from the emotion and human tragedy *"is like breaking up a band. The individual musicians don't rock in quite the same way. You keep the noise but lose the music"[11]*.

Her impassioned, albeit somewhat unilateral indictment of the controversial Narmada Valley Development Project[12], as a writer and an activist of human causes, reminds us also that development is everybody's business and ordinary people ought to have a decisive say about it. In other words, development should cease to be a monopoly of technocrats, bureaucrats and academicians and reach the market place. It belongs to the realm of democratic politics.

It is of course unacceptable to impose unbearable, and often unnecessary social harms under the pretext that they constitute the unavoidable costs of the progress. Yet, it is difficult not to build dams altogether in the absence of good alternatives to propose. In his Republic Day address, the President of India, K.R. Narayanan, tried to reply to Arundhati Roy and the different social protest movements, while acknowledging the accuracy and pertinence of many of their criticisms: *"factories will and must rise, satellites must and will soar to the heavens, and dams over rivers will rise to prevent floods, generate electricity and irrigate dry lands for cultivation. But that should not cause ecological and environmental devastation, and the uprooting of human settlements, especially of tribals and the poor. Ways and methods can be found for countering the harmful impact of modern technology on the lives of the common people. I believe that the answer to the ill-effects of science and technology is not to turn our back on technology, but to have more science and technology that is directed to human needs and for the betterment of the human condition"*[13].

The Realm of Politics

So the key to reconcile economic growth with social development resides in the realm of politics, the ability to give to the development process the necessary guidance in the form of a democratically evolved project[14] and to design a system of regulation of the public and private spheres of our lives.

The development potential of a country depends, first of all, on its cultural capacity to think endogenously about its desirable futures. Celso Furtado is right to emphasize the need to formulate development policies by explicitating the substantive goals to be achieved, instead of deriving them from the logic of means imposed by the accumulation process commanded by transnational enterprises[15]. Addressing the same question, Aminata Traoré, from Mali, has the following to say: *"To tame development, to prevent it from being used as a tool of social, economic and political transformation working to our disadvantage, it remains critical to give it a lot of thought and to practice it in relation with what we know, the resources we have, and a perspective which is ours, or in which we can at least recognize ourselves. Each facet of our existence allows for this work of redefinition and reorientation: education, health, food, housing, clothing, the State, governance, decentralization and, of course, the struggle against poverty"*[16].

As for the regulation of mixed economies and the finding of a compromise between need-oriented and market-led approaches, three questions must be addressed:

- the harmonization of the social, environmental and economic goals already referred to;
- the promotion of partnerships between all the stakeholders of the development process: the citizens and the organizations of the civil society, the

world of enterprises and a lean but operative State (the so-called *negotiated economy*); finally,

- the articulation of the development spaces from the local to the global, through the regional and national.

Special attention must be given to the interface between the national and the global economy. This is certainly the most sensitive point which requires not only national, but also international regulation. Globalization has been used as a pretext to promote across the board liberalization which reduces the chances of the weaker partners to resist the pressure of the overwhelming interests of the stronger partners. Equity in international relations calls for "rules of the game" biased in favour of the weak and not to formal equality among all partners. This principle seems fairly forgotten nowadays. It should be reinstated as the cornerstone of the reformed international system.

The Development Age is Still Ahead

To conclude, democracy is the foundational value. It ought to be interpreted in the strong way, giving a greater scope to what is known as *direct democracy,* affirming the centrality of human rights as the overriding law. As a matter of fact, as suggested by Amartya Sen, development can be equated with the expansion of positive freedoms and the effective appropriation of all human rights by all the people. In Johan Galtung words, *"democracy is empowerment, a giant effort to share more equally political decision-making, a decent livelihood, security from violence and cultural identity. To reduce democracy to electioneering is to lose the essence of it"*[17].

Development emerged some sixty years ago as an *idée-force* to guide the post-war reconstruction and, soon after, the decolonization process – undoubtedly the most significant geopolitical change of the century – to become, side by side with the preservation of peace, the cornerstone of the United Nations philosophy of action. Unfortunately, the gap between rhetoric and reality has widened in recent years, as the diffusion of the neoliberal gospel succeeded in undermining the very credibility of the concept. Yet, not only the developing countries of the South, but also the industrialized countries of the North need to reenter the development track and ensure the expansion of positive freedoms by promoting "three-win" solutions. Material conditions to move in this direction are better than ever. We have no right to fail in this endeavour.

Notes

1. The holocaust foremost, but also the German's earlier slaughter of Herreros in Africa, the Turks' killing of Armenians, the Hutu's of the Tutsis in Rwanda, the Croats' of Serbians in World War II, the Serbians' ethnic cleansing in Bosnia and Kosovo and now Russians' massacrous in Chechnya (see Ponting, C., 1999, The Twentieth Century: A World History, Henry Holt, quoted by Garry Wills, "A Reader's Guide to the Century", *The New York Review of Books,* July 15, 1999). On the overwhelming responsibility of the United States and other Western powers in not doing enough to prevent the genocide in Rwanda, see Solarz, S., Aronson, D. and Weissman, S., "Genocide in Rwanda: While Washington Dithered", *The International Herald Tribune,* 21 February 2000.
2. All the data from Garry Wills, op.cit.
3. In France, between 1896 and 1998, labour productivity went up sixteenfold, allowing a tenfold increase of the GNP with a working force only higher by 20 per cent and the number of worked hours per person almost halved (*Alternatives Economiques,* hors-série n°42, 1999).
4. UNDP, *Human Development Report,* 1999.
5. The U.S. inmate population doubled in ten years. 461 of every 100,000 Americans are now serving a prison sentence of at least one year. Although blacks comprise about 13 per cent of the U.S. population, they make up 50 per cent of the state and federal prison population (Jesse Katz, U.S. Prison Population Hits the 2 Million Mark, The *International Herald Tribune,* 16 February 2000).
6. The marxist vulgata does not differ in this respect from the neoliberal doctrine: the only thing that really matters is economic growth, the rest will follow.

7. Nor should one accept the extreme claim of some ecological economists that economic growth and development are oxymorons because the finite Spaceship Earth cannot support the exponencial increase in the natural resource-use. For these ecologists, in the long-term the only possible progress is of a qualitative nature through dematerialized production of services and aesthetic goods. This may be true in the very long perspective. We are not yet there. The tremendous *social deficit* has to be offset first and this will not happen without many decades of "three-win" economic growth. Let us not forget that the civilization of being presupposes an equitable sharing of having, as admirably condensed by Joseph Lebret in the following sentence: *civilisation de l'être dans le partage équitable de l'avoir.*

8. See on this point Sachs, I. (1999), "L'économie politique du développement des économies mixtes selon Kalecki: croissance tirée par l'emploi", *Mondes en développement,* tome 27, Bruxelles, pp.23-34.

9. The need-oriented and market-oriented components of the development strategy ought to be distinguished for planning purposes. An innovative approach in natural resource accounting and budgeting, using both physical budgeting and economic valuation, is being developed at present by a research team at the Indian Institute of Public Administration and Kalpavriksh chaired by Shekhar Singh.

10. Sen, A. (1999), *Development as Freedom,* Alfred A. Knopf, New York, p.48. For an earlier discussion of the same point, see Sachs, I. (1971), "A Welfare State for Poor Countries", *Economic and Political Weekly,* vol. VI, n° 3-4, january 1971, pp. 367-70.

11. Roy, Arundhati, "The Cost of Living", *Frontline,* February 18, 2000, p.65. This is the text of the Nehru Memorial Lecture delivered by the writer at Cambridge University on November 8, 1999 at the invitation of Professor Amartya Sen, Master of Trinity College.

12. Believed to be the most ambitious river valley development project in the world, it envisages building on Narmada and her 419 tributaries 2 multipurpose mega dams 28 other major dams, 135 medium and about 3000 small dams. It will affect the lives of 25 million people who live in the valley.

13. Address to the Nation on the eve of Republic Day, 25th January 2000.

14. In the meaning given to this word by Jean-Paul Sartre. To him, man was a project. A fortiori, human societies ought to spell out their project. Development rests, to a large extent, on the cultural ability of people to invent their future.

15. Furtado, Celso (2000), "Brasil: quando o futuro chegar", article to be published in a collective book on *Brasil: As Transformações do Século* (in preparation).

16. Traoré, Aminata (1999), *L'étau – l'Afrique dans un monde sans frontières,* Actes Sud, Marseille.

17. Sen, A. (1999), *op.cit.*

18. Keynote address, XVIth World Futures Studies Federation World Conference, Futures Bulletin vol.25 n°4, January 2, 2000. See also Friedmann, John (1992), *Empowerment: The Politics of Alternative Development,* Basil Blackwell, Oxford/Cambridge, Mass.

A Time to Act:
To Save Lives and
Promote Gender Equality

Nafis Sadik
Executive Director, UNFPA, New York, USA

Building a Consensus

When UNFPA began its work thirty years ago fertility had already started to decline in a few Asian countries, and there was little resistance in South and East Asia to the idea that family planning programmes might be useful policy tools. But even in Asia few countries had national population programmes and fewer still considered it among their priorities. African countries broadly perceived themselves as under-populated and tended to regard promoting family planning or even a discussion of birth rates as irrelevant to their economic development goals. A few were actively pro-natalist, others passively so. In Latin America, development theorists tended to regard population trends as dependent variables, not to be influenced directly: in any case strong Church influence in many countries inhibited discussion of family planning. In the English-speaking Caribbean, family planning was accepted but little discussed. In west Asia, the question was hardly raised. In 1969, the global population growth rate was at its historic peak, at 2 per cent per year. For developing countries the rate was 2.5 per cent per year and total fertility for these countries averaged six children per woman.

There was a great deal of doubt, even among experts, whether family planning could be successfully promoted in developing countries, or that family planning programmes would help to bring population growth rates down.

By 1974 and the World Population Conference, UNFPA had established its global presence, with $52 million per year in resources and programmes in 97 countries. As a trusted partner among countries of all ideological persuasions, UNFPA's annual budget grew to over \$125 million by the time it was ten years old, accepting voluntary contributions from over 100 countries.

UNFPA's partnership with donor and developing countries demonstrated that population is a "programmable" part of development strategy, and that population assistance can make a difference when effectively delivered without ideological connotations and in conformity with sovereign countries' priorities and values. These understandings have been critical in building today's global consensus on population and development.

Over the 30 years of UNFPA's work, population has changed from a highly divisive and controversial issue to one of the few development questions on which there is a detailed global consensus.

Programme experience has shown that family planning can be integrated into mother and child health care programmes. From this has developed the broader concept of reproductive health, which includes, not only care in pregnancy and childbirth, but prevention of unwanted pregnancy and protection against infection.

From this, in turn, have grown the connections to the broader ideas of reproductive health in the context of family and society: nurturing the girl child; care for the adolescent and empowerment for women. Gender equality is now perceived, not only as an aim of development, but as the context in which reproductive health can be guaranteed, personally and politically.

Men are full partners in women's empowerment and gender equality. They also have reproductive health needs that must be met, but men should also be expected to participate in protecting and promoting women's reproductive health. Gender equality extends to men's full participation in family life as well as to women's full participation in the life of the community and the nation. Achieving these goals will also contribute to the concomitant development goal of slower and more balanced population growth. Experience has shown that fertility falls when certain social development thresholds are crossed. Among the most important determinants are the level of women's education, their participation in the labour force and their access to reproductive health services.

In 1994 the International Conference on Population and Development (ICPD) approved a clear and comprehensive Programme of Action that recognises the interrelationship between population and development policies; programmes to achieve poverty alleviation and eradication; sustained economic growth in the context of sustainable development; education, especially for girls; gender equity and equality; infant, child and maternal mortality reduction; the provision of universal access to reproductive health services, including family planning and sexual health; sustainable patterns of consumption and production; food security; human resource development; and the guarantee of all human rights, including the right to development as a universal and inalienable right and an integral part of fundamental human rights. Quantitative goals were adopted in three areas: universal education, mortality reduction, and reproductive health.

At the Special Session of the United Nations General Assembly marking five years since ICPD, this consensus was renewed and strengthened in another landmark document, that articulated key actions that should be taken by governments, civil society groups and international community to fully implement the objectives and goals agreed to in 1994. New benchmarks to measure the implementation of ICPD goals were set:

- The 1990 illiteracy rate for women and girls should be halved by 2005. By 2010, the net primary school enrolment ratio for children of both sexes should be at least 90 per cent;
- By 2005, 60 per cent of primary health care and family planning facilities should offer the widest achievable range of safe and effective family planning methods, essential obstetric care, prevention and management of reproductive tract infections including sexually transmitted diseases, and barrier methods to prevent infection; 80 per cent of facilities should offer such services by 2010, and all should do so by 2015;
- At least 40 per cent of all births should be assisted by skilled attendants, where the maternal mortality rate is very high, and 80 per cent globally, by 2005; these figures should be 50 and 85 per cent, respectively, by 2010; and 60 and 90 per cent, by 2015;
- Any gap between the proportion of individuals using contraceptives and the proportion expressing a desire to space or limit their families should be reduced by half by 2005, 75 per cent by 2010, and 100 per cent by

2015. Recruitment targets or quotas should not be used in attempting to reach this goal.

- Recognising that the HIV/AIDS situation was worse than anticipated by the ICPD, the review agreed that, to reduce vulnerability to HIV/AIDS infection, at least 90 per cent of young men and women aged 15 to 24 should have access, by 2005, to preventive methods – such as female and male condoms, voluntary testing, counseling, and follow-up, and at least 95 per cent, by 2010. HIV infection rates in persons 15 to 24 years of age should be reduced by 25 per cent in the most affected countries by 2005 and by 25 per cent, globally, by 2010.

Achievements

Population and Sustainable Development

Nearly half of all countries have reviewed their policies in light of the new understandings of the role of population in development. More than one third have updated their population policies to be consistent with ICPD objectives or have integrated factors relating to health-care quality, gender equality and equity, and improvement of information systems into long-term development plans. Two thirds of all countries have introduced policy or legislative measures to promote gender equity and equality and the empowerment of women, including in the areas of inheritance, property rights and employment, and in protection from gender-based violence. New monitoring mechanisms and better means of collecting and using data have been put in place. Organizations of lawmakers, women, youth, traditional leaders as well as cultural, health and other advocates and policy makers are involved in population and development activities.

In developing countries, fertility has fallen by half since 1969. From almost six children per woman then, it is now under three children. As a result, population growth rates have begun to slow. This slowing of population growth was the work of many people over the last 30 years. Future achievements will depend on decisions taken now with regard to population and development policies and, in particular, on the universal exercise of the right to health, including reproductive health.

Reproductive Rights and Reproductive Health

Where only 15-20 per cent of women of reproductive age had access to modern, safe and effective means of family planning in 1969, more than half have such access today. The ICPD's broad-based approach to reproductive health is being implemented by an increasing number of countries. The rising use of family planning methods indicates that there is greater accessibility to family planning, and that more and more couples and individuals are able to choose the number and spacing of their children.

A total of 67 countries have made policy changes affirming a commitment to reproductive rights and reproductive health. Over 40 have incorporated this perspective in the provision of health services. Many countries have acted to improve the quality of reproductive health services. Nearly half the countries in the world have taken new measures to address adolescent reproductive health needs, often in collaboration with non-governmental organizations and the civil society sector. The Special Session of the General Assembly on key actions on the further implementation of ICPD calls for governments to include, at all levels, as appropriate, formal and non-formal schooling and education on population and health issues, including reproductive health issues.

Special measures are being undertaken to implement the ICPD call for all persons, irrespective of their conditions, to have access to basic health services including reproductive health and family planning services. For the first time in an international forum, expressed mention has been made of the plight of refugees, asylum seekers and displaced persons, in addition to that of migrants, with regard to reproductive rights and health.

All countries have taken some steps to ensure access to sexual and reproductive health information and services, including provision for the four central components – family planning, maternal health, prevention and treatment of sexually transmitted diseases, and towards a client-centered approach to meeting reproductive health needs.

The Empowerment of Women

We have seen remarkable progress in women's collective status and individual prospects over the last 30 years. The Platform for Action adopted by the Fourth World Conference on Women in 1995 reflected decades of effort by and for women. The advances, while incomplete, include improvements in educational enrolment and literacy; increased participation in the paid labour force; increased participation in management and administration; greater use of the voting franchise and attainment of political representation; legal action to establish and protect women's rights in marriage, inheritance and property; greater access to and control over resources through employment and micro-credit; stronger mechanisms for addressing women's rights issues as basic human rights concern; and recognition that gender-based violence is a social not a family matter. Many countries have revised laws and family codes to strengthen measures against female genital mutilation, rape, forced marriage, domestic violence, dowry murder, and "honour" killings. Fifteen African countries have outlawed female genital mutilation.

Progress in reproductive health since 1969 has directly contributed to women's empowerment. The ability to make informed choices about the number, timing and spacing of children accommodates women's need for education, which is often interrupted by early pregnancy or marriage; improves maternal and child health; and encourages balanced consideration of employment and family opportunities.

Despite severe resource constraints, experience has shown that an approach to development centered on individual needs and aspirations can create integrated programmes for sexual and reproductive health, advance the empowerment of women and mobilize new partnerships among governments and civil society.

Creating an Enabling Environment

The ICPD affirmed the crucial role that population policies and investment in the social sector play in creating the enabling environment for sustainable development. Over the past decade, the United Nations several global conferences – the Children's Summit, the Education Summit, the United Nations

Conference on Environment and Development, the World Conference on Human Rights, the International Conference on Population and Development, the World Summit for Social Development, the Fourth World Conference on Women, and Habitat II, further emphasized the importance of social sector investments.

The United Nations system embarked on a unified follow-up to these global conferences, to strengthen collaboration among United Nations organizations, including the World Bank and International Monetary Fund, in programmes to assist countries in achieving conference goals and the eradication of poverty. As part of this exercise, three task forces were established: (1) "Employment and Sustainable Livelihoods", (2) the "Enabling Environment for People-Centered Development" and (3) "Basic Social Services for All". The Task Force on Basic Social Services for All (BSSA) was an expansion of the Interagency Task Force on ICPD Implementation.

The products of the Task Force on Basic Social Services for All have been valuable to the new coordination reform initiatives of the United Nations, in particular, the United Nations Common Country Assessments (CCA) and United Nations Development Assistance Frameworks (UNDAF), now undertaken at country level. Earlier UNFPA had initiated, within the Joint Consultative Group on Policy (JCGP) comprising the five key funds and programmes of the United Nations, the first policy guides for the CCA – for common country data and situational analyses. Population programmes and those in other areas of social development can fit seamlessly together within such frameworks. Effectively coordinated policies and programmes lend new synergies, reinforce each other, and together can strengthen prospects for population stabilization, poverty eradication and positive economic and social change for a sustainable future.

Challenges

Thus, the 20th century has witnessed unprecedented changes in both population dynamics and the progress of human development. At the same time, much of humanity remains caught in a web of poverty, ill health and inequality. The coexistence of these divergent trends makes this a crucial moment of decisions about our future.

Poverty

The gap between rich and poor countries widens as well as the gap between rich and poor within countries. The effects of globalization have seen devastating dislocations. The financial crisis in Asia, for instance, led to severe cuts in public spending for basic social services; increased school dropouts, particularly among girls and the poor; and increased levels of unemployed, disproportionately affecting women. The financial cutbacks to public programmes have reduced the availability of social and reproductive health services, including family planning and have led to a rise in unwanted pregnancies and unsafe abortions with a concomitant rise in the risks to the lives of mothers and children. Globalisation affects a number of population and development concerns, increases stress on the environment, particularly in urban areas and already fragile areas from migration, and further aggravates deteriorating conditions with accompanying social, economic and environmental degradation for many.

The statistics are staggering, but they cannot begin to convey the extent or depth of human suffering. Today 2.6 billion people lack basic sanitation, 1.3 billion have no access to clean water, 1.1 billion lack adequate housing and nearly 1 billion have no access to basic health services. Approximately 600 million women die each year as a result of pregnancy and inadequate care during childbirth – 99 per cent occur in developing countries. 20 million unsafe abortions take place in developing countries each year and as many as 70,000 women die. While in developed countries 97 per cent of women have prenatal care, in developing countries only 65 per cent have such care. In developed countries 99 per cent of women have skilled birth attendants during delivery in developing countries this percentage is only 53 per cent. In developing countries 350 million women do not have access to a range of safe and effective family planning methods.

On 12 October 1999 we marked the day of Six Billion. World population is still growing at 78 million a year and it will start to decline only slowly in this decade. Young people, under 25 years of age, account for half of world population. Changing age structures will result in a higher proportion of people over the age of 60. It will rise from the current 10 per cent to 22 per cent by 2050. In developed countries it will rise from the current 20 per cent to 33 per cent over the same time span. These changes have major implications for meeting basic needs and assuring that more persons in extreme age groups do not become part of the "new poor".

The Elderly

In Europe, together with most industrial countries, birth rates are low and the proportion of older people is rising. At the same time the numbers of older people are increasing, because of longer life expectancy. For most industrial countries, the issue is how to mobilise the potential and meet the needs of older people. We will have to rethink our attitudes to retirement as people live longer and want to work longer too. Sixty is no longer the threshold of old age: for an increasing number of people it is the start of another 20 years of active life. The needs of the "oldest old", the over-80s, will also increase substantially over the next 20 years.

For industrial countries, this means an overhaul of the social security system and some redirection of health services. For most countries in Asia, Africa and Latin America, the extended family has been the main support of people in old age; but as populations become more urban, the extended family is not as close as it used to be. Older people are also living longer, putting an additional responsibility on their families. Most developing countries still lack the social safety net that industrial countries have, and for many it will be difficult to construct.

The Young

For most countries, however, this prospect is still on the horizon. Half the world's population is under 25, and there are over a billion young people between 15 and 24, the parents of the next generation. This new large generation of young people offers a unique opportunity to many developing countries. If they can be offered education, health care and meaningful employment, their contribution will spur rapid development in many countries.

But this generation is also uniquely at risk. The age at marriage in most countries is rising: at the same time, young people do not feel the constraints of earlier generations, and many are sexually active outside marriage. This has led to a rising rate of teenage pregnancy in many countries and an epidemic of sexually transmitted diseases, including HIV/AIDS. Half of new HIV infections are among young people.

This is a problem for all countries: but many are not yet willing to confront it. It is of course an uncomfortable and sensitive subject; yet it must be opened for informed discussion and action. The lives of young people, our future generation, are too important for us not to address their health and development needs and concerns.

Distribution and Migration

Globally, we are experiencing a changing distribution of world population.

- Whereas in 1960, 70 per cent of the world's people lived in the developing world, today the figure is 80 per cent.
- Urbanisation continues, with 60 million people becoming city dwellers each year. By 2030, it is predicted that nearly 5 billion people, over 60 per cent of the population, will live in urban areas.

International migration is moving near the top of the policy agenda in all regions, as the numbers of migrants increase and the issues they raise become more important. Migrants comprise 120 million people, but only 2 per cent of the population. Migrant workers send more than $70 billion home each year in remittances, and industries in some countries depend on their labour and skills. More and more migrants are women, almost 50 per cent in 1990, and many are vulnerable to exploitation and harassment.

Migration is an issue of particular importance in Europe with its many land boundaries and a wide variety of ethnic groups and economic situations. Over the last ten years, economic development has drawn European countries closer together; but this period of rapid international change and increasing personal mobility has also created tensions. At the same time, conflicts in the region have created a refugee situation not seen in Europe since 1945.

Increased mobility in Europe is paralleled by similar trends in other regions. The result has been considerable and continuing stress on international arrangements and understandings on migration, whether voluntary or involuntary. To address these concerns, we need better information on international flows and an informed international discussion of migration issues.

Gender

Between and within countries, the gaps between the rich and the poor are growing wider. In times of economic hardship, the poor are hardest hit, and women hardest of all. Poor health and education, active discrimination and violence contribute to women's poverty:

- Women are two-thirds of the world's 960 million illiterates. The "gender gap" is a fixture in many education systems – not because girls have less ability, but because they have less opportunity.
- More than half of all women will suffer some form of gender-based violence in their lives. Each year two million girls and young women are at risk of female genital mutilation.
- More than 585,000 women in developing countries die each year, and at least seven million women suffer infection or injury as a result of pregnancy. 70,000 women die every year from unsafe abortion. So far, the policy priority and the necessary resources for safer childbirth have not been forthcoming. The result is that pregnancy and childbirth are the greatest threat to a woman's health during her reproductive years.
- Of the nearly 175 million pregnancies each year, up to half are unwanted or ill-timed. Although contraceptive use in developing countries increased by 1.2 per cent annually between 1990 and 1995, the needs of about 20-25 per cent of couples are still not being met. Over 350 million women do not have access to a range of safe and effective contraception.
- Women are more vulnerable to a variety of sexually transmitted infections, including HIV/AIDS. With 11 new infections a minute, the pandemic is destroying lives and families and threatening development in sub-Saharan Africa and parts of the Indian subcontinent. Yet, women in many countries have neither services nor information to protect them against infection. In many countries women do not even have the right to say "No", even though they know their partner may be infected.
- Young women are especially at risk. Young women who do not know

225

their rights, and young men who do not know their responsibilities are a danger to themselves and to each other.

•   Women are excluded from political and economic life, and in some places they still do not have even legal recognition of their equal status in marriage, divorce, property and inheritance rights.

Together, these deprivations amount to gross abuse of human rights. The five-year review of the ICPD agreed that commitment to gender equity and equality must reach much further into all levels of society. Guaranteeing women's equality helps them to escape from poverty: and in doing so contributes directly to economic development.

Environment and a Culture of a Global Commons Community

The interface of the goals of the 1992 United Nations Conference on Environment and Development with ICPD goals may be one of the greatest challenges of all times. The increased recognition of the interdependence between human populations; the level and use of resources, for example, water, land, energy, air, forests, wildlife; a sustainable global commons; and the pace and change of economics and social condition, bring with it the responsibility to make choices today while we still have the ability to do so.

The key actions from the ICPD+5 review include a clear call to governments to intensify their efforts to equip planners and decision makers with a better understanding of the interrelationships among population; poverty; gender inequity and inequality; health; education; the environment; financial and human resources; and development. They also call on them to (a) draw attention to, and promote linkages among macro-economic, environmental and social policies; (b) intensify efforts to implement legislative and administrative measures about the need for sustainable production and consumption patterns; (c) to foster sustainable natural resource use; (d) to work concertedly to prevent environmental degradation; and (e) to implement programmes aimed at addressing the negative impact of environmental degradation on the high levels of maternal mortality and morbidity in some regions. The challenge still remains: to find a world that defines progress, not just in narrow economic terms, but in social, ethical and human dimensions, with safety and secure minimum needs for everyone, and with people and the planet in harmony.

Coordination and Partnerships

The ICPD Programme of Action represented a consensus among governments, but it recognized that giving practical effect to a concept of development centered on human aspirations and values would require collaboration among governments, civil society, and the international community. Partnerships are critical to the further successful implementation of the ICPD and other major conference goals.

Recent United Nations reform initiatives such as the CCA and UNDAF and the instruments of the Bretton Woods Institutions such as the Comprehensive Development Framework (CDF) and the Poverty Reduction Strategy Paper (PRSP), offer opportunities for policies and programmes through coordinated decision-making. The challenge is to maximize scarce resources through effective coordination and collaboration at all levels – national, sub-regional, regional and global.

Conclusion

It is necessary to:
Ensure that access to reproductive health, including family planning and sexual health is increased. This means making a concerted effort to reach the goal of universal access to reproductive health information and services as soon as possible and no later than the year 2015.

Integrate a gender-sensitive human rights perspective in reproductive health programmes. This entails creating an enabling environment to ensure a rights-based approach in which all people, women and men, can freely make reproductive choices and decisions.

Secure gender equality and empowerment of women. Empowering women and equipping them to be full partners in development is one of the best strategies to combat poverty.

Stem the HIV/AIDS pandemic and other sexually transmitted diseases. Interim benchmarks for reducing HIV/AIDS infection have been agreed by consensus at the special session of the General Assembly on the implementation of

227

ICPD five-year review. The international community must continue its support for research for a cure for this disease and it must assist developing countries in their efforts to curtail the spread of AIDS and other sexually transmitted diseases, and to respond to the consequences of AIDS-related morbidity and mortality.

Increase investment in the social sectors. Meeting the basic needs of the world's population (for clean water, enough food, secure housing, basic education and health care) is essential for eliminating gender and geographic inequity. Programmes such as the 20/20 Initiative must be placed in the context of broader development agendas which include undertaking reforms to promote economic growth, develop supportive policy and regulatory frameworks, and improve governance.

Utilise effectively operational partnerships to build country capacity. Partnerships should be forged among donor and programme countries, the non-governmental organisations, the private sector, parliamentarians, and religious groups, among others, in order to derive the maximum benefits from scarce resources for developing countries.

Mobilise additional resources. Current levels of overseas development assistance (ODA) fall far short of the amounts needed to achieve the goals of the global conferences. Declining levels of development assistance must be reversed. Urgent action is required on the part of both donors and developing countries to fulfill their financial commitments and to mobilize the resources required for accelerating the implementation of the programmes of action of global conferences. Concerted effort must be made to ensure that the available funds are used as effectively and efficiently as possible.

The need for a forum where all nations have a voice has never been greater. Such a forum is found in the United Nations. The consensus reached at the recent international conferences, under United Nations' leadership can attest to this. It is a place where there is a holistic approach to decision making. It is a place where decisions made, whether on economic or social issues, financial matters, trade, or human rights, are arrived at in a transparent and participatory manner. In many ways, constructive dialogue is the work of the United Nations, and building consensus *is* its reason for being.

The decisions we take now, while we still have choices, will have profound consequences for the future. This is the right time to act, to save lives, to act responsibly to future generations, and to fulfil the consensus goals so necessary to face the 21st century with confidence and a spirit of shared humanity for all.

Prisoners of the Global Market: Social Polarisation and the Growth of Poverty

Peter Townsend
Professor, University of Bristol, Bristol, United Kingdom

In the last 20 years wealth and poverty have become more and more polarised. This structural trend is destabilising world society and diminishing social cohesion and welfare in rich and poor countries alike. In the wake of the 1995 Copenhagen Declaration and Programme of Action, this was chosen as one of the key themes of the Copenhagen Seminars for Social Progress. It is the subject of this paper.

There are qualitative experiences and feelings across what Pierre Bourdieu has called "the social macrocosm" that accompany material poverty and magnify its meaning. As he points out, "using material poverty as the sole measure of all suffering keeps us from seeing and understanding a whole side of the suffering characteristic of a social order which (…) has set up the conditions for an unprecedented development of all kinds of ordinary suffering"[1]. The variety of action required defies terse summary.

The first part of this paper summarises the latest evidence. The second shows how some of the 1995 initiatives, particularly the recommendation for every country to draw up anti-poverty plans measuring both "absolute" and "overall" poverty, might be applied. The third goes on to show that investigation of the reasons for widening inequality and deeper poverty leads to the need for entirely new international as well as national policies. To achieve economic justice along with economic morality and economic participation a principled social strategy to guide everyday action has to be developed.

An Ominous Global Trend

The widening of living standards across and within countries began to accelerate in the final decades of the last century. The conventional wisdom had been that poverty would be diminished automatically through economic growth.

Plainly this has not happened. Among other things "trickle-down" was not working. Poverty had been placed at the top of the agenda of the World Bank as early as the 1960s. Despite the mixed story since then, of development, a succession of neo-liberal policies, crystallised around economic growth, human capital, extreme targeting of welfare, low taxation, deregulation and privatisation, have not succeeded in radically diminishing the problem. Without serious effort to analyse the reasons for policy failure, poverty was again lifted to the top of the World Bank's agenda. From 1990 onwards its reports on the subject multiplied[2]. The number of general, country-specific and methodological reports issued by the Bank every year that may be said to be poverty-related is huge. The Bank's publication priorities are also reflected in reports from the IMF and other international agencies, especially UNDP and by non-government organisations, especially Oxfam[3].

How can the accumulating evidence be generalised? Reporting in mid-1999 the UNDP found that income inequality had increased "in most OECD countries in the 1980s and early 1990s. Of 19 countries only one showed a slight improvement". Data on income inequality in Eastern Europe and the CIS "indicate that these changes were the fastest ever recorded. In less than a decade income inequality, as measured by the Gini coefficient increased from and average of 0.25-0.28 to 0.35-0.38, surpassing OECD levels. In China "disparities are widening between the export-oriented regions of the coast and the interior: the human poverty index is just under 20 per cent in coastal provinces, but more than 50 per cent in inland Guizhou". Other East and South East Asian countries that had achieved high growth while improving income distribution and reducing poverty in earlier decades, like Indonesia and Thailand, were similarly experiencing more inequality. The gap between countries as well as within countries has widened. The average income of the richest 20 per cent of world population was 30 times as large as of the poorest 20 per cent in 1960, but was 74 times as large by 1997.

Widening inequality has to be addressed at both ends of the spectrum. The pay of executives, and the disposable income and wealth of the richest people in the world has been growing at an astonishing rate. For example, "the assets of the 200 richest people are more than the combined income of 41 per cent of the world's people". The top three have more than the combined GNP of all 43 least developed countries[4].

The World Institute for Development Economic Research of the United Nations University (WIDER) confirms the trend. An econometric analysis of 77 countries (accounting for 82 per cent of world population), found rising inequality in 45, slowing inequality in 4, no definite trend in 12 and falling inequality in only 12. "For most countries, the last two decades have brought about slow growth and rising inequality.... Growing polarisation among countries has been accompanied by a surge in inequality between countries....Income concentration has risen in many nations of Latin America, Eastern Europe and the former Soviet Union, China, a few African and South East Asian economies and, since the early 1980s, almost two-thirds of the OECD countries". Since the early 1990s, "the international community has made the eradication of poverty its foremost development objective. Yet, the decline of poverty in the years ahead depends also on trends in income inequality, a fact which still attracts little concern by the policymakers. Much of the recent rise in income inequality must thus be viewed with alarm, as it may well prove to be incompatible with poverty reduction objectives"[5].

In the late 1980s inequality in the UK became fast-growing. In a book on *Poverty and Labour in London,* reporting a survey of London households, the term "social polarisation" was used to describe the trend, because it was far from being either small or temporary. In its scale and change of direction the trend was also unprecedented, certainly in the history of recorded measurement during the 18th and 19th centuries. Inequality was also growing in other European countries – including Belgium and Sweden – and in the US. In one respect the situation there was worse than in the UK. Average earnings of the poorest 20 per cent in the labor market had decreased significantly in real terms between 1979 and 1992[6].

There are differences between countries at comparable levels of average income. Major industrialised countries with the greatest inequality (as measured by comparing the richest and poorest 20 per cent of their populations) are Australia, the UK and United States (with a GDP per person ratio of 9.6:1, 9.6:1 and 8.9:1 respectively). These are the countries also with the largest proportions of the population with less than 50 per cent of the median income. By contrast there are industrialised countries like the Czech Republic, Japan, Spain, the Netherlands and Sweden, where the richest 20 per cent have only 3.9, 4.3, 4.4, 4.5 and 4.6 times, respectively, more income than the poorest 20 per cent.

Data put forward for the Third World countries are disputed, depending on the countries included and whether the 1985 criterion of $1 a day is applied. The World Bank estimates that those living below that figure in developing and transitional economies declined from 28.3 per cent in 1987 to 24.0 per cent in 1998. The scale of "income-poverty" – 1.2 billions "struggling to survive on less than $1 a day" – remains vast. If East Asia is excluded, the numbers living below this level in developing countries grew between 1987 and 1998 at an average rate of 1.5 per cent, adding 12 millions a year to the ranks of the poor. The continued use of the fixed standard of $1 a day was also severely questioned.

Neglected in the discussion is the substantial number of countries experiencing civil disorder and war. It is almost impossible to give any reliable information about their collapse into poverty.

After the disintegration of the Soviet Union at the end of the 1980s there was an even bigger growth in inequality in the countries of the Commonwealth of Independent States than elsewhere. The economic transformation had dramatic social effects, including increases in the rates of mortality for different age-groups in the 1990s[7]. In a visit to the Republic of Georgia in the former Soviet Union on behalf of UNDP, I found severe impoverishment – especially among poor families, sick and disabled people and pensioners, not only because of the collapse of industry but the erosion of unemployment insurance benefits, pensions and other benefits to levels worth a few pence a week[8].

The World Bank has acknowledged that the financial crisis of 1997-98 had increased poverty in the short to medium term. "The crisis has increased poverty in the East Asian countries, Brazil and Russia…[It] has engendered large costly movements of populations and sharp declines in standards of living for the middle classes. Urban poverty increased in all countries, particu-

larly the Republic of Korea…Real public expenditures on health and education fell in the crisis countries with a particularly severe impact on access to
services in Indonesia"[9].

Absolute and Overall Poverty

The structural trend is therefore established, and, with some fluctuations,
continuing. This explains the revived interest of the international bodies like
the World Bank, the IMF and UNDP in the problem of international poverty,
but it does not explain why the development policies that they and others put
in place, had so little success in more than 40 years, and whether the continuing and new policies are likely to do better. One explanation is the failure of
the international community to build a scientific consensus around definition
and measurement, and to identify precisely which policies have contributed
to the worsening or the alleviation of poverty, and by how much.

Some governments attempted for many years to sidetrack the problem altogether. In 1989 John Moore, as Secretary of State for the Department of
Social Security in the UK, stated that the problem did not apply to the United
Kingdom[10]. Only ten years later his successor, Alastair Darling, announced a
programme to undertake a poverty audit "and so place the problem at the top
of the nation's agenda". This illustrates the varied political reaction of disbe-
lief and procrastination of many governments around the world.

Poverty is a recognised evil but has lacked precise international definition and
a scientifically constructed remedy. The United States, for example, has its
own definition and measure, which the international agencies do not relate to
their priorities for development. Indeed, the amendments to measurement
recommended by the National Academy of Sciences seems to have served the
purpose of bolstering an independent American approach which is becoming
highly sophisticated as well as impenetrable from outside. Root and branch
reform on an avowed scientific or international basis has not been considered[11].

The World Summit for Social Development in 1995 was called because,
among other things, many governments were becoming restive with the lack
of progress in reducing the gap in living standards between rich and poor

countries and the persistence and growth of severe poverty. The text adopted in Copenhagen in March 1995 emphasised that the gap between rich and poor *within* both developed and developing societies was widening, just as the gap *between* developed and developing societies was also widening. Calling world attention to this dual structural phenomenon is perhaps the most notable achievement of the Summit.

The intention was to try to promote sustained economic growth within the context of sustainable development and by *"formulating or strengthening, preferably by 1996, and implementing national poverty eradication plans to address the structural causes of poverty, encompassing action on the local, national, subregional, and international levels. These plans should establish, within each national context, strategies and affordable, time-bound, goals and targets for the substantial reduction of overall poverty and the eradication of absolute poverty.... Each country should develop a precise definition and assessment of absolute poverty"*.

The two-level definition of poverty was designed to bridge First and Third Worlds and to afford a basis for cross-national measurement. Absolute poverty is defined as *"a condition characterised by severe deprivation of basic human needs, including food, safe drinking water, sanitation facilities, health, shelter, education and information. It depends not only on income but also on access to services"*.

Overall poverty takes various forms, including *"lack of income and productive resources to ensure sustainable livelihoods; hunger and malnutrition; ill health; limited or lack of access to education and other basic services; increased morbidity and mortality from illness; homelessness and inadequate housing; unsafe environments and social discrimination and exclusion. It is also characterised by lack of participation in decision-making and in civil, social and cultural life. It occurs in all countries: as mass poverty in many developing countries, pockets of poverty amid wealth in developed countries, loss of livelihoods as a result of economic recession, sudden poverty as a result of disaster or conflict, the poverty of low-wage workers, and the utter destitution of people who fall outside family support systems, social institutions and safety nets"*[12].

Accordingly, all governments were expected to prepare a national poverty eradication plan. In 1997 nearly a hundred European social scientists drew up a statement asking for an "international approach to the measurement and explanation of poverty". This urged the use of the UN's two-level definition. One example of what could be done was to build on national surveys of self-perceived poverty. A two level-measure was introduced into the 1999 poverty and social exclusion survey of Britain. This was carried out jointly by a research team from four British Universities and the Office of National Statistics. The results demonstrate that the Copenhagen approach is viable, and important, for rich countries. With modifications to the questionnaire the method could also be applied to the poorer countries[13].

Absolute poverty is perceived in the UK as large-scale. As many as 14 per cent of the sample (Table 1), representing 8 million people, said they had less income than the level they identified as being enough to keep a household like theirs out of "absolute" poverty. If the "Don't knows" are excluded, this figure becomes 17 per cent.

The income, after tax, said to be needed each week to escape *absolute* poverty averages £167 for all households. Informants gave estimates widely different from this average, but the great majority, allowing for type of household, were within 20 per cent of this figure.

Table 1

Income needed each week to keep a household of your type out of absolute and overall poverty (UK 1999)

	Absolute poverty	Overall poverty	General poverty
Mean income needed	£167	£237	£219
Don't know	13%	14%	13%
Actual income a lot above	46	34	31
A little above	20	22	27
About the same	7	7	12
A little below	7	9	8
A lot below	7	13	9
Don't know	13	14	13
Total	100	100	100
Number	1527	1527	1527

Perceptions of the poverty line varied by type of family, as would be expected. More lone parents than any other type of family (40 per cent) said they had an income below that needed to keep out of *absolute* poverty. Next were single pensioners (19 per cent) and couples with one child (18 per cent). Fewer couples of any age (11-12 per cent) and fewer couples with two or more children (7-8 per cent) perceived themselves to be in *absolute* poverty.

A larger proportion (22 per cent) – representing nearly 13 millions – ranked themselves in *overall* poverty. The proportion becomes 26 per cent if the "don't knows" are excluded. Although, as expected, the additions to the numbers came from every type of family, the additions were disproportionately high from families with children.

Table 2
Per cent of each type of household saying their actual income was lower than the mean income said to be needed by households of that type to keep out of absolute and overall poverty (UK 1999)

	Absolute poverty %	Overall poverty %	General poverty %
Single pensioner	19	26	21
Couple pensioner	12	18	15
Single adult	12	25	21
Couple	13	15	16
Couple 1 child	18	27	14
Couple 2 children	8	15	14
Couple 3+ children	7	27	13
Lone parent 1 child	40	44	46
Lone parent 2+ children	42	57	49
Other	9	19	11

In establishing "economies to serve human needs and aspirations" – an ambitious objective built into the 1995 World Summit – the research in the UK shows beyond reasonable doubt that the scale of needs in some rich industrial societies are perceived by their populations to be much larger than generally allowed in national and international discourse. When taken with reports from poorer countries, where comparable methods have been piloted, this two-level measure deserves to be extended internationally. It can take the form of self-perceived poverty, as in the illustration given here for the UK, but also "objective" poverty as measured by sets of indicators of deprivation and low income.

A series of surveys of poverty and social exclusion sponsored by the International Institute for Labour Studies, included three which drew on methods of measuring poverty previously tried in London. The three were reports on Tanzania, Yemen and Russia. A similar "standard of living" methodology also largely based on the categories adopted in the UK in the 1990s, was used to measure poverty in Vietnam[14].

Developing a New International Social Strategy

If measurement is arbitrary, it is impossible either to concoct the right policies for the alleviation or eradication of poverty, or monitor their effects closely. Thus criticism of the World Bank's adoption of the crude criterion of $1 a day at 1985 prices for the poorest countries, $2 a day for Latin America and $4 a day for the transitional economies, without regard to the changing conditions of needs and markets, has now become widespread[15].

In the early years the use of this crude standard was perhaps excusable for reasons of analytical convenience. In later years it has become less excusable, because the Bank and other agencies have had opportunities and resources to undertake extensive inquiries into the measurement of living conditions in relation to household income and assets. But in 2000 to go on using a "static" standard of need at 1985 (purchasing parity or currency equivalent) prices, unadjusted to changes in working practices, technologies and other aspects of living conditions becomes unreal. In every country people have experience of goods, activities and services that gradually disappear and of others that gradually appear. Some items once free have to be paid for. Sets of obligations as well as of consumer choices change, and often become more complex. Most people's needs, as well as the resources they possess to meet them, are determined externally by institutions beyond their powers to control. If change is normal, change in the construct of human need has to be conceived as normal too. And the way poverty is measured underpins every report on the subject.

Strategy is intimately connected with measurement. According to the most sophisticated independent reviews of operational strategies for poverty reduction by the Bank, such as that from the Christian Michelsen Institute to the Norwegian Ministry of Foreign Affairs the World Bank "has maintained a remarkably constant approach to poverty reduction throughout its 50-year history. Its assumption has always been to view development and poverty reduction as fundamentally an issue of economic growth". Its three-pronged anti-poverty approach of the 1960s has remained: broad-based economic growth; development of human resources, especially through education; and social safety nets for vulnerable groups[16].

An alternative model could consist of equitable tax and income policies, within an internationally sanctioned framework of socially responsible accumulation of wealth and income; an employment creation programme, sometimes described as labour-intensive projects to counter-balance job-cutting; regeneration or creation of collective, or "universal", social insurance and public social services – the "basic needs services" as ordinarily described; and accountability and a measure of social control of trans-national corporations and international agencies.

Challenging Liberalisation Programmes

The stabilisation and structural adjustment programmes that were advocated and supported by the international agencies, entailed the reduction of subsidies on food, fuel and other goods, retrenchments in public employment, cuts in public sector wages and other deflationary measures. According to many critics this generates recession but also distributional outcomes which are adverse in the poorer countries compared with industrialised countries, where wage systems are strongly institutionalised and self protecting, and where long-established social security has provided a better cushion for downturns in the economy. Unfortunately similar liberalisation policies to under-cut social insurance and social services are having comparable effects in an increasing number of industrial countries.

Policies to cut public expenditure, and target welfare on the poorest, for example through means-testing and the introduction of health care charges have increased inequality and perpetuated poverty, especially in countries where, because of globalised trade and growing influence of trans-national corporations, there has been a particularly rapid concentration of wealth.

It is significant that in some recent reports the Bank no longer highlights privatisation and extreme forms of targeting. It has admitted that poverty has tended to increase during recessions in Sub-Saharan Africa, Eastern Europe, and Latin America and not to decrease to the same extent during economic recoveries[17]. The fact that countries in East and South-East Asia are more sensitive to the encroachments of poverty also helps to explain the reactions of the international agencies to the financial crisis in those regions. The magic wands of liberalisation and structural adjustment programmes could no longer be waved, as they had been in Latin America and Africa and then in Eastern Europe and the Commonwealth of Independent States – and in similar strategic form in the industrial countries. The evidence is that poverty has increased sharply, especially in Korea, and a return to the former reduced rates seems an unlikely prospect for some considerable time.

Introducing Social Obligations for Transnationals

Poverty reduction policies have not taken any account of one structural cause of poverty. Because of deregulation and privatisation by Governments, often at the behest of international agencies, control of labour markets has veered away from states and towards transnational corporations. States in which the headquarters of the biggest trans-national corporations are located have acquired greater power to influence global economic developments.

In trade the emphasis on exports from the poorer countries was supposed to favour rural agricultural production, and diminish poverty by removing the imbalance between rural and urban living standards. This has not worked, partly because of the low wages induced by cash cropping, and the corresponding substitution of employed labour and technology for subsistence farming. This has also had a knock-on weakening effect on the vitality of urban markets. In many countries self-sufficiency in growing a range of crops has given way to a precarious dependence on sales from the export of those crops to finance the purchase of imports at affordable prices. Trans-national companies have exceptional power to cut the costs of what they buy and raise the costs of what they sell.

The growth of transnational companies is one of the greatest economic and social changes of the late 20th century. Only 25 countries of the world are now listed as having larger GDP than the annual value of the sales of the biggest transnational corporations. The top ten trans-national corporations (General Motors, Ford Motor, Mitsui, Mitsubushi, Itochu, Royal Dutch Shell Group, Marubeni, Sumitomo, Exxon and Toyota Motor) have bigger sales than the GDP of Malaysia, Venezuela and Colombia, and some of them more than Saudi Arabia, South Africa, Norway, Greece and Thailand. New Zealand's GDP is dwarfed by the sales of each of these corporations, and Australia's accounts for only about three times the value of the average sale of all ten.

The social policies of transnational corporations take at least two forms. On the one hand their internal policies, in relation to their senior staff and permanent and temporary workers scattered through subsidiary companies in many different countries, have to be explained. On the other hand, the larger role they play in contributing to social change, by influencing developments in world trade, government taxation and redistribution and investment, as well as recommendations for privatisation, also has to be explained.

There are serious shortcomings in both national and international company and social law in relation to trans-nationals. While capable of contributing positively to social development, one review found that few of them were doing much of consequence. The activities of some were positively harmful. Recent books on trans-national corporations have been assembling a case that governments and international agencies are going to find hard to ignore[18].

One feature of mergers between companies and the absorbtion of workforces overseas into the subsidiaries of corporations is not just the extension of the labour force accountable to management, but the elaboration as well as extension of the hierarchy of pay and rights in the corporation. There are many layers in workforces consisting of scores of thousands, sometimes hundreds of thousands, of employees working full-time, part-time, permanently and temporarily in 50, 60 or even more countries. Salaries at the top have been elevated, those at the bottom depressed.

This fast-developing occupational system deepens social stratification and introduces new social problems in every country. Ideas of supra- and sub-ordination are played out internationally as well as nationally and locally, and are carried over from one context to the other. This evolving hierarchy of power ramifies everywhere. All that has so far happened is that agencies like OECD have issued "guidelines" exhorting corporations to be socially responsible. In 1977 the ILO Governing Board put forward a declaration. This sought to exert influence upon governments, concluding that gradual reinforcement could pave the way for "more specific potentially binding international standards", turning codes of conduct into "the seed of customary rules of international law"[19].

Calling a Halt to Indiscriminate Privatisation

The international financial agencies have been eager to encourage privatisation, on grounds that this would enhance global market competition, weaken the intervening role of the state and reduce government taxation so that public expenditure in general, and public services in particular, would cost less and private companies would have greater freedom to manage their affairs as they wanted. But the agencies have thereby adopted a very narrow interpretation of the economic good, and have tended to ignore the fact that economic development is an integral part of social development.

World Bank advocacy of privatisation is explicit or implied in almost every published report of recent years – even in relation to poverty. The key text for the Bank's position was not published until 1997. The author is a development specialist who has advised many African countries on their privatisation programmes. The book covers a lot of ground and is testimony to the accelerating scale across the world of privatisation. It attempts to be dispassionate. But the arguments for public service and cooperative companies are largely absent, and no conclusions are drawn about the balance that might be struck between the public and private sectors in particular contexts and according to particular objectives. The historical reasons for the growth of public ownership and the welfare state during the 20th century are not debated. Certainly there is no dispassionate argument about alternative strategies[20].

In the analysis by a large number of experts much is made of the necessity of financial deregulation and the privatisation of insurance and the pension funds in order to create the right market conditions. The conflict of market insurance with the public interest in relation to the historical establishment of social insurance is not discussed.

The rapid growth of privatisation is not, even now, widely appreciated. In 1989 the gross annual revenue from the process was estimated to be $25 billions. In 1994 and 1995 annual revenue reached $80 billions. Over five years $271 billions were generated. By the mid-1990s the developing and "transition" countries accounted for much of the revenue[21].

Assets have often been sold extraordinarily cheaply – by market standards. Academic reviews, as in the UK, have failed to demonstrate evidence of privatisation being successful in terms of growth and price. There are examples either way[22].

The Shortcomings of Targeting and Safety Nets

In developing their structural adjustment programmes, first in Latin America and Africa, and then in the "transition" countries of Eastern Europe and the former Soviet Union, the IMF and the World Bank tried to balance the unequal social consequences of liberalisation, privatisation and cuts in public expenditure with proposals to target help on the most vulnerable groups in the population. For some years, and still to a large extent today, this has been presented in line with the principle of test of means. Even if coverage was not good, large sums of money would be saved, it was argued, if the near-to-poor were no longer subsidised by public funds.

Thus, a report for the IMF seeks to pin responsibility on the transition countries for a failure to transform universal services into targeted and partly privatised services. Unfortunately, this report fails to discuss the historical reasons for the development of these public and social services in the first place and especially their emulation of western European services. Ways in which former universal provisions might have been modified to allow market competition to grow but not create penury among millions were not seriously considered[23].

IMF loan conditions demanding lower government expenditures in the poorest countries have led to sharp reductions in general social spending at a time when the poorest fifth of the population in those countries have been receiving only about half their share of education and health expenditures – thus making access worse. This is evidence drawn from the IMF's own studies, which shows that "the poorest three-fifths of these nations are being excluded from whatever social "safety net" exists for education, health, housing and social security and welfare[24].

However, loan conditionalities affect economic security in other ways. There are cuts in the number of government employees and in their salaries, and there are private sector cuts and lay-offs, both of which are designed to raise cost-effectiveness in the world's export markets. Price subsidies for commodities such as bread and cooking oil are cut. Higher value added taxes that are advocated are regressive on income distribution.

In December 1987 the IMF introduced a fresh stage of its existing structural adjustment programme – the "Enhanced Structural Adjustment Facility" (ESAF). Of 79 countries eligible for these ESAF loans, on condition they complied with the IMF in setting "specific, quantifiable plans for financial policies" 36 had done so. Since World Bank aid also depends on fulfilling IMF criteria there is intense pressure on governments to accede. Critics have now concluded that countries which stayed out of the ESAF programme "began and remained better off by not accepting its advice". Those accepting the programme "have experienced profound economic crises: low or even declining economic growth, much larger foreign debts, and the stagnation that perpetuates systemic poverty". The IMF's own studies provided "a devastating assessment of the social and economic consequences of its guidance of dozens of poor nations"[25].

The problem applies sharply to rich and not only poor countries. The biggest struggle of the next years is going to be between restriction of social security, or "welfare", largely to means-tested benefits. Those who have assembled evidence for different European countries over many years point out that such policies are poor in coverage, administratively expensive and complex, provoke social divisions, are difficult to square with incentives into work, and tend to discourage forms of saving[26].

When structural adjustment programmes began to be applied to Eastern Europe and the former Soviet Union, in the early 1990s, it was clear they would compound the problems of poverty, following liberalisation. Social insurance, and social security generally, occupied a substantial part of the institutional infrastructures of these states, and the collapse of industry might have led to some external efforts to maintain at least a residual system in order to protect people, especially children, the disabled and the elderly, from the worst forms of destitution and even starvation. Unhappily World Bank and IMF teams lacked expertise in such institutions. They were also influenced by a prevailing ideology of the "short, sharp shock" following the collapse of communism. An additional factor was that social security systems were weak if not non-existent in the poorest developing countries, and the possibility that structural adjustment as applied to those countries was inappropriate in Eastern Europe.

From an anti-poverty perspective one analyst of events in the former Soviet Union concludes that "consideration of social policy has hitherto been dominated by fiscal considerations, which has led to radical proposals for reform of the pension and benefits systems which would have devastating consequences if they did not work as intended. The dependence of many households on age-related pensions and the inability of the majority of wage-earners to support even one dependent make the preservation of the real value of retirement pensions and the restoration of the real value and regular payment of child benefit much the most effective anti-poverty measures in a context in which the introduction of means-tested social assistance is completely unrealistic"[27].

A report from UNDP concedes the strengths of the former institutions of social security. "Policy-makers attempted to create a relatively egalitarian society free from poverty. Socialist income policy was based upon two main objectives: 1) To ensure a minimum standard of living for all citizens; and 2) To achieve a relatively flat income distribution" (...) Governments regulated overall salaries and fixed minimum wages high enough to ensure a basic standard of living (...). At the core of the social security systems were work-related contributory insurance programmes. The public came to expect that most social benefits would depend upon work-related factors such as years spent on the job and wages earned (....). Social insurance schemes were comprehensive. Pensions, like employment, were virtually guaranteed... Social insurance itself covered numerous exigencies, including accidents, sickness, parental death and child birth (...). Overall, means-tested social benefits were almost non-existent, representing on average less than 1 per cent of GDP. This was due largely to the inefficiency and high administrative costs associated with means-testing programmes". *The socially inclusive* advantages of these schemes was recognised. Thus, pension programmes "became a kind of contract between generations, whereby people invested their efforts in the collective welfare and were rewarded by a guarantee of supplemental income… Because social assistance allowances are very low in all transition countries, moving pensions towards means-tested social assistance programmes would push practically all pensioners into poverty"[28].

This is perhaps the first substantial acknowledgement from the international agencies of central elements of the welfare state. The authors claim there is a consensus for active labour market policies and work for social benefits as necessary components of the social insurance system. Funding should be both public and private forms of Pay-As-You-Go. "Categorical benefits should be offered to all in need, or at least to all those near or below the poverty line. It is very important to avoid providing support only to the "poorest of the poor" while neglecting the relatively poor". This plea for group or "categorical" benefits in place of means-tested benefits was qualified by a recognition that some such benefits could be conditional in different ways[29].

The Development of a New Strategy

The Declaration and Programme of Action agreed at the 1995 World Summit for Social Development in Copenhagen was in some respects ahead of its time. Agencies and governments alike have been slow to react to key recommendations – for example on annual anti-poverty plans and measures of absolute and overall poverty. In other respects the Programme is silent about major developments. Here I have tried to call attention to the paramount problem of social polarisation and the connected growth of transnational corporations and private-sector companies and services. Lack of reference to these developments may be remedied in the General Assembly review in Geneva in June 2000[30].

A succession of neo-liberal policies, crystallised around economic growth, human capital, extreme welfare targeting, low taxation, de-regulation of employment and privatisation have caused inequalities and poverty to persist and grow. A justifiable alternative strategy could take the following form:

1. Equitable tax and income policies, operating within an internationally sanctioned legal framework permitting "socially responsible" accumulation of wealth and income;

246

2. An employment creation programme. This would draw more heavily than at present on public investment, and would be designed deliberately to multiply labour-intensive projects to counter-balance market-induced job-cutting – that often indiscriminately worsens individual and community life in many countries. Conditions of employment for the low paid would also be internationally regulated;

3. Regeneration or creation of collective, or "universal", social insurance and public social services – the "basic needs services" as ordinarily described. This would involve introducing internationally sanctioned minimum wages and minimum levels of benefit; and

4. The introduction of greater accountability and social and democratic control over trans-national corporations and international agencies. Growing concern in the 1990s about the "democratic deficit" invites more energetic collaborative international action on a regional if not wider basis. There are of course many policies requiring to be developed under these headings if the damaging structural trend of social polarisation and growing poverty is first to be halted, and then reversed. There are two stages. At the first stage the critique has to be pulled together and made more forceful. This includes reformulating the measurement of poverty, social exclusion and unemployment and therefore reformulating the minimum standards of living, inclusion and employment that are to be acceptable in future. It includes the monitoring of specific policy impacts, for past decades as well as currently and prospectively, and determined fulfilment of international agreements. And it includes the mobilisation of new coalitions or alliances across countries – of parties, unions, campaigning groups, administrative departments and voluntary agencies – to question the conventional wisdom and promote an alternative strategy[31].

At the second stage measures for international taxation, regulation of transnational corporations and international agencies, reform of representation at the UN, and new guarantees of human rights, including minimal standards of income, have to be introduced and legally enforced.

Recognition of social insurance as one of the best means of building an "inclusive" society and preventing the slide into poverty, as well as contributing to social and economic stability, would represent one major step forward.

247

New legal and political institutions for social good in a global economy have to be built. A start would come with new international company and taxation law, combined with the modernisation and strengthening of social insurance and more imaginative planning and investment in basic services like health and education, so that they reflect international and not just national or regional standards.

At the beginning of the 21st century the prospect of mutual self-destruction within societies that are becoming more and more unequal is a pressing reality, and countervailing measures have to be taken urgently. Collaborative scientific and political action to establish a more democratic and internationalised legal framework to protect human living standards must be the first priority.

Notes

1. Bourdieu P. et al (1999), *The Weight of the World: Social Suffering in Contemporary Society,* Cambridge, Polity Press.
2. World Bank, *World Development Report 1990: Poverty,* Washington, 1990, *Implementing the World Bank's Strategy to Reduce Poverty: Progress and Challenges,* Washington, 1993, *Poverty Reduction and the World Bank: Progress and Challenges in the 1990s,* Washington 1996; *Safety Net Programs and Poverty Reduction: Lessons from Cross-Country Experience,* Washington 1997; *Poverty Reduction and the World Bank: Progress in Fiscal 1996 and 1997,* Washington 1997; *World Development Report 1997: The State in a Changing World,* Washington and New York, Oxford University Press 1997; *India: Achievements and Challenges in Reducing Poverty,* Washington 1997; *Global Economic Prospects and the Developing Countries 1998/99: Beyond Financial Crisis,* Washington and New York, Oxford University Press 1999; *The World Bank Research Programme 1999,* Washington 1999.
3. Oxfam, *Poverty Report,* Oxford, Oxfam, 1995; and Oyen E., Miller S.M. and Samad S. A., eds., *Poverty: A Global Review: Handbook on International Poverty Research,* Oslo, Scandinavian University Press, 1996; and Guidicini P., Pieretti G. and Bergamaschi M., *Extreme Urban Poverties in Europe: Contradictions and Perverse Effects in Welfare Policies,* Milano, FrancoAngeli, 1996.
4. *Human Development Report 1999,* New York and Oxford, Oxford University Press, 1999 p. 3, 36, 37, 38, 39.
5. Cornia G.A., *Social Funds in Stabilisation and Adjustment Programmes,* Research for Action 48, UNU World Institute for Development Economic Research, 1999.
6. Townsend P., with Corrigan P. and Kowarzik U., *Poverty and Labour in London,* London, Low Pay Unit, 1987; and Townsend P. "Poverty and Social Polarisation", in *Eurocities, Cities and Social Policies in Europe,* Barcelona, Ajuntament de Barcelona, 1991; and *The International Analysis of Poverty,* Hemel Hempstead, Harvester Wheatsheaf, 1993.
7. Cornia G.A., *Liberalisation, Globalisation and Income Distribution,* Working Paper No. 157, Helsinki, Finland, UNU World Institute for Development Economic Research, 1999; and Cornia G.A. and Pannicia R. eds., "The Mortality Crisis in Transitional Economies", Oxford, Oxford University Press, 1999; and Clarke S. *New Forms of*

Employment and Household Survival in Russia, Coventry and Moscow, Centre for Comparative Labour Studies and the Institute for Comparative Labour Relations Research, 1999; and Nelson J.M., Tilly C. and Walker L. 1997), *Transforming Post-Communist Political Economies,* task force on economies in transition, National Research Council Commission on Behavioural and Social Sciences and Education, Washington D.C., National Academy Press.

8. Townsend P. "Poverty in Eastern Europe: The Latest Manifestation of Global Polarisation", in Rodgers G. and Van der Hoeven eds., *New Approaches to Poverty Analysis and Policy – III: The Poverty Agenda: Trends and Policy Options,* Geneva, International Institute for Labour Studies, 1995: and Townsend P., *A Poor Future: Can we Counteract Growing Poverty in Britain and Across the World?,* London, Lemos and Crane, 1996; "Ending World Poverty in the 2 1ˢᵗ Century", in Pantazis C. and Gordon D. eds., *Tackling Inequalities: Where are we now and what can be done?* Bristol, Policy Press, 2000.

9. World Bank, *Global Economic Prospect and the Developing Countries – 2000,* Washington 2000, p. VII.

10. Moore J. (1989), *The End of Poverty,* London, Conservative Political Centre, 1999.

11. Citro C, F. and Michael R.T., *Measuring Poverty: A New Approach,* Panel on Poverty, National Research Council, Washington D.C., National Academy Press, 1995.

12. UN, *The Copenhagen Declaration and Programme of Action:* World Summit for Social Development, New York, UN, 1995, p. 57, 60, 61.

13. Bradshaw J., Gordon D., Levitas R., Middleton S., Pantazis C., Payne S. and Townsend P., *Perceptions of Poverty and Social Exclusion,* Report on Preparatory Research, University of Bristol, Centre for International Poverty Research, 1998.

14. Townsend P. and Gordon D., "What is Enough"? in House of Commons Social Services Committee, Minimum Income, *House of Commons 579,* London, HMSO, 1989; Gordon D. and Pantazis C., Breadline Britain in the 1990s, Aldershot, Ashgate, 1997; and Kaijage F. and Tibaijuka A., *Poverty and Social Exclusion in Tanzania,* Geneva, IILS, Research Series No. 109., 1996; and Tchernina N., *Economic Transition and Social Exclusion in Russia,* Geneva, IILS, Research Series No. 108 1996; and Gore C. and Figueiredo J.B., *Social Exclusion and Anti-Poverty Strategies,* International Institute for Labour Studies, in

250

conjunction with UNDP, Geneva, IILS, 1996; and Davies, R. and Smith, W., *The Basic Necessities Survey: The Experience of Action Aid Vietnam,* Action Aid, London, 1998.

15. Vandermoortele, J. *Absorbing Social Shocks, Protecting Children and Reducing Poverty:* The Role of Basic Social Services, UNICEF Working Papers, New York, UNICEF, 2000.

16. Tjonneland E.N., Harboe H., Jerve A.M. and Kanji N., *The World Bank and Poverty in Africa: A critical assessment of the Bank's operational strategies for poverty reduction,* a report submitted to the Royal Norwegian Ministry of Foreign Affairs by the Christian Michelsen Institute, Oslo, Royal Ministry of Foreign Affairs, 1998; and Psacharapoulos G., Morley S., Fiszbein A., Lee H. and Wood B., *Poverty and Income Distribution in Latin America: The Story of the 1980s,* World Bank Technical Paper No. 35 1, Washington DC, the World Bank, 1997.

17. Huther J., Roberts S. and Shah A., *Public Expenditure Reform Under Adjustment Lending:* Lessons from the World Bank Experience, World Bank Discussion Paper No. 382, Washington D.C., the World Bank, 1997.

18. Kozul-Wright R. and Rowthorn R., *Transnational Corporations and the Global Economy,* Helsinki, Finland, UNU World Institute for Development Economic Research 1998; and Lang T. and Hines C., *The New Protectionism: Protecting the Future Against Free Trade,* London, Earthscan Publications, 1994; and Deacon B. with Hulse M. and Stubbs P., *Global Social Policy: International Organisations and the Future of Welfare,* London, Sage, 1997; and Hoogvelt A., *Globalisation and the Postcolonial World: The New Political Economy of Development,* Basingstoke, Hampshire and London, Macmillan, 1997; Kolodner E., *Transnational Corporations: Impediments or Catalysts of Social Development?,* Occasional Paper No. 5, World Summit for Social Development, Geneva, UNRISD, 1994; and Korten D. C., *When Corporations Rule the World,* London, Earthscan, 1996.

19. ILO, *The ILO Tripartite Declaration of Principles Concerning Multinational Enterprises and Social Policy – Ten Years After,* Geneva, ILO, 1998.

20. Guislain P., *The Privatization Challenge: A Strategic, Legal and Institutional Analysis of International Experience,* Washington D.C., World Bank, 1997.

21. Lieberman I.W. and Kirkness C.D., eds., *Privatisation and Emerging Equity Markets,* Washington D.C., The World Bank and Flemings (1998).

22. Parker D. and Martin S., *The Impact of Privatisation,* London, Routledge, 1997.

23. Chu Ke-Y. and Gupta S. eds., *Social Safety Nets: Issues and Recent Experiences,* Washington D.C., International Monetary Fund, 1998.

24. Kolko G., "Ravaging the Poor: The International Monetary Fund Indicted by its own Data", *International Journal of Health Services,* Vol. 29, No. 1, pp. 51-57, 1999.

25. Ibid, p. 53

26. Oorschot W., *Targeting Welfare: On the Functions and Dysfunctions of Means-Testing in Social Policy,* Budapest Conference on Developing Poverty Measures: Research in Europe, 1999.

27. Clarke S., op.cit. p. 240.

28. UNDP, *Poverty in Transition,* Regional Bureau for Europe and the CIS, New York, UNDP, 1998, p. 90-109.

29. Ibid, p. 105.

30. UN, *Further Initiatives for the Implementation of the Outcome of the World Summit for Social Development,* Report of the Secretary General, Preparatory Committee for the Special Session of the General Assembly, 17-28 May, New York, UN, 1999.

31. Townsend P., with Donkor K., *Global Restructuring and Social Policy: An Alternative Strategy: Establishing an International Welfare State,* international seminar on Economic Restructuring and Social Policy, sponsored by UNRISD and UNDP, United Nations, New York, 1995, Policy Press, Bristol, 1996.

Mutual Learning as an Agenda for Social Delevopment

Tu Weiming
Professor, Director, the Harvard-Yenching Institute, Cambridge, USA

As we are confronted with a new world order, the exclusive dichotomy of capitalism and socialism imposed by the Cold War super powers is woefully inadequate for understanding the rich texture of the emerging global community. Intent on offering an alternative global paradigm, Francis Fukuyama and Samuel Huntington proffer two facile generalizations: "the end of history" and "the clash of civilizations". The two positions are seemingly contradictory readings of the human condition: an optimistic assertion that fundamental ideological divides no longer exist and a cautionary note that cultural, especially religious, differences are the major sources of international conflict.

It seems evident that the liberal democratic countries (Western Europe and North America), fueled by the market economy, have now set the stage for a radically new global transformation. It also seems plausible that challenges from, for example, the Confucian and the Islamic cultural zones may impede this process. Yet, should we take the trajectory of Western culture's impact as a sort of historical inevitability? Both positions evoked above are predicated on the assumption that the current working dichotomy is still "the West and the rest". Is this conceptual framework adequate for enhancing social development as an international joint venture?

If social development is seen as an aspiration and a promise for human flourishing, we need to address the fundamental ethical and spiritual issues confronting the global community. The old triumphant or confrontational Western mindset is counterproductive. The United States in particular, can take the lead in transforming itself from primarily a teaching civilization – especially in reference to East Asia since Second World War II – into a learning culture by considering some critical questions:

Which way is more congenial to social integration, viewing ourselves as isolated individuals or as centers of interpersonal relationships?

Even if we use quantifiable material conditions to define and measure our well-being, can we afford to cut off ourselves from the spiritual moorings of our cultures?

If success is solely measured as wealth and power to the exclusion of other goods, such as social capital, moral influence and exemplary teaching, how can we transmit cherished values to the next generation?

How can we expect others to respect our way of life, if we disregard what they themselves regard as meaningful and worthwhile?

Can our society prosper without inculcating in individuals a basic sense of duty and responsibility in addition to rights-consciousness?

Can we afford to focus our attention on the rule of law without emphasizing civility and trust in ordinary daily social intercourse?

Can liberty as an intrinsic value generate a humane society without distributive justice?

Can instrumental rationality alone right inequality without sympathy and compassion?

Should our culturally pluralistic world deliberately cultivate shared values as a common ground for organic social solidarity?

As we become more keenly aware of our earth's vulnerability and the depletion of natural resources, what steps must we take to preserve her?

Such questions suggest a much needed communal critical self-consciousness among the reflective minds of the world. We may be witnessing the very beginning of global history rather than the end of history. And, as we approach 2001, the United Nations-designated year of Dialogue Among Civilizations, this new beginning must take the desire for mutual reference as its point of departure. Our awareness of the danger of civilizational conflicts rooted in ethnicity, gender, language, land, class, age, and religion, makes the necessity of dialogue particularly compelling. If we envision development in social as well as economic terms, we recognize that globalization is not homogenization. Rather, it both intensifies and undermines various forms of localization. We should accept a plurality of models of sustainable development and emphasize the ethical and spiritual dimensions of human flourishing as integral parts of our development strategy.

A perception of development shaped by modernization as a unilinear progression and defined exclusively by quantifiable material gains is too simplistic to reflect the complexity and diversity of human flourishing. Surely, eradicating absolute poverty is one of the highest priorities of any global approach to social development, but even here, the enabling factors are political, social, cultural and legal as well as economic. This requires a more sophisticated vision of how different spheres of interests are interconnected nationally, regionally and globally.

Just as no local interests, no matter how compelling, should override national interests, regional and global interests must not be subsumed under national interests. Even if we assume that the United States alone can exert hegemonic influence in the global community, the really enduring American strength lies in "soft power" – moral persuasion – as well as military might. Social capital, the cultivation of cultural competence and the enhancement of spiritual values, is as important as economic capital, the cultivation of technical competence and the enhancement of material conditions.

The politics of domination is being replaced by the politics of communication, networking, negotiation, interaction, interfacing, and collaboration. The strong 1960's belief that "modernization would wipe out cultural, institutional, structural and mental differences and, if unimpeded, would lead to a uniform modern world" is no longer tenable. Since globalization engenders localization and indigenization as well as homogenization, cultural, institutional, structural and cognitive differences actually shape the contours of the modernizing processes. In consequence, traditions are constituent parts of modernity and modernization can assume different cultural, institutional, structural and mental forms. The thesis of convergence, meaning that the rest of the world will inevitably converge with the modern West, has been modified.

In the eighties, the thesis of reverse convergence was strongly implied, if not clearly articulated, by new modernization theorists as the result of East Asian economic dynamism. The ideas of "Asian values", "network capitalism", and "the Asia-Pacific century" were advocated as an alternative to modern Westernism. However, the observation that the engine of development had shifted from the Atlantic to the Pacific was premature. The 1997 Asian financial crisis forced a new interpretation. Authoritarianism and crony capitalism were identified as the cultural, institutional, structural and mental causes: Asian financial institutions had suffered from lack of transparency, public accountability and fair competitiveness. As the economies of the Asia-Pacific region begin to recover, East Asia will likely reemerge as the single most important reference and perhaps as a counterpoint for Western Europe and North America again.

If, instead of reverse convergence, "multiple modernities" had been presented as an explanatory model, the implications of East Asian modernity would have been far-reaching. East Asia has been deeply influenced by Western Europe and North America and its accelerating modernity is mainly the result of the Western impact. Yet, the shape of life of East Asian peoples is significantly different from that of Westerners. The possibility of being modern without being Western suggests that, under the influence of East Asia as well as West Europe and North America, Southeast Asian societies, notably Malaysia and Indonesia, may become modern without necessarily being European, American or East Asian. By implication, Latin American, South Asian and African forms of modernity are, in principle, realizable.

Is the vision of multiple modernities merely wishful thinking or practicable guide for social development? The Copenhagen Social Summit was committed to support full employment, promote social integration, achieve gender equality and equity, and attain universal and equitable access to education and primary care. If these are realizable aspirations for the global community, rather than privileges and entitlements of the First World, every country is, in both theory and practice, capable of human flourishing according to its own specific conditions. The mobilization of indigenous cultural recourses for capacity building is a precondition for such an endeavor.

East Asia is a case in point. Can East Asian political and cultural leaders be inspired by the Confucian spirit of self-cultivation, family cohesiveness, social solidarity, benevolent governance, and universal peace to practice responsibility in their domestic affairs? This question concerns us all. As Chinese, Japanese, Koreans, and Vietnamese emigrate to other parts of the world, can they share their rich cultural heritage? This question is important not only for East Asia, but for the United States, Canada, Australia, and the European Union.

The commitment to "accelerate the development of Africa and the least developed countries" is predicated on a holistic vision of human flourishing and a realistic model of interdependency. If we consider ethnic, cultural, linguistic, and religious diversity as a global asset, Africa should not be characterized by the HIV epidemic, poverty, unemployment and social disintegration alone. It should also be recognized as a rich reservoir for human spirituality and the wisdom of elders. The African Renaissance, symbolized by the geological and biological diversity of the tiny area around Capetown (said to be comparable in richness to the vast area of Canada) ought to be a source of inspiration for a changed mindset that addresses social development as a global joint venture.

The development of Africa is important for us because, without a holistic sense of human flourishing, we cannot properly anchor our sense of security, let alone well-being in the global community as a whole. The acknowledgment that there is a "multiplicity of modern societies around the globe" and that it is arrogant to proclaim our own cultural supremacy is a significant step toward mutual referencing among societies. We cannot help African societies to accelerate their development if we prematurely conclude that they have nothing to teach us. Indeed, the celebration of cultural diversity, without falling into the trap of pernicious relativism, is profoundly meaningful for global stewardship.

As the rise of Confucian East Asia suggests, traditions are present as active agents in modernity; in fact, the modernizing process has assumed a variety of cultural forms. Modernization originating in Western Europe has powerfully transformed the world in one dominant direction. In its inception, however, it was already a mixture of conflictual and even contradictory trajectories. Even if we overcome the conceptual difficulty of generalizing European cases as paradigmatic manifestations of modernity, we must still treat North American modernity as a separate case. The story of modernization as a master narrative contains several versions of globally significant local knowledge. Now that East Asia's local knowledge is added to the story, it seems reasonable to anticipate an increasing number of normal or even exemplary modernities from other parts of the world. Fruitful comparisons across geographic, linguistic, ethnic, cultural, and religious boundaries will enrich our understanding of social development as a holistic program for human flourishing.

The common practice of "learning from the West", deemed absolutely necessary for survival by East Asian intellectuals and political leaders, will certainly continue but the need to broaden the horizons of reference cultures is obvious. As "mutual referencing" progresses, East Asia can benefit from civilizational dialogues with Latin America, South Asia, the Islamic world, and Africa. I have been advocating in Beijing and throughout Cultural China that it is in China's best interest to take India seriously as a reference society. This will significantly broaden China's symbolic resources in understanding her own indigenous traditions, such as Mahayana Buddhism and religious Daoism and help her better appreciate the modern relevance of religion. If China can recognize Tibet as an enduring spiritual tradition and a venerable cultural heritage, not only will her international reputation significantly improve but also her domestic ability to promote social integration.

In the United States and, by implication, the modern West, the need to transform America's arrogance as a teaching civilization into the humility of a learning culture is predicated on a global vision of social development. We should accept the dictum that the more powerful, wealthy and influential nations are, the more obligated they are to enlarge the well-being of the global community. Strong and rich nations, as beneficiaries of the international system, are obligated to see to it that the least developed countries benefit from their international policies. The isolationist mentality that advocates national interest as an ultimate justification for global action is, in the long run, detrimental to domestic social solidarity. The protectionist approach is self-defeating because it eventually undermines the very system that has generated and sustained its prosperity.

East Asian intellectuals have been devoted students of Western learning. In Japan, European and American tutelage has played an important role in modernization. Japan's ability to learn from the West without abandoning indigenous resources for national and cultural identity, helped this country to become one of the most developed in the world. The West, on the other hand, has not felt compelled to learn from the rest of the global community. This asymmetrical situation is particularly pronounced in United States' relationships with East Asia, notably China. To remain a strong international leader the United States needs an elite educated to be well-informed global citizens.

The time is long over due for American educators and politicians to rekindle a cosmopolitan spirit. The United States' assumption of the role of a tutor for democracy, market economy, civil society, and human rights in East Asia since World War II has been instrumental in developing an international vision. Although an implicit hegemonic mentality in this vision was unhealthy, it had the potential of evolving into true internationalism. However, as the anti-Communist ideology fades and East Asia assumes a greater role in global business and politics, a more wholesome American presence in East Asia is partnership. Implicit in partnership are recognition, understanding and appreciation. Although the obligation to address this asymmetry is mutual, the United States, as the stronger and wealthier partner has greater resources to improve the situation effectively and equitably.

America's current isolationist and protectionist mentality, a reflection of the politics of domination, cannot be transformed by top-down political will. Change can only occur through mobilization of social forces, including nongovernmental organizations. Public intellectuals in government, media, business, the professions, labor, religion, and advocacy movements – for example, environmental protection, gender equality, racial harmony, or human rights – as well as the academic community should take responsibility for facilitating a new agenda to discuss the American vision of and contribution to the global community. Given America's habits of the heart and fragmented political prospects for increasing American internationalism are not particularly encouraging in the short run.

At the Copenhagen Social Summit in 1995, heads of State or Government from 117 countries pledged to implement 10 commitments to alleviate poverty, promote employment and ensure social integration. This obviously newsworthy item received scant attention and was substantially overwhelmed by trivia from Los Angeles during the O. J. Simpson murder trial even in some of the nation's leading international journals. This fact alone clearly cautions against any naive optimism. Nevertheless, pragmatic idealism and a cosmopolitan spirit are also defining characteristics of the American mind. American officials as well as scholars and experts have been at the forefront in ensuring that structural adjustment programs include social development and increasing resources allocated to social development. The possibility of an authentic American internationalism is still there.

The emergence of a new communal critical self-consciousness among public intellectuals will better facilitate American participation in strengthening cooperation for social development through the UN and help realize inspiring leadership on the global scene. In the eyes of East Asian intellectuals, the strength of the United States as a model of modernity lies in vibrant market economy, functioning democratic polity, dynamic civil society, and culture of freedom. The Enlightenment values, such as liberty, rights consciousness, due process of law, and dignity of the individual, are evident in American economy, polity, society, and culture. Yet, unfortunately, American life is also plagued by inequality, litigiousness, conflict, and violence. The American people could benefit from a spirit of distributive justice in economy, an ethic of responsibility in politics, a sense of trust in society, and, above all, a culture of peace. Among the developed countries, the United States is noted for openness to change, willingness to experiment and flexibility. Somewhat liberal immigration policies, admittedly often dictated by economic need and political expediency, are clear indication of the evolution of the United States into a microcosmic "united nations". Multiculturalism and ethnic diversity are integral parts of the American way of life. The best of America is seen in a spirit of tolerance, co-existence, dialogical interaction, and mutual learning across race, gender, age, class, and religion. If the American mindset evolves to encompass responsibility, civility and compassion as well as freedom and rights and take a global perspective in defining national interest, the United States can significantly enhance the UN agenda for social development.

Appendix

Seminar Participants and Resources

Chairman

Mr. Poul Nielson
Minister for Development Cooperation (Denmark)   1996-1998
Mr. Torben Brylle
Under-Secretary, Ambassador, Ministry of Foreign Affairs
(Denmark)   1999

Participants

Dr. Khalid Alioua
Minister of Social Development,
Solidarity and Employment (Morocco)   1996
Mr. Ole Mølgaard Andersen
Economist, Ministry of Foreign Affairs (Denmark)   1998
Mr. Osman Bakar
Deputy Vice Chancellor, University of Malaya (Malaysia)   1998
Mrs. Cynthia Bautista
Executive Director, University of the Philippines (Philippines) 1997, 1999
Mr. Christian Balslev-Olesen
Secretary General, Danchurchaid (Denmark)   1997, 1998
Mrs. Birgit Breuel
Ambassador, General Commissioner for EXPO 2000
(Germany)   1996
Mrs. Joan Burton
Former Minister, Dublin Institute of Technology (Ireland)   1996, 1997

Dr. Mapopa Chipeta
Minister of Foreign Affairs (Malawi)   1997
Mr. Nils Christie
Professor, University of Oslo (Norway)   1999
Mr. Clifford Cobb
Senior Fellow (USA)   1999
Mr. Jean-Michel Collette
Former International Civil Servant (France)   1999
Mr. Andrea Giovanni Cornia
Director, WIDER, Helsinki, Finland (Italy)   1999
Mr. Bob Deacon
Professor, University of Sheffield (United Kingdom)   1998
Mr. Nitin Desai
Under-Secretary General, United Nations Secretariat,
New York (India)   1996, 1997
Mr. Zephirin Diabré
Former Minister (Burkina Faso)   1997, 1998
Mr. Julian Disney
President, ICSW, International Council for Social Welfare
(Australia)   1998
Mr. John D'Mello
Professor, St. Pius College, New Delhi (India)   1999
Mr. Poul Engberg-Pedersen
Director, Centre for Development Research,
Copenhagen (Denmark)   1997, 1999
Mr. Gosta Esping-Andersen
Professor, University Pompeo Fabra, Spain (Denmark)   1999
Mr. Richard Falk
Professor, Princeton University (USA)   1997, 1998
Mr. Aurelio Fernandez
Permanent Mission of Spain to the United Nations,
New York (Spain)   1999
Mr. Aldo Ferrer
Professor, Buenos Aires University (Argentina)   1997
Mrs. Vigdis Finnbogadóttir
Former President (Iceland)   1996-1999
Mr. Michael K. Francis
Archbishop, Archdiocese of Monrovia (Liberia)   1997

Mr. Mario de Franco
Minister fo Agriculture (Nicaragua)   1997
Mrs. Geraldine Fraser-Moleketi
Minister for Welfare (South Africa)   1996
Mr. Bjørn Førde
Secretary-General, Danish Association for
Development Cooperation (Denmark)   1998
Mr. Robert Gamer
Professor, University of Missouri (USA)   1999
Mr. Berhane Ghebray
Former Minister (Ethiopia)   1997
Mr. Ion Gorita
Ambassador, Permanent Representative of Romania to
the United Nations (Romania)   1998
Mr. Xabier Gorostiaga
Rector, Universidad Centroamericano, Managua (Nicaragua) 1996
Mr. Clive Hamilton
Executive Director, Australia Institute (Australia)   1999
Mrs. Faith Innerarity
Director, Ministry of Labour, Social Security
and Sport (Jamaica)   1998
Mr. Hisanori Isomura
President, Japanese Cultural Centre, Paris (Japan)   1996
Mr. Vyacheslav Ivanov
Professor, University of California, USA (Russia)   1998
Ms. Elizabeth Jelin
CONICET, Argentina (Argentina)   1998
Mr. Donald J. Johnston
Secretary General, OECD, Paris (Canada)   1996
Mr. Jänis Jurkäns
Member of Parliament (Latvia)   1997
Mrs. Gloria Kan
Chief of Branch, United Nations Secretariat,
New York (USA)   1999
Mrs. Salma Khan
Director General, Bangladesh Institute of Management
(Bangladesh)   1997

Ms. Ida Elisabeth Koch
Senior Researcher, The Danish Centre for Human Rights
(Denmark)   1999
Mr. Lars Kolind
General Manager, Oticon (Denmark)   1996
Mr. Robert Lamb
Director, TVE International (United Kingdom)   1999
Mr. John Langmore
Director, United Nations Secretariat, New York (Australia)   1999
Mr. Poul Henning Larsen
Chief Statistical Adviser, Uganda (Denmark)   1999
Mrs. Marju Lauristin
Professor, Tartu University, Estonia (Estonia)   1996
Ms. Flora Lewis
Journalist, Paris, France (USA)   1998
Mr. Bernd Marin
European Centre for Social Welfare Policy and Research,
Vienna (Austria)   1999
Mr. Peter Marris
Professor, Department of Architecture and
Urban Design, University of California (USA)   1998
Mr. Ray F. Marshall
Former Secretary of Labour, University of Texas (USA)   1996
Mr. Thandika Mkandawire
Director, United Nations Research Institute for
Social Development, Geneva, Switzerland (Sweden)   1999
Mr. James W. Mubiru
Acting Commissioner for Statistics, Uganda (Uganda)   1999
Mr. Saad Nagi
Professor Emeritus, The Ohio State University, USA (Egypt)   1998, 1999
Mr. Deepak Nayyar
Professor, Centre for Economic Studies & Planning,
New Delhi (India)   1999
Mr. Arkadii Nekrassov
President of Association of Social Workers (Russia)   1997
Mr. Thomas R. Odhiambo
Professor, Managing Trustee, Nairobi (Kenya)   1997

Mr. Fred Opio
Executive Director, Makarere University (Uganda)   1997
Mr. Abdul Magid Osman
Chairman, Banco Commercial e de Investismento,
Maputo (Mozambique)   1997
Dr. Devendra Raj Panday
Former Minister of France, Chairman,
Nepal South Asia Centre (Nepal)   1996
Mr. Kwame Pianim
Director, New World Investment Ltd. Accra (Ghana)   1996, 1999
Mr. Giandomenico Picco
Chairman and CEO, GDP Associates Inc., USA (Italy)   1996, 1999
Ms. Margo Picken
Center for International Studies, LSE (United Kingdom)   1999
Mr. Dennis Pirages
Professor, University of Maryland (USA)   1999
Mr. Michael Remmert
Administrator, Council of Europe, Strasbourg (Germany)   1999
Mr. Koos Richelle
Director General for International Cooperation,
Ministry of Foreign Affairs (Netherlands)   1996, 1997
Mr. Gert Rosenthal
Permanent Mission of Guatemala to the United Nations,
USA (Guatemala)   1999
Mr. Mandivamba Rukuni
Professor, University of Zimbabwe (Zimbabwe)   1997, 1999
Mr. Ignacy Sachs
Professor, Ecole des Hautes Etudes en Sciences Sociales,
Paris (France)   1999
Mrs. Nafis Sadik
Executive Director, United Nations Population Fund
(Pakistan)   1999
Mr. J. Stanley Sanders
Lawyer (USA)   1996-1998
Mr. Ismail Serageldin
Vice President, The World Bank (Egypt)   1997
Mr. Mihaly Simai
Professor, Institute for World Economics, Budapest (Hungary) 1999

266

Mr. Zola Skweyiya
Minister for Welfare and Population Development
(South Africa)   1999
Mr. Dirck Stryker
Director, AIRD, Boston (USA)   1999
Mrs. Barbara Sundberg-Baudot
Professor, Saint Anselm College (USA)   1999
Mr. Dae-Won Suh
Ambassador, Deputy Permanent Representative of
the Republic of Korea to the United Nations
(Republic of Korea)   1998
Mr. Osvaldo Sunkel
Professor, Unversidad de Chile, Santiago (Chile)   1999
Mr. Bengt Säve-Söderbergh
Secretary General, IDEA (Sweden)   1998
Mr. Lars Thygesen
Director, Statistics Denmark (Denmark)   1999
Mr. Peter Townsend
Emeritus Professor of Social Policy, University of Bristol
(United Kingdom)   1999
Mr. Pierre Elliott Trudeau
Former Prime Minister (Canada)   1996
Mr. Tu Weiming
Professor of Chinese History and Philosophy, Director,
Harvard-Yenching Institute (USA)   1996-1999
Mr. Pierre Uhel
Vice President, Asian Development Bank (France)   1998
Mr. Varujan Vosganian
Member of Parliament, Union of Armenians in Romania
(Romania)   1996
Mrs. Linda Wong
Professor, City University of Hong Kong, China (China)   1999
Mr. Daniel Yona
Minister of Finance (Tanzania)   1997
Mrs. Zuo Huanchen
Vice Mayor of Shanghai (China)   1996

Royal Danish Ministry of Foreign Affairs

Mr. Peter Brückner
Ambassador, Former Under-Secretary for Multilateral Affairs   1996
Mr. Torben Brylle
Under-Secretary, Ambassador   1997-1999
Ms. Ellen Margrethe Løj
Ambassador, Head of the South Group   1996-1998

Secretary

Mr. Jacques Baudot
Special Adviser (France)   1996-1999

Assistants

Mr. Lars Zbinden Hansen	1996
Mr. Tobias Holmstrup	1998, 1999
Ms. Camilla Bang Petersen	1999
Ms. Dorte Falkenberg Villumsen	1997, 1998

Resource Persons

Ms. Cynthia Hewitt de Alcantarra
UNRISD, Geneva, Switzerland (Mexico)
Mr. Ole Mølgaard Andersen
Economist, Ministry of Foreign Affairs (Denmark)
Mr. Frank J. Aguilar
Professor, Harvard Business School (USA)
Mr. Martin Beaumont
DESCO, Lima (Peru)
Ms. Grace Bediako
Statistics Division, United Nations Secretariat, New York

Mr. Michael M. Cernea
Professor, (USA)
Mr. Leif Christoffersen
Noragric, Agricultural University of Norway (Norway)
Mr. Clifford Cobb
Senior Fellow (USA)
Mr. Jean-Michel Collette
Former Civil Servant (France)
Mr. Andrea Giovanni Cornia
Director, WIDER, Helsinki (Italy)
Mr. John D'Mello
Professor, St. Pius College, New Delhi (India)
Mr. Edward Dommen
Professor, Geneva (Switzerland)
Mr. Poul Engberg-Pedersen
Director, Centre for Development Research (Denmark)
Mr. P. Gopinath
Director, International Institute for Labour Studies, Geneva,
Switzerland (India)
Mr. Clive Hamilton
Executive Director, Australia Institute (Australia)
Mr. Gorm Harste
Professor, Department of Political Science, Aarhus University (Denmark)
Mrs. S. Nazik Izik
Statistical Adviser (Turkey)
Mr. Yusuf Izik
State Planning Organisation (Turkey)
Mr. John Langmore
Director, United Nations Secretariat, New York (Australia)
Mr. Poul Henning Larsen
Chief Statistical Adviser, Uganda (Denmark)
Mr. Jakob Magnussen
Copenhagen Business School (Denmark)
Mr. E.S.K. Muwanga-Zake
Statistics Department (Uganda)
Mr. Deepak Nayyar
Professor, Jawaharlal Nehru University, New Delhi (India)

Mr. J.P.R. Ochieng'Odero
ICIPE, Nairobi (Kenya)
Ms. Margo Picken
Center for International Studies, LSE (United Kingdom)
Mr. Dennis Pirages
Professor, University of Maryland, (USA)
Mr. Peter Pruzan
Copenhagen Business School (Denmark)
Mr. Mandivamba Rukuni
Professor, University of Zimbabwe, Zimbabwe (Zimbabwe)
Mr. Ignacy Sachs
Professor, Ecole des Hautes Etudes en Sciences Sociales, Paris (France)
Mr. Norman Scott
Professor, The Graduate Institute of International Studies, Geneva,
Switzerland (United Kingdom)
Mr. Mihaly Simai
Professor, Institute for World Economics, Budapest (Hungary)
Mr. Dirck Stryker
Director, AIRD, Cambridge (USA)
Mr. Lars Thygesen
Director, Statistics Denmark (Denmark)
Mr. Peter Townsend
Emeritus Professor of Social Policy, University of Bristol (United Kingdom)
Mr. Andrew Whitley
Chief, Office of the Secretary General, UNCTAD (United Kingdom)
Mrs. Linda Wong
Professor, City University of Hong Kong, (China)

Background Papers

Mr. Frank Aguilar
"Corporate Interest, Ethics and the Common Good", 1996
"Opening Access to the Market, a Case Study", 1997
Mr. Clifford Cobb
"The Role of Indicators of Progress and Regress in Social Development", 1999

Mr. Jean-Michel Collette
"Empirical Inquiries, National Income Measurement and the Assessment of Social Progress in Western Europe: A Historical Perspective", 1999
Mr. John D'Mello
"Towards an Ethical Culture for a Global World", 1998
Mr. Poul Engberg-Pedersen
"The Political Economy of Democratising the International System", 1998
Mr. Gosta Esping-Andersen
"Social Indicators and Welfare Monitoring", 1999
Mr. Clive Hamilton
"Notes on Defining and Measuring Social Progress and Social Regress", 1999
Mr. Gorm Harste
"The Paradoxes of Risk Society: Political Thinking of Tolerance and Solidarity Under Conditions of Globalisation", 1996
Mr. John Langmore
"Employment Strategy: Overcoming Obstacles to Work for All", 1997
"Political Culture and Institutions for a World Community", 1998
Mr. Deepak Nayyar
"Globalisation: What Does it Mean for Development?", 1996
"Democracy, Markets and People in the Context of Globalisation", 1997
"From the World Economy to a World Community: Some Questions and some Reflections", 1998
Mr. J.P.R. Ocheing'Odero
"Winners and Losers in the Integrated Economy: The Case of Africa", 1997
Mr. J.P.R. Ocheing'Odero & Mr. Eric B. Orina
"The Contour of an Alternative to the Current Process of Integration in the World Economy: An African Perspective, 1996
Ms. Margo Picken
"Human Rights and Foreign Policy in the 1990s", 1999
Mr. Dennis Pirages
"A New Planetary Bargain: Towards Ecologically Sustainable Social Progress", 1996
"States, Markets, and Social Progress", 1997
"Globalisation without Governance: Poverty and Pathogens", 1998
Mr. Peter Pruzan and Mr. Simon Zadek
"Socially Responsible and Accountable Enterprise", 1996

Mr. Mandivamba Rukuni
"Political Culture and Institutions for a World Community:
Some Reflections", 1998
Mr. Ignacy Sachs
"Developing in a Liberalized and Globalizing World Economy:
An Impossible Challenge?", 1996
"People's Livelihoods in Real Economy", 1997
"Citizenhood: Local, National, Regional and Planetary", 1998
Mr. Norman Scott
"Main Features of the Functioning of the World Economy", 1996